A Simple Extraordinary Life

my Journey from Anxiety to Peace

Terry Gall

A Simple Extraordinary Life: My Journey from Anxiety to Peace
Copyright ©2018 by Terry Gall

Scripture quotations marked NIV are taken from the *Holy Bible, New International Version*®, NIV® Copyright © 1973, 1978, 1984, 2011 by Biblica, Inc.® Used by permission. All rights reserved worldwide.

Scripture quotations marked TPT are from *The Passion Translation*®. Copyright © 2017, 2018 by Passion & Fire Ministries, Inc. Used by permission. All rights reserved. ThePassionTranslation.com.

ISBN 13: 978-0-578-40342-7
Printed in the USA.

In loving memory of
Franklin Delano Maus

Contents

Prologue

*I*t's as if I suddenly wake up from a deep slumber, stunned and quite surprised at where I now find myself. Feeling a bit off kilter at how fast these sudden feelings have taken me to that place in life where my thoughts are drifting back in time, musing about how quick the passage of time catches up to a person. Years have gone by, never to be captured again. Passages of time, some peaceful and fun filled. Other pieces of time have been antagonizing, endless and slow while yet others have passed so swiftly they leave me breathless.

I envision life's first measurable and tangible passing of time to be somewhat like watching a peaceful and meandering creek; languid waters winding slowly along the banks of our lives at a serpentine snail's pace. Time that seems limitless, its bends and turns that will go on forever, last forever. I have visions of young children at play with no worries of tomorrow, their youthful thoughts filled with play of endless summer days. Possibilities and dreams filling their hearts and minds giving way to their teenage years, captured with the notion they are invincible. Eventually some will become harried young mothers, overwhelmed with the demands of young children, feeling as if they'll be stuck in those years that will never end. Others will be in jobs that give them no satisfaction, the slow tick, tick, tick of the clock of monotony and drudgery that makes the years drag by. The lucky ones will be those who love every stage of life they find themselves in making the years of their lives pass ever too swiftly and with an ease others will envy.

The irony is that somewhere along this seemingly endless journey of life, time will start to take its place, its toll. The essence of time takes on new meaning, years become many and our slow meandering creek has turned into the raging waters of a fast river that somehow surprises you with its swiftness, catching you off guard. The clock is ticking and an alarm feels like it's about to go off. It is here, this place, that I now find myself in, at the threshold of realization that life is coming at me at a much faster pace than it ever did before. Time has had a way of tricking and deceiving me into believing that I have endless amounts of disposable time. Never before did I imagine I would feel my life speeding by at this pace. Time is slipping; summer days seem more fleeting. Memories are becoming distant.

Pondering on these thoughts I ask myself, what became of all that time, all the years I have lived thus far? Did I just slip through life, caught unaware, and with no conscious thought or regard to what impact my life might of have had to those around me? I would like to think I haven't been entirely devoid of that thought.

Knowing I can't recapture the past, slow down time, or wishfully have a much-wanted do over of time, it is these thoughts that turn myself to the present. While good memories are being stored up and treasured, time is becoming too limited to waste on regrets or bad memories that want to linger. It is such a cliché phrase, "time is short", but oh how true it is. Instead I would rather put my focus on the rest of time that's been granted to me. My thoughts then wander to another set of questions.

If there is still time for me to bestow or impart something worthwhile to those around me, and if so, what would that be? What, if anything, from this simple life I have lived could I use to accomplish this? Who is it in my life that had the power to change and impact it? Is there any wisdom to be gained by the telling of my experiences that can be divinely passed on to others so that they might grasp today what it took near a lifetime for me to grasp?

I've heard it said that everyone has a story. Could it be that my story would have something useful or beautiful in it? However small or large the impact could be on someone, if a life such as mine can be changed, what, if anything in my story could change yours? It is these thoughts that compel me to tell my story, to put pen to paper and stretch myself beyond anything I've ever done before.

Beginnings, Cardboard Boxes, & One Amazing Event

CHAPTER

1

*I*t goes without saying; age is only relevant to how people view you.

Take for instance if you were to ask some of my younger grandchildren they would tell you sixty is super old.

Some would say super duper old, and some, when they want to be especially sweet to me whisper softly in my ear. "Gramma, you're not old!"

"Oh you think so, do you?" I snickered.

They smile sweetly and look into my eyes. "Yeah, you're not old."

"Yeah sure if that's what you think, you are so funny but I don't think that's the truth!" I grinned at them and their feigned innocence. "What do you want?"

To them, time stretches endlessly before them but I feel like the clock is ticking rather fast these days. All I know is that when they tell me I'm not old, it makes me want to give them anything their little heart desires, for I wish I could make time stand still.

My eighty-three year old mother and my eighty-three year old mother-in-law would wistfully view sixty as still relatively young. Ask me directly though and I will be sure to say, no doubt about it, I'm getting old. The mirror so rudely reflects this every time I walk by and see a reflection of a full head of gray hair staring back at me. My vanity took a real bruising the day I decided I was just too tired of the constant upkeep it took trying to color my hair and keep all my nasty gray hairs from showing. I tried hard to avoid the inevitable fact; but it was a losing battle, those wiry and wild gray hairs were fast multiplying by the day. I wasn't too happy about the fact I couldn't easily conceal them anymore.

I'm starting to look more and more like my mother every day. In fact, one day not long after I let my hair go a hundred percent gray, while out shopping, I thought for sure I saw my mom in the store, and went to go say hello to her. How stunned I was when I suddenly realized I had been looking at a reflection of myself in the mirror on the far wall. *Well how incredibly rude,* I thought, *inside I still feel much younger than what that image in the mirror is telling me!*

I can't deny it, for sure there is absolutely no question in my mind, the hard cold truth is; age is catching up to me rather quickly these days. Time seems to go buy so fast these days, and it's impossible to make it slow down. It's hard to fathom as I slowly digest this fact. *When did I get this old and how did this many years go by so fast?* Now I know, Lord willing, I still have a lot of life left but it doesn't stop me from wishing I could go back in time and slow some parts of my life down so I could have savored them more. I guess that's part of the foolish living we do when we are young, feeling as if we have a lot of time left yet to live or accomplish life's goals. It's not something we usually spend a lot of time and energy thinking about. We don't realize we should slow down, and learn to enjoy and savor the seasons of life we are in. No amount of wishful thinking will be getting any of our seasons back.

My own wishful thinking might have something to do with having married young at the age of seventeen, and birthed all four of my children before the age of twenty-seven. When the birth of my fourth child rolled around, I was already feeling too old and used up to be having more children. It is hard for me to comprehend that by then, I'd already felt I'd lived a lifetime.

Looking through the lenses of my life, there are those parts of my life that seem like nothing but a fuzzy blur, while yet other parts seemed to play out with endless cruelty. But here I am, finding myself wanting to jump too far ahead of myself and get to the part of my story that I am most anxious to tell, about the significance of vast amounts of time that stretched into years that were lost by myself, ever so foolishly. Those times can only be told by going back to the beginning where this life of mine all began. My greatest and deepest wish is that you would be able to fully understand the beauty of all that wasted time, being restored by the One who has made my life worth living.

There was nothing remarkable about my beginnings. I entered this world just like every other ordinary person did, born into an average young American family on September 6[th,] 1957. I was born in a small American town, Benson, Minnesota and I was the firstborn to my parents. Well I like to say I was the firstborn since technically, I was born an hour or so before my twin brother. Having twins was a surprise to my parents. At birth I weighed 4 lbs. 15 oz., quite a bit smaller than my twin brother. Due to my small size they kept me at the hospital for two weeks before they released me to go home with my parents, my brother went home a week earlier.

My parents who both grew up in rural Minnesota had each come from large families. Both of them had been raised on their parents' farms towards the end of the great depression era in their respective small towns that they were both born in. My father's family heralded fifteen children, Dad being second to the youngest, and my mother's family had twelve children in it. I'm guessing large families were pretty normal in those days and especially for that area where they came from since the children would just become a large part of the labor force for their sprawling family farms.

When we were kids, mom would tell us stories about growing up on the farm.

"When I was a kid, I loved to run barefoot through the fields as a child, squishing the cow patties between my toes."

We'd screw up our nose and loudly exclaim. "Ewe that is disgusting!"

"What else do you remember?"

She would look away trying to remember things she could tell us.

"Well sometimes what we used to call hobos would come around looking for work. They wanted a hot meal but they would never eat until they finished the work up my dad would give them to do. They were just honest out of luck folks, it was right after the Great Depression and times were still hard for a lot of people."

"Were you scared of them when they showed up at your house?"

"No, not really." She'd then go on to tell us about how poor there family was. "I had to bring cold sliced potato sandwiches to school sometimes because it's all we had."

"Yuck, that sounds awful!" our noses wrinkled at the thought.

"They weren't that bad."

I think she liked to tell us that story of those potato sandwiches so we'd be more grateful for what we had.

Stories both my parents told us of all the endless weeding of the family's vegetable gardens, the early morning rising while it was still dark out in the frigid cold of a Minnesota winter to milk their cows, and all the other stories they told of the hard work they did on their families' farms made me ever so grateful we didn't have to live the farming life while I was growing up.

About all I can remember hearing about my mom and dad's courtship was that my mother who was waitressing at a café waited on a dashingly handsome young man than soon told her he was going to marry her someday. Now I have a sneaky suspicion he saw a cute girl and was flirting, but who knows, because soon after, at the age of nineteen my parents married. Two years later my father would get drafted into the military.

After his basic training in the army and some other specialized training he had, he was shipped off to Germany where he drove tanks. Many years later he would tell us stories of the war torn streets and the bombed out buildings he saw while they drove their tanks through the streets of the German towns they were patrolling. He also told us about some mischievous things they did with their tanks, but I won't tell them. I'm sure lots of those young men away from their families during those years got into mischievous activity, so Dad was no different from them. He did tell us though that he thought Germany was a beautiful country and that some of our ancestry is part German. We used to joke that maybe that's why most of us could be pretty stubborn at times; it had to come from somewhere.

While stationed in Germany, Dad's father had suddenly passed away, so the army let him come home for some morale leave. He left Germany to come home, boarding a big ocean liner that crossed the Atlantic sea. While crossing the ocean the sea became very rough. They had encountered a severe storm and the large ship was rocking and rolling, listing side-to-side in the violent seas. Many around him were lying in their bunks with severe seasickness, their faces fraught with worry. My father says he remembers making a promise to God that if he survived this ocean crossing and got home safely he would do what most people say at such a time as this, be a better person, do something good with his life, and all the usual promises one makes when they are in fear for their life. Of course, once they made it safely home and his feet landed on solid ground, that promise was quickly forgotten. After his morale leave he went back to Germany and served out his remaining time.

My parents had been married for five years before they had their first children, the surprise twins, my brother and I. The story I've been told that really changed our course as a family began when I was about two years of age. My father who had been lured by all the many grandiose stories told to him from an older brother of all the plentiful game, fishing, and trapping to be had in a wild and beautiful place called Alaska that his brother now lived in, packed up his own little family and decided he would move us all there also.

My father had already left the farming life and his love for hunting and fishing made Alaska sound pretty appealing to him. Our family at that time consisted of five people; my dad, my pregnant mother, me, my twin brother and our younger sister, who was only a year and four days younger than us twins. Dad packed everyone up into their car, pulling a trailer loaded with all their possessions and preceded to start driving up the infamous Alcan Highway, the only road to and from Alaska.

A Simple Extraordinary Life

Back then, in the late 1950's, the highway to Alaska, the Alcan, was a long, winding, dusty and somewhat treacherous gravel and dirt road that stretched through the providences of Canada. I have memories of a child years later, traveling that road when our family would take a trip back down that highway to go see our relatives in the lower forty-eight states. The clouds of dust from traveling for days on that gravel road would seep into the car, making us feel dirty and thirsty, resulting in all of us becoming very cranky. When we would finally hit pavement after the long and weary days of those dirt roads, it was paradise, feeling sure this must be what the good book tell us it will be like when we reach the gold paved highways of heaven at the end of our life.

Well over fifty years later, it is now completely paved, and much of the tight winds, curves and steep hills have been taken out to be a much safer and more comfortable drive than it used to be all those years ago. There will always be the occasional scattered road construction zones and highway crews, doing the endless maintenance and repair of the over thirteen hundred miles of the Alcan Highway. Parts of this highway go through the frozen tundra riddled with permafrost, resulting in some very bad frost heaves. You have to slow down greatly to miss the heaves or weave around them, or else you'll jar yourself silly and possibly do damage to your vehicle. But still, it seems like a cakewalk these days compared to those old and very dusty traveling days we once had. During the short summer months the highway is always busy with the many tourists who travel to come see this beautiful state of Alaska and experience its wonders.

Many mountain passes have to be crossed driving this highway and it was there in one of those mountain passes, on my parents' virgin trek to Alaska that my dad was caught driving, in the middle of a snowstorm.

He found himself contemplating what to do. He was sure that the trailer he was pulling behind the car was going to jackknife in the snow, and take the car with all of us in it and plunge us over the embankment. In anticipation of the worst, he instructed my mother.

"If the trailer starts to go over the cliff, be ready, grab the kids and be ready to jump out of the car!"

My Journey from Anxiety to Peace

Now I wonder, *just how was mom supposed to wrangle three small kids, her pregnant self, and get out of the car in time?* I'm sure this is something Dad never quite completely thought through. I'm pretty sure Mom was unbelievably scared at the prospect of having to jump and Dad probably had white knuckles from trying to keep this scenario from happening. Miraculously, they ended up making it through the snowy pass without incident except for probably gaining a few gray hairs and maybe becoming a little wiser, breathing a sigh of relief when they finally made it safely all the way to their new home, in the great state of Alaska.

Our family moved into a single wide mobile home trailer in an area called Spenard, in the most populated city in Alaska, Anchorage. My mother having given birth to another boy, now had four little children under the age of four. My father worked some odd jobs till he landed a job with the United States Post Office delivering and sorting mail. Because he was an avid hunter and fisherman and ran trap lines in his spare time, Mom would be left alone a lot with us kids in this new place. Not knowing many people she would be quite lonely. Eventually though, my parents would meet people and make some new friends. It was about this time that I started to gather my own memories.

One of my first vivid memories happened one cold winter day. My parents and their friends were visiting inside our trailer home and I had wandered outside to the porch where I proceeded to do what many young kids have learned the hard way not to do in the cold of winter, lick the tantalizing and glittery ice off the metal railing. There I was, my tongue firmly stuck to the icy railing, frantically trying in vain to yell, to alert someone, anyone to my dilemma. What seemed like an eternity had passed while my tongue burned, too afraid to pull myself away lest I leave all the skin of my tongue there on the ice cold railing. I heard a lot of laughing and carrying on inside. *Is anyone going to realize I'm gone?* Eventually someone finally took notice and realized I was gone and went to look for me.

To my great relief, my dad had come out to the porch and found me and my tongue glued to the freezing metal railing and proceeded to pour warm water over my tongue to release it. *Boy oh boy, did that hurt!* I learned a lesson the hard way never to be repeated again. That was an easier lesson to learn than some other life lessons I had that I tended to repeat, over and over - but here I am again, getting ahead of myself.

CHAPTER

2

I was a very timid, extremely shy, and introverted child. It didn't take long in my young life before all these inherent personality traits would become like a crippling noose held tight around my neck. Traits that constantly made me feel like I was trapped in a cardboard box with only small eye holes that I could view the vibrant life of those around me, those more fortunate than I; who had no box of fears that encased them, crippling them, stopping them from walking freely around seemingly unencumbered. My box of traits was bothersome, unwieldy, something I longed to shed but instead carried around with a hateful vengeance.

I found myself in constant struggles fraught with anxiety and panic, resulting in many stomachaches brought on by the fear I had of people and being put in any situation that was out of my comfort zone. My comfort zones were extremely and sadly, very limited. My twin brother in comparison, at least in my jaded and obscured eyes, seemed to be much more outgoing than I, and at a young age it didn't take me long to become envious of the difference in personality we seemed to have. Whereas I seemed to always be strangled by my fears, he didn't appear to me, to struggle in that way. Wanting to be something different than myself, it wasn't long before I started to torture myself with thoughts of how I was lacking, leading to low self-esteem and what was the beginnings of leading myself down the destructive path of jealousy.

A Simple Extraordinary Life

Watching my twin, he always seemed much more talkative and at ease around people than I was. I found it very intimidating and extremely hard to talk to people, and the byproduct of that was I didn't have a lot of childhood friendships because I found it so difficult to engage with people, even those my own age.

Memories were starting to accumulate in my young life and the memories that caused me pain and distress were the ones that took on a life of their own, wanting to stay lodged deep in my battery bank of memories, trying hard to crowd out the pleasant and good ones. Those were the memories that started to form and shape what I thought about myself and others and the life around me.

By the time I was old enough to start kindergarten, having barely turned five years old, we had moved into a house in the Muldoon area of Anchorage. My mother was pregnant again and I remember a few days before school was to start, she walked my twin brother and I to the elementary school. The purpose of this walk was to show us the route we were to take the first day of school when we'd walk together alone to school. We had to walk down the road from our house and then cross a busy main street, then go down another quieter side street to get to the school.

The first day of school had arrived. My mother set us off that morning to walk to school together with explicit instructions.

"You wait for your sister when school lets out." She looked over at my brother. "I want you to walk home together!"

I don't remember anything about what happened during that first day of school, but the memory and feeling of what happened at the end of the school day still seems seared in my mind.

The school bell rang, signaling the end of school for the day and all of us were let out of our classrooms. Noisy children were flooding through the doors to the outside, glad to be free. I was ready to walk home at the end of the school day, but nowhere in the crowd of kids that surrounded me, making me nervous, could I see my brother. I searched and searched the sea of unfamiliar faces and couldn't find him. Very quickly panic started setting in, quivers of fear assaulting all my senses.

I could feel big fat tears forming and escaping, embarrassing me as they made their sticky wet tracks down my hot and angry face. Furiously I wiped them away, trying hard not to cry. The crowds of children were thinning out fast as I frantically continued to search for my brother's face, but still I couldn't see him anywhere.

By now I was in full-fledged panic mode, frustrated that I couldn't remember on my own, the way to walk home. The school was situated at the end of two roads that formed a "V", ending at the school. I peered up and down at both of those roads and neither one looked familiar to me. I stood there and waited and waited, trying to think what to do. I started to walk a few steps up each road but couldn't bring myself to the decision to go any farther than just a few yards.

I just wasn't sure. *Which one is the right road?*

Distraught and seething with anger at my brother I continued to look around. *How could he just leave me here alone when Mom specifically told him not to?*

I felt like stomping my foot with righteous indignation. *He had better get in big trouble for leaving me here all alone!*

Far too timid to seek out any help I just stood there, afraid I was going to vomit out of sheer anxiety. I kept darting my eyes back and forth down both roads, hoping I could remember which road was the right one that would lead me home. I tried in vain to gather up enough courage to take myself down one of those roads more than just a few steps but I couldn't muster up much of anything other than more panic, anxiety and anger at my brother.

What seemed like an eternity had passed while I stood there, sheathed in my misery. No one else was left in the schoolyard but me. Left alone, I peered again down the road and here coming down it was a motorcycle with a rider, headed towards the school. The man on the motorcycle approached me and asked me if I needed a ride home. Violently shaking my head no I stepped back, deathly afraid of this stranger.

He asked me again stating, "Your mother sent me", but still I refused and he left, motoring his way back up the road.

A Simple Extraordinary Life

I stood there shaking in fear, and still alone.

A little while later the motorcycle comes back up the road again towards the school. By now, I was sweating with fear as he approached me again.

"You sure you don't need a ride home, your mother said it was okay; she asked if I could please give you a ride home."

My head shook no, my voice strangled in anxious silence, my throat parched dry with fear. The motorcyclist shook his head, resigned I wasn't going to go with him and left again. I felt a small measure of relief at his leaving, but still I couldn't figure out what to do. *How am I going to get home?*

Time passed infinitely slow as I stood there, desperately wondering what to do if it turned dark, struggling to figure out how I was going to find my way home. Over and over in my head my thoughts raged that my brother had forgotten about me.

He was supposed to have waited for me! His actions made it more evident to me. *I mustn't be important enough to matter anything to him or he would have remembered to wait for me!*

I wanted to kick myself, overcome with humiliation as I stood there feeling incredibly dumb that I was too stupid to remember the way home. These thoughts were only adding to my already preconceived notion that he, my twin brother, was in my fragile mind, worlds better than me. Crippling ways of thinking about myself were on a fast track, telling me that I was unworthy of much thought or care. Standing there crying, my heart was filling up fast with hurt, my pride bruised just thinking about the injustice of it all. I looked up one of the roads and started to see a figure, slowly walking towards the school. I wanted to run away, so afraid that another stranger might approach me.

Squinting hard, I looked again and realized it wasn't a stranger, it was my nine month pregnant mother. Relief set in as I watched her slowly but surely making her way down the road; she was coming to get me.

My Journey from Anxiety to Peace

"When your brother came home without you, I asked a man who was riding by on his motorcycle if he would come here to the school and see if you were here and give you a ride home." She panted as she told me this while we walked home.

I don't think she was too angry that I wouldn't get on that motorcycle; she more than likely knew that I wouldn't. A day or two later my new baby sister was born. The next day of school my brother waited for me and I eventually learned the way home. I don't ever remember getting an apology from my brother. Looking back now, I realize that about this time of my life was when I had started a journey that would take me down what would be a detrimental road, heading down a very rocky path of unhealthy thinking about myself. I was picking up pebbles in the bottom of my shoes, irritating and when not removed would eventually cause a very sore spot on the bottom of my foot. Amassing pebbles of hurt that I didn't get rid of made for some very confusing thoughts I would eventually store up about myself, eroding any sense of a normal and healthy self-confidence I should have had.

Not long after that incident of being left alone at school, another tangible memory of mine that contributed even more to this type of wrongful thinking about myself had occurred. It would take me even farther down that rocky path of piling up hurts and wounds that would linger; skewing my perceptions and my thoughts, leaving its nasty marks in the sea of memories that I was accumulating. It was easy for my young and impressionable mind to harbor feelings of loss of self-worth, far too easy.

We were still living in the house in Muldoon. It was a hot summer like day, so it was probably close to the end of a school year. My brother and I, along with some neighborhood kids, had walked home from school only to find the house locked up and my parents not yet at home to let us in. This in itself was unusual but we couldn't do anything about it other than wait for them to come home. We were extremely thirsty from the heat and the dust kicked up by the dirt road we had just walked up, and I badly wanted something to drink.

My twin brother extended his arm to me. "Here, have this, it's a can of 7up!" His friend stood by as he offered me the can.

I mumbled, "Thanks!" and took a large swallow from the can.

I was very gullible and never did the thought cross my mind to wonder where they got that can of 7up.

"Oooh-gah...ecch!" Gagging and sputtering as I tried to spit this horrible taste out of my mouth while my brother and his friend just looked at me laughing and laughing while I wretched and spit.

They had peed in the can before offering it to me.

I became so angry and incredibly hurt that they thought it was so funny to deceive me in such an awful, horrible way. Feeling no shame in their laughter, it only furthered the feelings for me that I didn't matter much to them. Especially hurt that my own brother, someone who was supposed to love me would do something like that to me and not seem to be sorry for it. Again, I became angry at myself for being so dumb and so gullible. I was fast learning a way of thinking that would only seek to hinder me later on in life. I couldn't seem to let these things go. These hurt feelings and bruised pride were starting to fester. Instead of learning to let them go like water off a duck's back, they settled deep within, poking and prodding, eroding any small feelings I ever had of any self-worth, reminding me of how inferior I would always feel.

Poisonous roots were growing inside my cardboard box, polluting the air around me, competing with what little joy in life I could find. Getting tangled in the roots of feeling inadequate and unworthy; jealousy, resentment and anger were easily forming frown lines upon my face right beside the laugh lines.

As a young child how could I understand the forces that were willing me to buy into the lies I believed about myself? *I'm not as smart and funny and likeable as my brother*. Every other kid I met or knew, I always felt was better than me. Always feeling awkward and horribly shy, I somehow thought I had received the short end of the stick when it came to my brother and me. Constantly caught up in comparisons of myself with others, and in my eyes, I never seemed to quite measure up.

In elementary school this was only reinforced by classmates who couldn't wait to see after the teacher handed back our work papers, which twin, my brother or I, had the better-graded paper. Never could I comprehend why my classmates thought this should define who I was, or who was supposedly the better twin based off some silly school paper. Even though I was physically small and extremely quiet like a mouse, deep inside, oh how I could rage.

I am my own person, not part of my brother! Why can't people see that?

I had never felt any extra special connection to him even though he was my twin and it confused me when others alluded that I should. Thankfully, somewhere around second or third grade the school separated us into different classrooms so my anxiety about constantly being compared to my twin brother by my classmates reduced some.

School life became mostly a sea of anxiety ridden moments in time for me. Panic would quickly overtake me if the teacher called on me or even said a name that sounded remotely like mine. Instantly I would break out in a sweat and get that familiar gut wrenching stomach ache, accompanied with those cramps that meant for sure I'd have to make a dash to the bathroom. There was one time though that I remember feeling good about myself in class, managing to accomplish something no one else in the class could do.

My second grade teacher Mrs. Forgery, who secretly we all called Mrs. Froggy, had inadvertently dropped something inside a jar and couldn't get it out. One by one the kids in my class tried to put their hands down in the jar and retrieve the item for our teacher but their hands were too large.

Mrs. Forgery looked at me. "Terry, do you want to try?"

I stepped up to the jar to take my turn. Miraculously my small hand fit down in the jar. With a small triumphant smile on my face I pulled the item out and handed it to my teacher. Unusual pride filled me; finally there was something about me that was good, my small hand. My elation didn't last long though before I was back in the confines of my cardboard box.

I'm really amazed that I somehow managed to pass every grade, year after year, having never once spoken in front of, or rarely inside a school classroom. I always avoided all group school projects the best

I could, I got pretty deft at that. Not once did I give a speech in the required high school speech class. I would prepare the speech required for homework, lamely thinking that maybe, just maybe, I could bring myself to get up in front of the class and give my speech. It never failed, when the time came for me to give my speech, that same familiar fear would overtake me.

The speech teacher looked at me. "Do you have your speech ready?"

"No." I would sheepishly tell the teacher as I ducked my head, "I'm not prepared."

Immediately I would be overcome with guilt. *I just lied; I'm not supposed to lie.*

I think the teacher took pity on me, never once did he force me to give even one speech, just barely giving me a passing grade for the class. Home would be the only place where I felt I could escape to and feel more relaxed, not having to deal so much with my many anxieties.

Being so timid I hardly had any friends in grade school or middle school, but finally by high school I had found two friends. The three of us were just about as shy as the next and together we limped through those first awkward years of high school, only to have one of my friends in the tenth grade move to another state.

This left me with my one and only other friend I would have.

CHAPTER

3

ot all my childhood memories were the ones that I held close to me in unjustifiable anger or make me wince at their memory. Although I did have plenty of those, I also have my share of memories that make me smile. Memories I find lighthearted and amusing, and those memories that were just part of my growing up years.

For reasons I'm not sure about we had moved from our house in Muldoon back to the trailer in Spenard. We were living here on March 27, 1964, Good Friday, when a 9.2 magnitude earthquake shook south central Alaska. My recollection of this event at around six and a half years old was that we, meaning my dad, two brothers and sister were sitting inside the car at the local Piggly Wiggly supermarket parking lot when the earthquake hit. My mom and youngest sister were inside the store shopping for groceries.

My mother never has, and still doesn't to this day have a driver's license, her being the nervous sort; we have all thought it was probably for the best. Because she didn't drive, the norm would be that my dad would wait in the car with some of us kids while my mother would take one or two of us into the grocery store with her while she did our family's weekly grocery shopping. This trip she only took my baby sister in with her.

A Simple Extraordinary Life

There we were, Mom in the store shopping while us kids that were left under the care of my father, sat in the back seat of the car trying our best to be good and patient so Dad didn't have to turn around and get after us. The car suddenly started wildly jerking around and bouncing up and down on its rubber tires, giving us kids what we thought, was a good and fun ride.

When the car had finally stopped bouncing around, us kids giggled and squealed. "Dad, do that again!"

"Aaah, I can't", Dad answered not explaining why.

"Come on Dad, do it again!" "That was fun!"

As kids we were totally unaware that it had been an earthquake that had shook us around and made our car bounce around so easily like a pogo stick. We didn't even know what an earthquake was! My dad had stayed calm, though I'm sure he was filled with worry about my mom and sister caught inside the grocery store while the ground shook and rolled for about five minutes.

Mom was slightly trembling as she excitedly told us. "It was shaking so bad, cans were flying off the grocery shelves all around me so I laid in the aisle over top your baby sister so she wouldn't get hit! It lasted so long!"

Electricity was knocked out for a few days after and people were melting snow for drinking water. Days later after the earthquake, I heard whispers from the adults around me of something they referred to as aftershocks, and how scared people were getting because of all these aftershocks. My father told of how one day while he was at work down at the main post office at the airport, they were sorting mail and another aftershock shook the building. A lady Dad worked with became very scared.

Shaking her head she announced. "That's it! I'm not doing this anymore."

She left work, walked straight over to the airport, boarded a plane and flew straight out of Alaska not even bothering to go home and pack a suitcase.

My Journey from Anxiety to Peace

The adults continued to whisper around us, thinking we children couldn't hear them talking. They told stories about how houses with people in them had vanished, washed out to the muddy gray waters of the Cook Inlet, never to be seen again. There were stories of how the side of the JC Penny department store downtown fell and crushed someone in a parked car, killing them. We overheard stories about how some streets had buckled and were left with giant cracks and sink holes from the violent rolling of the ground. Boats had washed up to shore, piling up in heaps of destruction in places far away from where we were here in Anchorage, like Seward and Kodiak Island because of the tsunamis. Whispers were heard of all the different devastation both close and far the earthquake had left in its wake. Because I was still pretty young I didn't really understand the full toll the earthquake had taken on the city of Anchorage and its surrounding areas. The earthquake had caused over 311 million dollars in damage.

In my young mind at the time it had all sounded more like storytelling to me. I just vividly remembered what seemed like an awfully fun amusement ride in the back seat of the family car.

Other blurry memories and faint recollections come to mind of our family going to a friend's cabin one winter somewhere and all of us kids sledding on big wooden toboggans down the surrounding snow covered slopes. Fuzzy memories of fast rides, careening down the hill and flying in the air over top the astonished adult's heads that were standing in the middle of the road, watching us as we landed on the opposite side of the road where we continued to go screaming down the snow covered hill, only to crash in a heap down at the bottom of the deep snow covered slope. What really sticks in the recesses of my mind is that upon crashing I had flown through the air and hit my tail end hard, making it sore for months afterwards. It was my sore backside that I remember the most.

Growing up, we had two bicycles to share between my brothers and sisters, a pink bike and a blue bike. Two bikes between all of us kids always ended up with squabbles.

"It's my turn!" my younger brother yelled at my twin brother who was on the blue bike.

He glared at him, "No it isn't!" egging him on as he drove the blue bike past him.

"Give me the bike!" he said even louder.

"No!"

He yelled out the ultimate threat at him, "I'm going to tell mom you're not sharing!"

"Just ride the pink bike, no one's using it!"

"No! I'm not getting on the pink bike!" he huffily started walking towards the house. "I'm telling!"

"FINE, HERE take it!" he shouted as he threw down the blue bike in the dirt in the backyard, stalking off angry that he had to share.

My brother stomped over triumphantly and picked up the bike from the dirt, hopped on, and took off riding down the streets of our suburban neighborhood. Sometimes I'd pick up the pink bike and follow him, but usually I preferred to ride alone. In solitude I'd pedal the bike as fast as I could and feel the faint breeze on a warm sunny day as it lifted my thin and wavy long brown hair while I drove back and forth on the street in front of our little house. Sometimes we would ride through our small neighborhood, down a little dirt path that connected us with the next neighborhood over from us.

We'd ride those bikes through the neighborhoods with a few other neighbor kids; then over to the little convenience store that was at the four corners of two intersecting highways nearby to buy some sweets with our rare money we had in our pockets.

Our eyes were greedy as we walked the candy aisle of the convenience store. "What are you going to get?"

"I don't know, maybe gum and a candy bar."

"I like watermelon gum, and an Almond Joy, no maybe a Three Musketeers, oooh it's so hard to decide!"

"I think I might have enough money to get five pieces of candy!" my brother said as he perused the hard candy selection.

"Here, help me count my money!" he said as he fished his money out of his dirty jeans pocket.

Once we had purchased our goodies we would devour them on the bike ride back home.

One of my father's new friends managed that convenience store for a while. We didn't get to go there but a few times. Our parents weren't too thrilled about us going that far away and having to cross a busy highway. We just might have snuck over there to the four corners convenience store a few times when we weren't supposed to, the appeal of the assortment of candy and candy bars too much for us to ignore; disobeying the wishes of our parents. It never dawned on us that we would get caught since it was my dad's friend who would ring up our purchases and mention our sneaky visit to his store to our father.

Many of my childhood memories included my uncle Bill. He was the brother of my father that had talked my dad into moving our family to Alaska. I recall him being around a lot, especially when he and his family had lived close to us in Spenard. Uncle Bill also worked for a while for the United States post office. I remember that because one day he was over at our house and my baby sister had wandered over to him. Seeing the familiar blue pants of his uniform she yanked on his leg, and he picked her up. It wasn't until she finally looked at his face when he said something that she realized he wasn't Dad. Then she started to cry. You could definitely tell my dad and Uncle Bill were brothers they looked so much alike, and the older they got even more so. They both were very handsome men. This is very evident looking at all the old black and white photos and all the faded dog-eared photos of them in color when they were young men. They could have easily been mistaken for old movie stars I thought, with their dark wavy hair and smoldering good looks as they posed for the camera.

My uncle Bill and his family were pretty much the only relatives I would know growing up. We did have the occasional visit from my dad's mother. I remember as a child watching her at the dinner table; she would put her food in very small piles on her plate never letting any one food touch the other foods on her plate. *I guess I'll try that.* I imitated that for a while but didn't see what the advantage about it was, so I soon

31

returned to it being okay to letting my food touch. Her hands looked just like my fathers, other than noticing these few things I don't know if I ever spoke a word to her. If we wanted to see relatives our family had to make the trip back to Minnesota; and that was a very rare event. Both of my grandfathers died before I was even born, so I really never had any grandparents I had a relationship with, being that I only saw my grandmothers a few times. I had a large extended family of uncles and aunts and cousins that lived in the lower forty-eight states, but I didn't really get the chance to know any of them. Only my uncle Bill and his family that lived here in Alaska, the reason he happens to be in so many of my memories.

Uncle Bill was an ingenious sort and a self-made entrepreneur. One of his many endeavors was that he built track swamp buggies. He and my dad, along with a group of hunting buddies would take these swamp buggies way out in the woods of Alaska to hunt with. They would venture out into the woods with Uncle Bill's swamp buggies traversing over the moss covered, sparsely treed tundra, where rivers and streams would have to be crossed, way back in the mountains in the middle of nowhere to hunt, mostly for moose. Those swamp buggies were a source of some of the stories the men would often tell; of the breakdowns they'd have and how they would eventually fix them while out in the back woods of Alaska hunting.

One such story they would tell was how they were forty miles back in the woods when a track on one of their rigs broke. Out of the hunting group that were there ready to hunt for their families winter supply of moose, my father was singled out to be the one who was going to have to hike out the forty miles, and get the needed part to fix their broken rig. He then would need to hike back in those forty miles with the heavy part so they could repair the rig, and get them and their gear back out again.

Dad shook his head as he paced around. "Boy that is going to be a really long walk! You sure there's no way to fix it? I'll probably have to be gone for a few days getting the part."

"Well, I - don't know, hmmmm" Uncle Bill mumbled as he walked around staring at the broken track. He seemed lost in thought as Dad asked him again if he thought they could fix it.

Dad sure didn't relish the thought of what it would mean for him if they couldn't figure something else out. It would be an awful lot of hard hiking through the tundra and take a very long time. Trying hard to avoid this scenario the other men put their heads together again along with my reluctant Dad and Uncle Bill and managed to come up with an idea of how they could jerry rig a temporary fix. The fix lasted long enough to get all of their hunting party and the rig out of the woods, saving my dad from what would have been a very long and arduous hike.

As a child I was always glad to see my dad return from his many hunting trips. When we saw him drive up we'd all run outside to happily greet him. Dad would always be wearing his sweat and dirt stained tan hunting hat on his head, his scratchy blood stained green wool pants and one of his red plaid wool shirts, sporting a week's worth of stubble on his face that he always thought was great fun to give us kids whisker burns with.

"Hi there, did you miss me? Dad laughed as he stroked his burly cheek against our soft one.

"Ouch!" I said trying to act incensed as he massaged his face next to mine.

"Daaad!" "That tickles!" We'd all squeal with mock outrage as he rubbed his whiskers over our faces one by one. We loved it all the same; Dad was home!

I often wonder if the era that these men were born in caused them to be the way they were, tough reliant men, able and willing to take on many a daunting task. Uncle Bill was a genius of sorts; he could build pretty much anything he put his mind to. He had his own concrete plant at one time in his life, running it out of the Matanuska Valley where he had eventually moved his family. He was a tough man who weathered some pretty bad accidents in his life. While working at his concrete plant one day he had fallen down one of the high conveyer belts where they would later find him hanging. He ended up with the surgeons having to put a metal plate in his head.

"You'll probably set off the metal detectors at the airport!" we liked to joke with him.

A Simple Extraordinary Life

It didn't take Uncle Bill long after his accident to be back working hard again.

He could run many kinds of heavy machinery. He also worked in construction and my dad eventually put my twin brother under his tutelage at about the age of 13. He spent his summers living during the week with my uncle's family while Uncle Bill taught him some of his skills. My brother would learn how to build houses and become a master himself at running heavy machinery. Eventually, when he got older he would become really good at running a bull dozer, grading ground and putting in driveways and foundations for houses in some pretty daunting places.

Dad and Uncle Bill had something in common; they both had fathered a set of twins. The only difference was that Dad's first children had been my brother and I; Uncle Bill's twins would be a boy and girl, the last of his five children born. My cousins, Uncle Bill's kids were very rambunctious, wild boys. My brothers would go out to their place where they lived in the Matanuska Valley and spend the night with them. When my brothers came home they would paint their stories, telling us of all the wild things they would do.

Their bright eyes showed their exhilaration. "They have these ropes hanging from the trees near a bluff!"

"We swung out on the ropes and we were so high up on the bluff we were swinging over the top of the trees that were way down below us!"

"I don't want you doing that!" Mom would say as she anxiously listened to their stories.

We'd find out later that some of their other rope swings they had scattered around the woods would take them soaring over a raging river that was close by their property. Some of their stunts were so dangerous that if they ever fell, they could be in real danger of breaking their bones or even losing their life. Mom wasn't too sure about letting them go over there very often if they continued to pull these stunts. One of my cousins even lost most of his vision in one of his eyes while foolishly playing around with firecrackers.

That same cousin would love to scare his mother silly by hanging out the door of her moving car, laughing as she drove down the highway. He was wild and fearless, giving his parents a run for their money so to speak.

My brothers always had stories of my uncle and aunt running around yelling, a hunk of hose dangling from their hand trying to catch my cousins so they could whip them; all the while my cousins would just run circles laughing at their parents as they tried to catch up with them. They tried hard to tame their children, but those visions of Uncle Bill and my aunt running around their yard trying to get after their kids would just set us all to laughing when we thought about it.

My uncle's wife was very intriguing to me. She wasn't as timid as my mother and she had no qualms about saying what was on her mind. I thought about how different they both were even though both of their given names were Eleanore, only my aunt never went by that name.

Sometimes she shocked me with what she would say but I got used to it. *Oh that's just Aunt Lilly, she's like that!*

She was from Austria; her family had been refugees that came to Alaska, sponsored by a family in Anchorage. Listening to her stories were even more intriguing to me.

"We would hear these sirens go off and have to go sit in these bomb shelters till the sirens would stop and it was safe to go back home."

She told us this and other stories of herself as a child growing up during the war torn years in Europe. Her mother would be around sometimes visiting for long periods of time with her, and my aunt always referred to her mother as "Oma". For many years I always thought that was her given name, never realizing that it really meant Grandma.

My aunt's distinct accent, which was so different from anything I was used to hearing made her seem almost exotic to me. She made backdrops and props for the local Nordstrom's display windows. It fascinated me when we were at their house and I could see all the finished props and partially made things she was working on sitting around for the window displays. The fact that she got paid to do this and that it was her job besides being a mother to her children was something I would ponder about. That fascination was probably what got me to thinking some about my far away future. The allure of wanting to become more and do more things in my life than just be an ordinary housewife who only stayed at home and took care of her family had started to take up space in my subconscious mind.

Who am I kidding, I'm not smart enough to do much, especially make stuff like all these pretty things! How does she figure out how to make this stuff, she's so smart and talented!

In the generation that my parents belonged to not many women worked outside of their home, so it made my aunt seem all the more interesting to me. I knew that I wished I could be just as crafty as my aunt and do what seemed like more exciting things in life than just those mundane things such as cooking and cleaning and taking care of children.

So there I sat observing, peering through the eye holes of my confining cardboard box. I watched and studied everyone around me; trying hard to capture everything I could and make sense of it all without being noticed. As quietly as I could, I usually hung around the perimeter of the room listening to the adults, especially enjoying the stories of the men that would gather with my father. Their conversations always seemed so much more interesting to me than the conversations of the women that would be gathered.

Maybe it had a lot to do with the differences between my mother and father. My mother was much more reserved than my dad was. My dad laughed and joked a lot, he loved to tell stories and was a big teaser.

It was hard to get a straight answer out of him a lot of the times. Especially hard if you wanted to know what time of the day it was.

"Dad what time is it?" I asked while trying to get a look at the watch on his wrist.

With a straight face he'd answer while he turned his arm away from me. "Half past kissing time, time to kiss again!"

"Daaad, what time is it?"

He'd grin. "I told you, half past kissing time, time to kiss again!"

"Just tell me what time it is dad!" my exasperation starting to show as I playfully tried to twist his arm so I could see his watch.

He wasn't about to give me the answer till I gave in and gave him a kiss first which in reality didn't bother me too much, it was a game we played.

When I had my own kids and tried to tell them the same thing when they'd ask me what time it was they would just look at me like I'd lost my marbles. But I had tender memories of my father always teasing me about what time it was.

Dad was always very physically demonstrative in his love to us kids, whereas my mother really was not. Though he could be a strict disciplinarian and I was afraid of him at times, I always knew he loved me. Just the fact that he told me often that he loved me and showed it to me in his many hugs and kisses, and that special twinkle he had in his eye when he looked at me, told me that he loved me. I can close my eyes and still feel the prickly scratch of his five o'clock shadow as I kissed his cheek while reaching into his arms to receive his hug, my hand that always reached out to pat his hard and slightly protruding stomach, and catch the faint whiff of his spicy aftershave that would tickle my nose. There was comfort and safety found within his presence. The twinkle of his eyes, that special look he always gave me that I knew was reserved just for me gave me the comforting knowledge that I was loved by him.

Dad would mushily look at me sometimes. "You're my Terry Lynn Daughter Maus!"

"Dad why do you say my name like that?"

He'd grin. "Because, that's what you called yourself when you were little!" "Terry Lynn Daughter Maus."

I never felt too old for receiving that coveted look he had for me. I was and am, still a daughter who loved being loved by her father.

Parts of my memories have to do with wanting to please my father, trying my hardest in every way I could. I looked up to him and wanted to be like him, maybe that's why he could crush my feelings sometimes like no one else could. There were things I loved about my dad and things I wished maybe he could be a little different about, but it's funny how most of my childhood memories revolved around him. I guess he was larger than life to me.

There is one childhood block of memory I have of my dad that has always stood out to me, impacting me greatly. In many ways, it would be the reason for the course my life would take and what would be the beginnings of the cornerstone of what I would eventually believe in.

One winter during my early grade school years, my father fell off the back of his mail truck hitting the hard packed ice, breaking his neck. I still remember him taking our families old black and white TV and putting it high up on a pile of empty boxes so he could see it, because the brace on his neck limited his movement. It seemed strange to have my dad around the house while he was off work recovering. Eventually the brace came off and he returned back to work, though he was left with severe pain that he would have to go to a chiropractor and an osteopath several times a week to try and find some measure of relief. The prognosis being, he would have to continue treatment and learn to live with the severe pain for the rest of his life. The after effects of his broken neck had left him with terrible pain he was desperate to be rid of.

About this time, my Uncle Bill started to talk to my dad about a new and different way of thinking, about religion and God. We went as a family regularly to a Lutheran church in town but I really have no recollections of it other than one day being with my dad while he was at the church, running a buffing machine across the tiled church floors. I've always wondered why I have no other memories of being there. Maybe this was because it left no significant impression on me or held nothing of importance to my childhood memories. My uncle had told my dad of a church he knew of on the outskirts of town that had a Bible school that was meeting on a week night. There at that Bible school they learned about the Bible and taught on how you can have a personal relationship with God. Uncle Bill talked of Jesus and salvation and a whole host of things that were new to my father.

"Come to the meeting with me." he asked my dad.

"I don't know, maybe."

"I'm telling you - it'll - it'll be fine!" Uncle Bill stuttered in his excitement. "We can learn a lot!" "I've been reading the Bible and studying what it has to say, there is a lot more to learn than what you believe in now!" "Here let me show you!" Uncle Bill said as he fingered through his Bible.

"Okay, I'll go with you." Dad said pensively.

It was here at one of those meetings that my dad's life was forever changed.

Dad knew no one there, other than his older brother, and no one knew him.

The man who was leading the Bible study told everyone gathered, "God has told a lady here that there is a person here who has broken their neck and God wants to heal them."

My father upon hearing this was astounded; how could anyone know anything about him? Dad says he remembers nothing else that was said that night. He didn't say anything to anyone at the meeting, but later discussed it greatly with his brother Bill.

"That person had what is referred to as a word of knowledge from God." Uncle Bill told my father. He then showed him in the Bible in Corinthians where the gifts of the Holy Spirit are listed, the message of knowledge one of them.

My father, desperate for some kind of relief from his pain and some prodding from his brother to go back to the next meeting to see what might happen, went back the following week. After the meeting was over my dad and his brother went up to the man who had spoken the week before of his broken neck.

My father nervously told him. "Last week, when you said there was someone here that had broken their neck and God wanted to heal it, well that was me!"

When asked if they could pray for him he accepted. While he bowed his head they laid their hands on him and prayed to God to heal his neck. While they prayed for him, my father said it was as if a heavy weight was lifted immediately off his neck, all the pain was miraculously gone and it never came back again in his lifetime. This amazing event in my father's life would begin to shape and form the next phase of accumulated memories for me. Drastic changes were about to come to our family.

We were about to enter a new and different time, and it wasn't going to be the same life as it had been before.

CHAPTER

4

Where previously I had no significant memories of being in church, now I was amassing many. It was also the beginning of a period of years where I would gather different memories and different outlooks about how I would start to view this new environment around me.

After my dad was completely and miraculously healed from all the after effects and pain of his broken neck, I now observed that he started to talk all the time with my Uncle Bill about God. They'd talk about how Jesus could save a man from his sins and make his life whole, giving his life new purpose. Significant and what seemed extraordinarily different talk than their usual banter about how to follow the teachings of Jesus and instead taking the Bible as the word of God in which you could pattern how to live your life. My father started going to those weeknight Bible study meetings and soon after, we as a family no longer attended the Lutheran church; we started attending this nondenominational church that held those Bible study meetings that Dad now attended.

Not long after we made this change to this different church my father would tell everyone how one night while he was fast asleep in his bedroom he awoke to an ethereal light coming from the foot of his bed and saw a hand outstretched to him.

"Come, come!" said a wondrous voice.

He immediately sensed and knew it was Jesus asking him to come to Him.

He leapt out of his bed running towards the light. "I'm coming!"

The light disappeared and never again did Dad feel the same as before. His life from then on was radically changed.

Going forward it seems like we were there at this new church anytime the doors were open. Sunday meetings, weeknight meetings, all different types of fellowship times; there was always something happening at the church, and we as a family would be there. Suddenly my little protected world of mostly my uncle, his family, and ours was being expanded to include all kinds of different people, and different settings.

My father felt convicted to start tithing, giving ten percent of his money to the church. This would mean some financial sacrifice on his part. He got rid of the new expensive family van we had, and bought a cheap old and very small two-door car. For a short time one of Dad's teenage nephews from the states had come to stay with us. We'd all pile into that car, all five of us kids and our older cousin in the back seat and head to church. When we'd bumpily cross the railroad tracks that crossed the highway whoever was sitting on my cousin's lap would usually hit their head on the low roof of the car.

There were a lot of us kids to keep track of at church and this was more apparent when one time we got home from church and realized my youngest sister wasn't with us. Dad got in the car and went back to the church where she had been inadvertently missed while my parents herded us all up. Rain, snow or sunshine we never missed church. My father made it his top priority now in his life to be there and learn all that he could about this new commitment he'd made to God.

Some of the new changes in family life included that my parents were constantly having people from the church over for dinner; company had been a rare occurrence before, so this was new. Our family was also going to other people's houses for dinner too. By now there were six of us kids, soon to be seven and it became a joke at the church that if someone had our large family over for dinner it was really something;

My Journey from Anxiety to Peace

I guess we were a bit of an oddity so many kids and all! My mom was used to cooking for a large family so to add a few more around the family table was no big deal, but that wasn't always the case in reverse situations. Along with being thrust into the new environment of going to people's houses for dinner, it also meant being introduced to different foods that I wasn't used to.

I remember sitting at the table while at a new family friend's house, watching the lady of the house cooking food for us and she was going to serve something I had never heard of, beef stroganoff, well at least not the type we ate. There were containers of sour cream on her counter waiting to go into the simmering beef on her stove. Sour cream was something that we had never tasted before or used in our cooking at home so this made me very leery. I was just sure, positive even, it would be something I would hate; after all it was something new and I was much more comfortable with the same old things. My eyes were as round as saucers as I watched her dump all those containers of sour cream into the pot. I looked at Mom with the question in my eyes. *What will I do?*

Now we were brought up with manners and knew that whatever was placed in front of us we would have to eat, and act like we liked it. It would never do to make a scene and act like we didn't appreciate it; there would surely be consequences to follow later at home if we did something like that. Home might be a different story, but never could we think that disrespect would fly at someone else's house. When it came time to dish up us kids plates, Mom made sure to put just a little bit of the sauce on our plain noodles so we didn't look like we didn't like what she had so graciously cooked for us. We all ate it, every bit of it that was put on our plates.

The fact that my parents heralded from the Midwest and grew up on farms meant that our meals usually consisted of a lot of hearty food. Lots of meat and potatoes, bread, soup, actually rather bland but tasty and filling food, but never anything spicy. Mom cooked what Dad liked and that's what we learned to like. Our vegetable palate was usually corn, green beans, carrots or peas. We had vegetable gardens where Mom and Dad would grow potatoes, green beans, carrots, peas, lettuce and radishes in. There was nothing better when as kids we were allowed to pull up fresh sweet carrots from the garden and wash them off with the garden hose and eat them; or pick the peas off the vine and pop those fresh peas from the shell and stuff them in our mouth. I hated gardening though. I never could stand having dirt on my hands; but regardless of my distaste of it, all of us had to work weeding and harvesting right along with our parents.

My mom, along with us girls help, would can hundreds of quart jars of vegetables for a winter's supply of vegetables that would later go on the family's dinner table. We'd all be sporting orange hands for days from cutting up the hordes of carrots it took to fill those jars. We had a little room in the basement lined with shelves that were filled with all those canned jars of vegetables. Along with vegetables, Mom also canned a lot of salmon from Dad's fishing trips. The pressure cooker on the stove would be used for days in the fall, the constant sound of the hiss from the pressure release valve filling the background noise of our busy household. One of our favorite meals, at least mine, was salmon patties with fresh creamed peas from the garden, and meatballs, man we ate lots and lots of meatballs!

Never was I more thankful though that I had already moved out of the house newly married, when my parents started raising chickens to butcher for meat. The smell of the dank wet feathers as they dunked those dead chickens in a huge pot of boiling water to loosen the feathers for plucking turned my stomach every time I happened to stop by their house while they were butchering their chickens. I would have never been able to eat that chicken if I had been the one to help do the butchering. Dad had raised some pigs for butchering a few times too, but again I was so thankful, this was after I had moved out of my family's house and these things didn't happen while I was still a child growing up in their home.

It would be much later in my childhood when we branched out a bit, deviating from our usual fare. It wasn't until a young couple that my dad had taken in to live with us, that we ever had anything like enchiladas grace our dining table. It was that young lady that taught my mom how to make them and we kids actually liked them, wonder of all wonders.

We started to eat things like tacos, but of course we drowned our meat in a household staple, ketchup. Even things like spaghetti and lasagna were starting to make more frequent visits to our family dining room table, but still no sour cream.

My little world was slowly expanding along with my taste buds.

Confusion,
Change,
&
A Crush

CHAPTER

5

From my corner of the living room where I sat quietly listening, much of the talk I now overheard coming from my dad, uncle, and his new friends centered on God, the church, and learning things from the Bible. There would still be the occasional telling of fishing and hunting stories thrown in, still lots of laughing to be had, but so much more talk about God now. My siblings and I saw changes in my dad we hadn't witnessed before, like him kneeling and praying in church, unashamed tears streaming down his face. He would read and study his Bible with a voracious appetite. He absolutely loved to talk to his friends and ask them questions about God and about what the Bible teaches and how it applied to our lives. I sat and observed it all.

Something else was strangely new and it was hard on our ears because we had to bare a lot of unwanted noise now; Dad had started to teach himself how to play the banjo. The beginnings of which were pretty awful for all of us to have to bear; being that the banjo is a very loud instrument, I just don't think there is any way to play it quietly. Dad eventually played his banjo well enough to join the other musicians that played the music for our singing and worship time during the church services. He joined them up on the platform sitting in the background picking away on his banjo, wearing these silver metal contraptions on the tips of his fingers. Dad sure loved his blue grass and country music, maybe that's why he chose the banjo. He would torture us kids with the style of music he preferred, playing it loudly from all of his old cassettes. To me, the worse it sounded the better he liked it.

For as long as I remember Dad had been a cigarette smoker and I recall hearing him talk with others now about how he didn't think God would want him smoking anymore, so he decided he needed to quit. He told my mother to hide his cigarettes where he couldn't find them. I thought that was kind of silly and strange. *What was she supposed to do if he asked for them when he had a craving, say no to him?* I had visions of Dad getting very angry with Mom if she didn't give him his cigarettes, but thankfully that never did happen. Dad would tell us how hard it was to quit. He was tempted in ways he had never been before, so tempted to pick up a cigarette and start smoking again. Complete strangers would offer him cigarettes or he'd find whole packs of cigarettes mysteriously lying in the streets when he walked his mail delivery route.

"Jesus, please help me! Take these cravings away!" Dad cried out as he sat in his mail truck during his lunch break.

Eventually he did and Dad never touched a cigarette again in his lifetime.

It was then, when he quit smoking that he started the habit of chewing a half stick of Wrigley's spearmint gum. Never a whole, always a half stick. He always carried his gum in his front shirt pocket; I could always see the bulge of it in his left chest pocket. Later in life when he started to have grandkids, he would dole out his half sticks of gum to them. They would line up after church services to get their half stick of Wrigley's spearmint gum from their beloved grandpa. He always made sure to have enough gum on hand for just these occasions; he'd garner a kiss and hug from them before handing them their half stick of gum. Mom bought his gum in bulk, those white gum wrappers forever a fond part of my memories.

I still had my usual hang-ups about being tremendously shy so I didn't make many friends in this new church environment. My comfort zone was always hanging out in the perimeter of the room, watching life around me feeling like I was forever caught in the sidelines entrapped and encased within my box. Always stuck, too timid to every really enter the life around me, instead watching wistfully from the sidelines, fervently wishing I could at least gather up the courage to attempt to try. I was firmly entrenched in my fears of people and too painfully shy to conjure up much of anything that would get me to even remotely change my limited capabilities of how I interacted with people.

So instead of entering the life I wished for, I watched and listened embedded in those sidelines hearing a lot of new things I had not heard before, especially in church. As I sat observing everything in church I would also hear many scriptures from the Bible that were being read and taught on, making me start to form different and new ways of thinking and believing for me. Some parts of my new thinking were good, others not so much. Because I didn't fully understand or comprehend all of the teachings I was hearing, I ended up taking too literally to heart, some of the passages of scriptures and teachings I heard. In my limited understanding this would only serve to hinder and confuse me later on down the road.

There were new experiences, new activities to go to. The church held both winter and summer youth camps that my brother and I would attend. The youth camp was situated outside of Anchorage by a very stale and stagnant lake called Edmonds Lake. During the summer camps when the kids would go out canoeing in the lake, there always managed to be those "accidents" of tipping the canoes in the shallow and stinky green muck that permeated the bottom and the edges of the lake. This always resulted in much hooting and laughter when some unlucky soul would come back up from the bottom of the lake, covered in that disgusting slimy and awful smelly green mud. Luckily since I didn't know how to swim, I never went out in the canoes and avoided being dumped in that nasty foul stuff.

During the winter youth camps, we did a lot of sledding down a long sledding trail someone had bulldozed down the mountain, a sledding trail that was much too straight and steep to be very safe. At the bottom of the hill it dumped out to a big bog that we would go screaming across on the frozen ice on our sleds or big inner tubes. Sometimes some poor unfortunate kid would break their leg or ankle, or get a tooth knocked out. Eventually they had bulldozed in some curves in the sledding hill to slow our sleds down and cut back on the sledding accidents.

It was here at one of these youth camps I had what I would say, my first real encounter and tangible feeling of my own experiencing God. One evening after one of the nightly meetings all of us kids had gathered around and were praying. I noticed that some of the kids around me were quietly praying in a strange way that I later learned was called speaking in tongues. I felt my heart longing. *Whatever these kids have I want it!* Even though I didn't understand it or know what was going on around me, I knew there was a sweet and calming presence around me that I wanted and longed for. Before I knew it, I had my head bowed and my heart was longing, my lips were speaking on their own in a language I didn't know. It was a wonder to me. *God I think I feel your presence, so you must be real.*

It was also at these youth camps that I started to hear about things that were strange and frightening to me. Some of the girls would whisper in the cabins where we slept at night, and talk about demons and Satan. They would tell stories they'd heard, probably gleaned from some adults or other older kids talking. Stories like how they'd heard people talk about how sometimes they would hear toilets flushing in the night even when they knew no one was in the restroom. They'd go on with their other creepy stories that set me to shaking. Upon hearing these things my heart started to fill with terror and fear. I tried in vain not to listen to any more of their strange and scary talk but by then I was convinced. *If God is real so must Satan and his demons be real.*

I was still quite young and the ensuing problem I had, I hadn't yet come to any kind of real understanding of who God really was, and that He overcomes all evil. I never asked anyone the questions that ran through my childish and fearful mind. I was much too timid and strangled in my own fear of people to ask anyone any questions so that I could find the answers I sought, or needed to hear. To do so would mean talking with people, something I found way too hard to do. Confusion over many things started growing within me, compounding my already perverted ways of thinking about myself and the view I had of others, and even worse yet, my views about God and what He thought about me.

Over the next few years I would learn more from listening to the sermons and teaching around me, not always, but sometimes clearing up some of the questions I had. Still I had several fundamental and troubling aspects left in my life. For one, because I was always so down on myself and practically hated everything about myself, especially the anxiety and extreme shyness, I couldn't seem to accept that God could or would truly care all that much about me. Number two, I was still deathly afraid of evil. Satan, demons, hell, anything that portrayed spiritual darkness made me consumed with fear. I hated to watch any movie or TV shows that would depict these sorts of things, finding that my anxiety and fear would quickly start to take hold of me. It would boggle my mind that these kinds of things didn't bother some of the other kids as far as I could tell. There was nothing "make believe" about them, I knew in the depths of my young heart they were real, just as real as I knew God was.

The transformation I was witnessing in my father's life proved that to me, God was very real.

CHAPTER

6

*O*ur family had grown again; there were now seven children in our family. I knew we were considered somewhat of an oddity since not too many families we knew or even saw had anywhere near that many children. It felt normal to me growing up since it's all I had ever known. Being one of that many also meant that sometimes I would be left craving the attention I could have received if there had been less of us kids.

Some of those feelings overtook me, spilling into jealousy over my twin brother and Dad's relationship. My father spent much of his time and attention with my twin brother. He took my brother everywhere with him, his fishing and hunting trips and running his errands. Dad also spent a lot of time teaching him something or another by having my brother work with him on all of his many projects around the house that he always had going on. Like I've said before, these things held more interest for me than the typical "woman" things. Possibly why they held more interest for me is because they involved my father, a person I continually wanted to be with and around.

Around the time my father was healed from the after effects of a broken neck and our family started attending our new church we had moved into a small ranch house in the Sand Lake area of town. Dad started to expand our small three-bedroom house. He framed a bedroom for him and Mom behind the small garage and closed in the outside patio to make a new dining room. With the help of my brothers he dug out half the crawl space under the house, buckets of dirt coming up the hatch door that led to the crawl space till he got enough room down there to move around, and pour a concrete floor. Eventually the room would hold a pool table. It was pretty tight quarters but many games of pool were played down there. My brother moved his bed down there under the steps leading down, I think more to get his own room than anything else. I recall Dad repainting the whole outside of the house with these large stiff paintbrushes a new bright blue color.

Timidly I asked. "Dad can I paint with you?" "I'll do a good job!"

He sighed. "Okay, go get another brush over there next to the other paint can by the side of the house."

Thrilled I quickly ran over and picked up the paintbrush he was talking about and dipped it in the can of paint he gave me to use. I stood next to him and brushed that bright blue paint on the house, tickled as pink that I was spending time with Dad doing what was considered more one of the boys' chores.

The birth order in our family had been, girl, boy, girl, boy all the way down the line. Chores and duties in our house were broken up by what were the girls' chores were and what the boys' chores were. We girls got the chores that were considered the more womanly things: cooking, cleaning and taking care of the little ones. My brothers took out the trash and did the yard work and of course worked with my Dad on all the many projects he always had going on. Something that in my mind the boys should enjoy because it meant you were with Dad. *So what if it was work!*

I struggled with envy because the boys' adventures included getting to go on the many fishing and hunting trips with Dad, and be involved in all the planning that went along with that. We girls stayed home with Mom who didn't seem to ever go anywhere near as exciting as the boys, because she didn't drive. It was probably due to more of a generational thing because in much later years my Dad started taking my younger sister on his hunting and fishing trips, but by then I was grown, married, and had moved out of the house.

Just listening to the boys tell their stories of being on boats going down rivers or riding on those swamp buggies sounded like so much fun. Their laughter and jokes about things that would happen on those trips and of course all the subsequent bragging on who caught the biggest fish or who shot the biggest moose, just made it seem like I had to be missing out on something.

Although I longed for these adventures as a child, I might not have been able to bring myself to actually go if the opportunity had arisen. The men's stories of hearing bears in the night when they retold their many hunting stories or of seeing bears in the rivers when they fished had already scared me enough. I wanted to cover my ears when they told those stories. I wasn't too keen on going anywhere near the woods, I was pretty sure there would probably be bears around that would want to chase me down and eat me and I never wanted to encounter one!

It was somewhere in this time frame where I remember having my first good memory thinking I had finally managed to please my father and capture some of my much-coveted Dad's attention. I'm sure it wasn't that I didn't please him, or he intentionally didn't give me all the attention I craved; I just had a very twisted and illogical idea that I wasn't worth much attention. *Nothing I do really stands out to warrant it, does it?* I mean after all I was quiet, I tried hard not to be observed or noticed, always sitting in the corner absorbed within the confines of my box. My thoughts had already been formed at a young age to have that kind of negative bend to them.

But there was this time when just a look from my dad meant the world to me. While cleaning up the kitchen one evening after dinner I was doing the dishes and putting away the dry pots and pans. As I bent over putting the pans in the lower cupboard where they belonged I heard my mother bring my father over.

She whispered, pointing at me. "Look at what a good job she's doing".

Dad beamed. "Yes, she is!"

A Simple Extraordinary Life

They didn't think I heard or saw either of them but when I saw Dad grin and get a look in his eye that said he was pretty pleased, I was thrilled. It was just a little thing, but it would speak volumes into what I thought would make me a good girl, or later on a virtuous woman, or a good wife.

I took notice how well my mom took care of my dad. She was always cooking and cleaning. He bragged on her abilities to others. He loved a clean house and loved her cooking, especially her homemade apple pies. That seemed to be the best thing he would brag about, those apple pies. If Mom wanted to do something special for Dad, it was make him an apple pie. Dad's eyes would twinkle in delight at mom when he saw an apple pie sitting on the counter cooling the lingering scent of cinnamon still in the air. Mom was speaking his love language. It didn't hurt any that we got to eat them too; they were delicious! Mom always got up in the morning to get Dad off to work, make his coffee and cook his breakfast and pack him a lunch. If he was going on a fishing or hunting trip she would prepare all the meals and pack them for the group. She always kept his shirts ironed, his uniforms for the post office cleaned and looking sharp. She mended our clothes, kept us kids clean and kept the laundry done. She always worked hard, and my dad appreciated all of it, of that I had no doubt.

Dad couldn't properly say Mom's given name Eleanore, instead saying Elnore. He always had a hard time pronouncing certain words and sounds but his pronouncing of my mother's name was like hearing his pet name for her. Though to me my parents seemed like opposites in a lot of ways, I knew dad loved her very much.

It was a lot of hard work for my mom having that many children, and the laundry was never ending! Long before there was such a thing as a steam iron I can remember Mom setting up the ironing board and sprinkling the wrinkled clothes with water from an old glass bottle that had a sprinkler top , roll them up and set them aside before she would then start the tedious process of ironing them piece by piece. Later on when I got old enough to handle the iron I got the dreaded pleasure of that chore. I never liked ironing much and when I got older and had my own household and husband, it didn't bother me too much if my husband had to iron his own shirt once in a while. Of course I mostly did it because I would feel guilty that I wasn't taking proper care of him, but later on I learned the neat trick of throwing the wrinkled clothes back in the dryer with a wet washcloth for a few minutes to get the wrinkles out. I still despise ironing.

Mom's Saturday nights always consisted of getting everyone bathed, clean pajamas donned, our ears cleaned and our fingernails trimmed. Dad would help; we'd line up waiting our turn to get our fingernails clipped by him. Sunday morning church clothes were laid out, and we girls would sometimes get our hair put up in those spongy pink rollers you had to try to sleep on all night long just so you could have curly hair in the morning. We didn't have much in the way of nice things but we always looked as presentable as possible. Dad took pride in his large brood. His quiver was full, very full and he was teased about it, but I could always tell Dad was proud about it. He loved us all very much.

Snippets of all these memories would play into what kind of a young wife and mother I would be. I was becoming quite proficient, even at a young age at all those "woman" duties, cooking and cleaning and I could do them well. So well that while barely a teenager my mom decided she could put me completely in charge of the household while she left for a week and went one summer to a church held children's camp, and become a camp counselor for the week. There were eight of us kids now, mom having given birth two years before to their last child. Seven siblings and my father would be under my care. I cooked all the meals, cleaned the house, did the laundry and watched my younger brothers and sisters. The heaviest responsibility that made me pretty nervous was making sure my dad got up to go to work at his job he still held at the post office. Since Dad had never been able to hear an alarm clock, I had to set my alarm, get up and then go wake Dad up.

Tentatively I stood at his bedroom door listening to the loud snores behind it. I stood there for a minute, nervous about waking my father up. Turning the knob I tiptoed over to the form that was my sleeping father debating just how to wake him. Feeling awkward about the whole thing I finally just reached out and touched his arm beneath the sleeve of his white t-shirt, lightly shaking it.

"Dad, Dad it's time to get up." I softly whispered, my voice sounding to my ears like an awkward intrusion.

He rolled over blankly staring at me at first before he answered. "Oh, ah - okay."

I crept back out of his bedroom hoping he'd crawl out of bed and not fall back asleep. Thankfully he would get out of bed much easier for me than he would for my mom.

While Dad was getting ready for work I would make a sack lunch for him, brew the coffee to fill his large metal thermos he took to work with him, to which I would add his required "just a smidgen of sugar," hoping I got the amount precisely right. Next was to make his usual breakfast of two slices of toast with strawberry jelly that he would carry out the front door with him on a small plate with his thermos of coffee tucked under his arm. Hearing him walk down the front steps on his way to work, relief crossed my face that I hadn't blundered by burning his toast or forgetting something I was supposed to do for him. By now usually one or more of my siblings would wake up and my day of cooking, babysitting, and cleaning would begin.

I felt strung out trying to keep up with my youngest brother who was a very busy and active toddler. I would get so frustrated trying to keep track of him while I worked on the household chores. He could and would disappear in the blink of an eye. I'd look out the window and there he'd be on his little red tricycle down by the busy highway at the bottom of the hill from our house. Frantically I'd drop everything and run down the hill after him before he got run over by the traffic, only to have him turn around and do it again later. Afraid of how much trouble I'd be in if anything was to happen to him while in my charge, by the second and third time he'd done this stunt I picked up a switch from the side of the road and paddled his bottom on the way back up the hill hoping I could get across to him not to scare me so by taking off again.

"Don't do that again!" "You have to stay by the house!" I said with exasperated punctuation because he didn't seem to be listening to me. My face turned red. "Stay- Up- Here!" "If you go down to the highway again you're going to have to stay in the house for the rest of the day!"

My Journey from Anxiety to Peace

By late afternoon already feeling tired and drained, dinner had to be made and I always made sure to make something my father would like. After dinner it would be time to wash the enormous amount of dishes it takes to cook and feed that large amount of people. Next it would be time to make sure the little ones had baths to wash all the summer dirt off them and then put them to bed. After all that I would then fall into bed myself, exhausted.

I pulled up my covers and sighed. *This is going to be a very long week!*

I was ever so thankful for Friday when my mom came home.

Given the choice of what chore I could choose it was always to cook. For some reason I liked to cook. That chore would be the one I would choose, since the one who did the cooking didn't have to do the dishes. Washing the dishes was the other kitchen chore we could choose and I didn't like it near as well as being creative and learning how to cook different things. Dirty dishes were always the same thing, day in and day out. Sometimes though, my father didn't always appreciate my cooking endeavors and trying out new recipes.

Dad was a creature of habit; he liked the same things cooked the same way every time. I remember one time after perusing through the Better Homes and Garden cookbook, breading the pork chops Mom had left out for dinner with crushed saltine crackers before frying them. When we sat down to dinner he rudely announced to Mom that I had ruined the pork chops, because there was no gravy to go with them. Well, without his meaning to, he had hurt my feelings and I ran to my room crying my eyes out.

"FRANKLIN!" my mom loudly exclaimed.

That was how she talked to my dad when she thought he had stepped over the line or done something she didn't approve of.

"What?" he looked at her trying to play innocent.

Poor Dad, he could hardly figure out what he had done, why I would be so upset. I guess he thought he was just making an obvious statement. He came to my bedroom and tried to apologize, but by then it was too

61

late, I couldn't stop crying because no one could hurt my feelings more than him. I had a very sensitive disposition when it came to my father; I so wanted to please him. It wouldn't be the first or the last time either that my feelings would be crushed by him.

Dad had gone fishing with my brothers and they brought home a bunch of fish that needed to be cleaned and filleted. I was already struggling with jealously that I never got to go with him on these excursions. We all gathered around the newspaper covered dining room table to clean fish. Chewing on my bottom lip in concentration I tried my best to learn how to filet the fish so Dad would be proud of me. I was making a huge mess of my fish. Dad pointed it out to me that I was ruining the meat and just like that, there I went again, tears and torrents of sobbing, shoving off my chair and running off to my room crying so upset that I couldn't seem to do anything right. My dad would try to make up with me but I was too upset. Darn it I thought. *I was trying my hardest to be as good as my brothers and Dad were at filleting fish!* My father never knew quite what to do with me and my uncontrollable crying fits. I could tell it made him uncomfortable but regardless he always tried to assure me he loved me. Still, I had this innate need to please him.

That childhood need to please and try to always do my best controlled me.

Later as an adult what I thought was the right way to run a household would later become almost an obsession with me. Clean and orderly houses, meals on the table, kids watched after, laundry always done. Rarely did I take the time to just play with my children, my anxious thoughts kept me from enjoying them like I should. *I must cook, clean, work, be doing something that I deem productive or I am being lazy.* Obsessed and uptight I didn't know how to relax, my mind always in turmoil. I would constantly pick up my children's toys all day long because it would drive me crazy insane to have things out of order. Multi-tasking came easily for me, baking pies while cleaning the house top to bottom, laundry going all the while watching my children was normal for me and I couldn't understand other women who struggled with doing more than one thing at once.

My Journey from Anxiety to Peace

If I couldn't control what was going on deep inside me with my constant anxiety and fears and hidden wounds, maybe I could control things on the outside around me to make me feel better. I couldn't, just couldn't let my kids have wax left in their ears or have dirty and long fingernails, or a house that was out of order. I was obsessive about it and heaven help my children, if they walked by me and I noticed wax in their ears! Immediately I would take to them with a Q-tip or my fingernail and get rid of that nasty stuff. I constantly hounded them about cutting their fingernails and combing their hair or cleaning their rooms.

I religiously made up my bed every morning or it would make me anxious to see it unmade. It was disorder, and I didn't like disorder. My children's unmade beds were a sore point with me. They saw no use to having their beds made since they were just going to crawl back in them every night, so what was the point? It was a chore getting them to make their beds so eventually I had to let it go; but I could only handle it by keeping their doors closed so I didn't have to see their messy unmade beds. Our childhood experiences and how we perceive things can shape much of whom we become as adults. I was no exception. If there is one regret I have now it's that I couldn't find it within me to ease up, relax and take the time to spend with my children instead of always worrying about having an immaculate house.

I felt uptight, tense and helpless to stop the insanity that would overtake me. My husband would be incensed with me at times because of my obsessions. If dinner was over and I was doing the dishes I would hover over him, ready to take that glass he was still drinking from away the second he took his last swallow, so I could wash it.

"You done yet with that glass?" I asked him annoyed.

"No, give me a minute!"

Impatience was eating at me as I loudly sighed. "But I'm washing the dishes now!"

He looked irritated at me. "I'll bring it in to the kitchen when I'm done!"

"But I'll be finished with the dishes before you do that!" perturbed that a lone glass would be sitting dirty in the sink.

A Simple Extraordinary Life

At least now many years later we can laugh about it; I've learned to leave his glass alone, and a few dirty glasses in the sink doesn't drive me quite over the edge the way it used to. I still tend to have obsessive tendencies but they have lessened quite a bit. Towels need to be hung straight, pillows on the couch just so. Too many things out of place, too much clutter and I find myself getting uptight and have to talk myself down, telling myself it's okay, a little disorder is okay. I'm sure you get the drift about how these obsessions could cause me anxiety. I've learned to just accept this about myself and just straighten things up. I go over and straighten that towel up that hubby just hung up, shake my head and smile about it, and feel better that I've established a more peaceful order around me.

Anxiety and panic would so easily overtake me and be something I would constantly deal with much of my life. One such memory comes to mind. I was a young mother out shopping one day at a small indoor mall in town. Having finished my shopping I exited the large doors and left the mall. Walking out to the parking lot I couldn't find my car in the place I was sure I had parked. I started to panic, wildly looking around, sudden fear overtaking me. Sure that someone had stolen my car, I took out my phone to call my husband who was at work. I was in the habit of calling him at work one to two times every day, but in my state of panic I couldn't remember his work phone number. All those old fears of being left alone at school, wondering how I was to get home, came flooding back.

Tears stung my eyes. *Why can't I remember that stupid phone number?* I bit my lip as I racked my brain trying to remember. *How dumb am I? I know that number; I call it every day!* Panicking as I wildly looked around my heart pounding violently. *Where is my car?* I went back into the mall and tried to calm myself and stop my tears.

Eventually I managed after many errant tries to get the right combination of numbers right and get a call through to my husband. In tears I told him what had happened, that I couldn't find my car.

"Someone must have stolen it!" my anxiety making my voice shrill.

Calmly he asked me, "You're sure that is where you parked it?"

"Yes, ah I think so." I answered him as I tried to back track in my mind. "I'm pretty sure it is."

Talking to him helped soothe my anxiety and I realized, I had come out the wrong door; there my car was across the parking lot right where I had left it. On my way home from the mall I stopped at a different store and bought myself an address book that I could always carry around in my purse with every one's phone numbers and addresses. In the future I had to use it many times. I still to this day have trouble if I have to think quickly, or someone asks me my phone number. Even with pizza deliveries I'll feel foolish when I have to put them on hold so I can get out my address book and give them my correct address.

These days I have less episodes of this kind of panic but back then it was a regular occurrence, and in my childhood panic was my constant friend.

CHAPTER

7

Much of who I had become as an adult and what I was like go back to things that either traumatized me or left wounds and scars upon my heart as a child. By never dealing with these things or letting them go, they instead compounded my already polluted thinking.

After a few years of attendance at our family's new church, I would have one of those traumatic experiences that is still very vivid in my memory. Outside forces were hard at work wanting me to remain in mute silence, kept locked up in a sea of suffering and fear, crippling me even more than where I already was. I descended into an even further downward spiral of what was a strangling and heavy silence of my voice. The weight I carried of constant anxiety, doubt and fear only got worse.

Somewhere around the end of grade school near the first few years of being in our new church I was awakened during the night to something I'll never forget. I shared a bedroom with one of my sisters. We slept on bunk beds, me on the top bunk, my sister on the lower bunk. Dead asleep one night I was suddenly awakened to a sinister laughing noise that resonated from somewhere down the hallway, its eerie sound wafting into my bedroom. Immediately, even as a child I knew that I sensed an evil presence in my bedroom. Again, I heard that awful noise. *Where...Where is that coming from?* Fearfully looking around I glanced out our open bedroom door down the hall and saw what I can only describe as a floating, screeching, hideous thing, which appeared to me, to be carrying what seemed to be some kind of thick blanket.

Awful terrifying noises were coming from it. I found myself frozen, caught in an awful and indescribable fear while it cackled and laughed with a menacing sound. It looked at me and came running towards me, throwing that blanket at me and then ran back down the hall screeching its horrible laugh. I had a very real, physical sensation of a heavy weight come over me. Then this thing, this apparition would come running back, throw that blanket on me and run back away again, laughing and screeching back down the hallway. I was wide-awake and consumed in shaking fear. My breath caught in my throat, I couldn't seem to make a sound while it would come back and throw this thing over me, again and again. The weight was getting heavier and heavier, suffocating me with this awful feeling.

My heart was racing, I couldn't believe my sister heard none of this and was sleeping right through all of it. I had heard enough in church to know there was good and evil. This was pure evil what was happening and what I was seeing and feeling. In my limited knowledge I kept thinking, if I can just say the name of Jesus, I could make it go away. I tried over and over to emit some kind of noise. *Say the name of Jesus*, but I couldn't find my voice. My next thought was I need to get to Dad; but he was asleep in his bedroom. This meant I would have to go down the hall to get to him. I lay there in bed sweating profusely, waiting for a long time between appearances of this creature to get up the courage to get to my father.

Finally, there seemed to be a longer pause between assaults. Leaping from my bed my heart wildly pounding, I closed my eyes and ran as fast as I could in complete fear that I would run head first into this thing, this evil, evil thing. I barged into my parents' bedroom, crying and trembling, shaking in fear, waking them up. I'm not sure what I told my father had happened, but I remember him praying with me and just being in Dad's presence calmed me enough that I later returned to bed. I didn't see that creature again that night.

This was a pivotal and crucial time in my life. Something happened during that experience. Battered and harassed with an evil force that wished me to remain in the throes of silence and anxiety. Forces that wanted me to continue to accept lies about myself, heap even more wounds that I would hold close to the very core of my being and continue to skew my thinking, putting blinders on my eyes and robbing me of ever having any kind of peace.

You see the worst pain and deepest wound I had yet to experience was coming, not far over the horizon.

CHAPTER

8

My father and mother continued to be very involved in the church. Much of our family life centered on it. My dad continued to attend the church's evening Bible classes and somewhere between four to five years of constant attendance at this church he came home one day, and dropped a bombshell.

"I think God wants me to become a pastor." Dad said to us while we all looked at him in shock, question marks in our eyes.

This was a huge surprise and sudden shock to us all, our father a pastor? Immediately we peppered him with our questions speaking over top of each other.

"When Dad?" "When?"

"Dad where are we going to go to?" my brother asked.

"What…what church?" more than one of us asked.

How is this possible, my father? Places were mentioned that he might go to pastor at, places like the villages of Bethel or Nome. I was aghast at the idea he might uproot us and take us to a faraway native village. *Those places are dark and cold places and way up north, I think we would be about the only white people there!* Of course I had no idea what they were really like, but this is what I was sure of. I didn't like that idea at all, and panic was setting in at what possible changes were coming. Changes I was sure not to like.

Paramount to some of my new fears and high on my ever increasing list of fears is that I also had been hearing a lot of scripture and teaching in the past few years about what the Bible said about leaders in the church; instructions about government structure within the church and requirements of its elders and pastors. The one that resounded in my head the most was that elders and pastors were to have their children in order. This struck a new kind of fear in me. *How am I ever to live up to the expectations that people are going to expect of me?* I was sure now that Dad was going to become a pastor, everyone's eyes were going to be watching me and this made me extremely nervous and uncomfortable. My mind whirled, how was this shy and awkward girl ever going to survive under that kind of scrutiny? I wanted to find a rock, crawl under it and hide from the kind of upcoming and unwanted examination I was sure I would endure.

By now I had entered junior high. Leaving Sand Lake Elementary to go to Mears Junior-High School for the seventh grade was its own special kind of hell for me. Naïve as I was, I was in shock, they actually had a smoking lounge for the students inside the school atrium that was used by both the junior high and high school students. Having just left from a pretty mild grade school it was a jolt to my senses, boys and girls making out in the hallways and kids using rampant profanity. I felt very much out of place and it was hard for me to understand this new world of junior high.

Having grown up pretty sheltered, my social times centered on the church and its functions so pretty much the only people I was ever around were Christians or *church* people. Being thrust into this new and scary environment only served to heighten my anxieties. Lunch break was the worst. The school cafeteria was always busy with swarms of students. Because there were never any empty tables I could go sit at by myself and try to stay invisible, and since I didn't have any friends to join, I would stand in the perimeter of the room trying to covertly eat my sack lunch, hopefully without being noticed.

My Journey from Anxiety to Peace

To add even more fuel to the growing fire within me, shoving me even further into self-doubt, I was very late developing, every young girl's nightmare. It only served to humiliate me further by having one of our neighbor's daughters, who was my age, hand me a bag of her training bras that she had long outgrown, embarrassed because I was nowhere near even needing one yet. I spent most of the next years of my school life every day no matter the temperature, always wearing a coat. It rarely came off. It was my security blanket that helped me hide my insecurities. Getting wrapped up in my lack of self-confidence and fast becoming overly concerned with material things that I thought would make me more likeable became a new issue for me.

Since we were a large family only relying on my father's income there usually wasn't much extra spending on frivolous things. Our clothes would be a lot of hand-me-downs or very limited. For a budding teenage girl who now felt the pressure that maybe she wasn't near as pretty as all the other girls, or she didn't have all the choices in clothing or the newest trend in clothing made me want to withdraw into my shell even more. From the time I started earning my own money babysitting, I always spent it on clothes.

My new purchases were very important to me. No more did this ring true when once I came home from church to find my newly purchased clothes missing.

I frantically looked around my room extremely upset. *Where are my new clothes?* Devastation filled my thoughts. *I bought those clothes with my own money!*

It was later discovered that a young girl from church had come up to our house, which was next door to the church at that time and had come into my bedroom and had taken my new clothes where they lay, neatly folded up on a chair next to my bed. I felt bad for the girl, she had even less than I did, but that didn't stop me from being angry about it. Somehow my parents made sure my new clothes were returned to me. From then on I made sure not to leave my prized possessions out in plain sight again. This new obsession on material things had started a few years earlier.

A Simple Extraordinary Life

There was one other family at the church we attended that was like our family, they too had a lot of children, the associate pastor's family. They had several girls around my age. All the girls at church started talking about an upcoming youth function where everyone that was going would be dressing up for the event. I knew that the associate pastor's girls along with many other girls from the church were going to this function. It was going to be a fancy affair, at a fancy place and serve a fancy dinner. The pastor's girls were going to get their hair done at a salon for the event. All the pastor's girls were getting new dresses and shoes, just like every other girl that planned on attending. *Every girl but me!* Someone gave my mother a handed down frilly chiffon dress for me to wear, it was pale pink.

Mom handed me the dress. "Here try this on."

I drug my feet as I shuffled to my room to try that dreaded frilly thing on.

"Come out here and let me see it!" yelled my mother.

I felt extremely awkward as I hesitantly walked into the living room so she could see me.

"I think it looks nice!" my mother exclaimed.

I shrugged my shoulders knowing it wouldn't matter if I liked it or not, it was the only choice I had to wear. Pink was a color I despised and the dress was way too frilly for my tastes.

"Hold still!" mom said as she tried to pull up my hair into a ponytail on top of my head. She wrapped pieces of my ponytail into curls that she pinned to my scalp. Mom was trying the best she could to put my hair up in a fancy do before I went and put on that fluffy pink dress the night of the event.

Since I had no good dress shoes, my mom had scraped up enough money to buy me a pair of white lace up canvas tennis shoes. Just the idea of going to this thing was terrifying to me. I think maybe my parents were making me go.

My cheeks were enflamed in embarrassment all night, feeling horribly awkward in my frilly pink dress. *If I can just sink as far into my chair as I can, maybe I won't be noticed.* I sulked in my chair, envious of everyone else, their easy laughter, and the girls that could seem to attract the boys; jealousy fairly oozing from my pores as I sat there, hating myself. *I can't wait for this evening to be over!* It was sheer torture sitting there waiting for it to end when one of the older male youth leaders had come over to me.

"You sure look nice tonight!" he said.

I felt he was just taking pity on me and tried to sink even farther into my chair, willing this horrid evening to come to an end. No way did I believe him or think he might have been genuine with his compliments. From then on I always wanted something new to wear for special events or holidays, I wanted to be like everyone else who I envied.

Easter Sunday, May 24, 1970, I was twelve years old and at the end of my seventh grade school year, the day my father became an ordained pastor through the church we attended. I wasn't young enough to just easily adapt to this new change and wasn't old enough to have the maturity to work through this new change without having some consequences. These changes would affect my future outlook and many myriad responses and feelings I would have towards people, especially people from the church.

The church Dad was ordained from had started to what they called "plant" other offshoot congregations in other areas of the state. Eventually they would also plant churches out of state too. There was one such small congregation in an area called Peters Creek, which was about a forty-minute drive away from Anchorage. In the beginning this small congregation met in a Quonset hut that was formally an old military building that had been moved onto the church property to be used for them to meet in. There really wasn't much in Peters Creek but a gas station and a few scattered houses. You could go to another small community that was in between there and Anchorage, Eagle River and get groceries at the only grocery store there. We visited this church in Peters Creek a few times and soon, I was to find out why.

My father had told his pastor he felt called to go pastor this church in Peters Creek. Since it already had a pastor they both agreed to keep it between themselves and pray about it. Not much time had passed after their initial conversation when the current pastor at Peters Creek came and told Dad's pastor that he felt he was to turn his church over to my father.

By this time the congregation in Peters Creek had built a small concrete block building that was pretty dark and dingy, much of it not yet finished. Our family visited this church in that little block building. The interior walls had clear visqueen sheeting covering up the pink insulation stuffed between the studs of the walls. Bare light bulbs that didn't give off near enough light hung from sagging electrical wires from the ceiling, the bathroom nothing but a porta-potty in a room that had no door, just a heavy curtain for privacy. Nothing was finished or painted, including the outside of the building. It had a furnace that blew black soot all over the few rows of chairs in the room for the congregation to sit in. The atmosphere seemed gloomy and depressing to me. I could hardly believe it. *This is where Dad is taking us to pastor at?*

I must confess the truth here. I didn't get all that upset since it was sounding and looking so much better than a village in the remote parts of Alaska. I was concerned about the bathroom situation though, that I remember well. My youngest sister at the time was near two years of age and still in diapers. One service while we were visiting my sister got restless.

Mom handed me my young sister. "Terry take your sister up to the neighbor's house and watch her there till the service is over."

Dutifully I answered her. "Okay mom."

I grabbed my sister's pudgy hand and led her outside into the sunshine, then hoisted her up on my hip and headed to the neighbor's house. It was a young couple's place that came to the church where I was to go. It just so happened when I nervously stepped into the house it surprised me to see there was a young teenage boy there also watching that couple's young child.

My poor sister's cloth diaper was sagging, needing desperately to be changed, but I was too embarrassed to do that in front of this boy. I also really needed to use the restroom, another thing I was too embarrassed to do, use these strangers' restroom. *I am not doing that, especially in front of this cute boy!* I felt so awkward and tongue-tied the entire time around him so I was relieved when the church service was finally over. I still needed to pee but there was no way I was going to use that porta-potty at the church in a room that had no locking door! I was miserable; my embarrassment had resulted in a very long drive back home to Anchorage for myself, and fairly certain that I might just possibly burst.

My mind was whirling, thinking hard during that long drive home about this new place we were moving to. The best part of it I could see, there was a family there already a part of the congregation with a boy my age that had caught my eye, that cute boy up at the house where I had been watching my little sister, and I was fast developing a crush on him. That little fact I kept a tightly guarded secret! *Maybe this new move wasn't going to be that bad after all.*

At a rather fast pace things started to fall into place for us to make the move to Peters Creek. My parents sold their house in Sand Lake and a double wide trailer was bought to be moved onto the church property for a parsonage. We all thought it was pretty nice since it was all brand new and filled with avocado green and gold furnishings, which made it seem pretty fancy and elegant at the time. My dad and brothers spent the summer between my seventh and eighth grade year clearing land and building a cement block foundation to put the trailer on that would eventually get finished out as a day light basement; until that happened we had a three bedroom house, all the boys in one room and all us girls in the other.

That summer we made the move from Anchorage to Peters Creek. My mother was pregnant with her eighth child. Adding our large family to this small congregation took the numbers up to about thirty-five, forty people. My father took over pastoring the church and immediately started fixing up the place.

It was us kids' duty to go down and dust the furnace soot from the chairs before every service so people wouldn't get their pants and dresses dirty. We didn't like much going down there; it always seemed dark and creepy until Dad started making progress on fixing the place up. The best improvements made to the place were real flushing toilets, with a boys' and girls' bathroom that had actual locking doors on the bathrooms. Dad hung sheetrock, installed bright fluorescent lights, painted the inside walls white and the brick exterior blue. Eventually we got a new furnace that didn't blow black soot all over.

It was sure different getting used to my father being the one at the front of the church congregation conducting services. He was song leader, gave the announcements, led us all in prayer, and preached the sermon; he did everything. I can still see him in my mind's eye, standing up there behind the small podium with his dark hair that he wore with a curvy wave, a suit on, usually with a bolo tie and wearing his cowboy boots. He would open his Bible that had many highlighted verses from doing his studies and take out his handwritten notes he used to preach from. I imagine I can smell the strong scent from the Old Spice cologne that he always wore, wafting through the air towards the chairs that the small congregation sat in. My father who got his GED while in the military because he had never finished high school had become the great student of his Bible, ready to lay down his life and humbly lead us all. I was in awe of him.

Dad still held his job with the United States Postal Service commuting to Anchorage during his first few years of pastoring. He wanted to make sure the small congregation could afford to pay his salary before he quit his postal job. Dad worked hard, essentially two jobs. One of which besides pastoring his flock included fixing up the church building, which was no small task. He was always doing continued maintenance and janitorial duties on the building and the surrounding church property. This would also include the parking lots, which he kept graded smooth in the spring through fall, and in the winter he would plow the snow from the driveways and church parking lot.

He was always sweeping the sidewalks to the building.

"It's important to keep the sidewalks clean for the people who come to church." Dad said looking at us and pointing out a lesson he'd hope we'd understand.

This included dutifully clearing the snow and ice from them in the winter months. Nothing was ever beneath him to do; he did it gratefully and cheerfully. Cleaning up the building after services and picking up the discarded bulletins off the floor he would always joke with us giving us more of his wisdom.

As Dad bent over picking up the trash and bulletins off the floor and chairs he grinned at us while he worked. "If there are no pigs in the pig pen then the stalls would be clean!"

We'd snicker with the idea he had just called the people pigs, but we knew that's not what he meant. He was quoting scripture.

When the congregation grew and we needed more room he did much of the physical work on all the new building additions. He spent hours and hours of his time building oak church pews for the new auditorium. Mom and some other ladies from the church upholstered them in a light blue fabric. Always without grumbling and a smile upon his face he looked out for what was in the best interest for the church and its people, sacrificing much and never making much more than a meager salary.

While Dad was still working at the post office he started to share his beliefs, especially with a particular younger coworker about Jesus. He invited his coworker to come to church, and told him what time the service would be on Sunday at Peters Creek Chapel. When his coworker came visiting church one Sunday and saw my Dad leading the music he was surprised; but nothing prepared him for his astonishment when my dad put down his banjo, took out his Bible and started to preach. My father had never once told him that he was pastor of the church. His coworker and wife would soon accept Jesus into their lives and join our congregation. Soon after, they decided to move from Anchorage to Peters Creek. While waiting for their new single wide trailer to be delivered and set up that following spring, he and his wife moved in with our family at the invitation to do so from our Dad. They would have their first child while living with us.

They would be just one of the many families or single people my father eventually would take into his home for extended periods of time.

CHAPTER

9

*I*t was humble beginnings; the start of my father's pastoring at this little church we now as a family were part of.

Music at our little church consisted of my father on the banjo and my twin brother on the organ. As I sang along to the song my father was leading I had my own thoughts about the music. *This isn't exactly the best sound!*

My brother had been pretty much forced to learn to play that instrument much to his own chagrin. It had started out first that it was I who was to learn how to play the organ or piano, long before our family came out to Peters Creek to live. While we were going to the church in Anchorage the lady at our church who was the piano player would come to our house and give me lessons. I had learned a few hymns and songs that I could barely play, reading the music from a learner's piano book. One weekend my dad was invited to go preach by his good friend at the church that his friend pastored in Kenai, a town about four hours away. My father for some reason got it in his head that it would be a good idea to have me play my few songs I had learned. Our family would make the drive to Kenai, spend the night and Dad would preach on that Sunday. Dad told me to pack my music book.

I got so agitated and extremely worried. There was no way I would ever get up in front of that church and try to play.

I cried and begged my father. "Please Dad, I don't want to!" I was just sick to my stomach in fear.

He sternly told me. "Bring your book, you're going to play."

No amount of pleading, begging or crying was changing his mind. We loaded up in the family van and started the drive to Kenai. My mind whirled in panic, how was I ever going to get out of this. I was afraid to go against my father's wishes but I also knew I would never, ever get up in front of them and play. I knew deep down I would defy him out of sheer anxiety and I had bad visions of how this was going to play out. Sitting in the backseat of the van I had myself so worked up in panic I thought I was going to throw up for sure, my stomach churning as it was. But providence smiled down on me. There, going through the mountain pass on our way to Kenai we drove into a bad snowstorm. Dad had to turn the car around and take us back home. I was so overcome in relief, thankful that I had been spared for what was sure to have become an ugly situation.

My lessons continued. Most of the church music they played and sang at church had no written music and was played by ear. Trying hard, my music teacher tried to teach me to play by ear but I didn't have the natural ability to play anything by ear. I knew when I played a bad note, that much was obvious, but I had no idea of where to go, what note to play from there. One day my music teacher was getting pretty frustrated with me when my twin brother happened to walk by, she pulled him down to the bench and had him try. It was soon apparent he had that natural gifting. My music lessons went by the wayside, which was just fine with me! My brother though, became the new guinea pig for music lessons. Our pastor played the accordion and the organ and since my father greatly admired and revered him I guess that made him think it would be a very spectacular idea to have my brother learn both of those instruments.

Dad and his pastor had become best friends that would last a lifetime. Dad considered it a great privilege to take him fishing, always supplying all the poles, gear, boat, and even Mom's packed lunches. Later on in years they would even take vacations together along with their wives. His pastor had a great sense of humor and they loved to tell jokes together and laugh and laugh. Even though in many ways they were quite different from each other he was one of my father's most treasured friends.

The associate pastor also became one of my father's lifelong best friends and one of his hunting and fishing buddies. Their shared hunting trips decreased in the years following our move to Peters Creek where Dad had a lot of other new hunting buddies, one of which, would become the father-in-law to two of my siblings. In successive years because most of us kids would find our spouses from the families that attended our church, there was a lot of joking that would go around how intermarried we were. It was a wonderful way I thought to live your life, everyone felt connected to each other and lots of love was shared among us.

Somehow this friendship between my dad and his pastor must have been an influence to my father's way of thinking when it came to what instrument he thought my brother should play. I do remember many battles between my father and brother getting him to practice his instrument, especially the accordion. Eventually he was able to lay that aside and concentrate on the organ. He actually was pretty good at playing the organ but what young teenager would willingly choose that instrument? He sure didn't, so much later on he would teach himself to play the guitar. So there in our humble beginnings was my brother, a very young teen playing the organ alongside my dad strumming his banjo in front of the congregation, making what was supposed to be, a joyful noise unto the Lord. *Man I am so glad it isn't me who has to be up there!*

This new move our family made to Peters Creek would also mean a new school for me as I entered the eighth grade. I felt slightly a little more at ease than I did the prior year because this new school would be much smaller than the previous one I had attended. Still though, I struggled with being anxiety ridden most of the time.

It was sometime during this next year or so while barely at the cusp of entering young womanhood at the tender age of about 14, the memory of the hardest and most painful thing I would endure would take place, leaving its scars that would haunt me for many long years to come.

The Dirty
Looking Glass

CHAPTER

10

$\mathcal{A}$fter I had finished out my seventh grade school year that gave me nothing but nightmares, it was refreshing to be away from all that everyday pressure and enjoy what was a rather blissful summer in this new place we had moved to.

My brothers, sisters and I spent a lot of time outdoors exploring our new surroundings. There happened to be a state campground nearby, next to a creek adeptly named Peters Creek where we would take walks to, having discovered trails through the woods that led to a canyon upriver. One afternoon my parents left me in charge of my siblings while they went to town to do some shopping.

"Come with me, I want to walk up to the canyon" My twin brother asked me.

"No, I can't I'm supposed to be watching the kids!"

"Come on, we'll be back before mom and dad get home, they can watch themselves!" he tried to assure me.

"No, I'll get in trouble!"

"Come on," my brother begged. "Please, pretty please?" he persistently begged while he wiggled his eyes at me.

I finally gave in to his pleas, even though I knew it was a stupid thing to do since I was supposed to be watching my brothers and sisters.

The fact that he wanted me to go do something with him was rare, so it was hard for me to say no to him.

Nervously I trudged up the trail following him, begging him to turn back so we could get back home before Mom and Dad got back from town.

"We need to go back now!" I pleaded with my brother.

By now we had hiked into the woods so far I was afraid I wouldn't find my way back alone. I continued to plead with him to turn around. Finally he turned around and there on our trek back we ran into our silent and very angry father. My stomach churned as I followed quietly behind my dad, fuming that I had let myself be persuaded to go with my brother. I knew by how angry my father was, there would be no getting out of what I knew was coming. That was the last time I ever got spanked by him. Humiliated by being spanked and angry at myself that I couldn't stand up to my brother and tell him no, I didn't want to go with him, knowing full well we'd get in big trouble if caught filled my thoughts.

Why do I have such a hard time saying no to him?

Mixed emotions struggled to find their place within me when I thought about my brother: jealousy, anger, love, envy, and adoration. The list went on and on.

During the late summer evenings we played many games of kick the can with the neighbor kids outside in our yard and in the nearby woods by our house, until Mom would call us back into the house for the night. We were enjoying ourselves, playing outside long past our normal bed times, the warm summer sun still high in the sky late at night. Sadly summer came to an end and in the fall we started school. Even the beginnings of my eighth grade school year seemed quite idyllic for someone like me. It seemed like we were starting to make friends with the family up the road that attended our church. It just so happened to be that their oldest boy was the one who had caught my eye earlier, making this new move for me a little bit easier since I had developed a crush on this new and cute boy.

My Journey from Anxiety to Peace

During the summer maybe it wasn't too difficult for my new crush to be friends with us, the pastor's kids, because no one else was around to see it. I noticed that he seemed to be quite popular and had quite a few friends at school. I wasn't all that surprised that when in school he didn't act like he knew us very well, he more than likely kept it a hidden fact that his family attended our church, or any church for that matter. He did have a bit of a bad boy reputation at school, but this didn't stop my crush at all, and that was part of the problem. Immature, sheltered from worldly ways, I was very naïve, whereas he, was far from it. He was a charmer, good looking and had a lot of natural charisma. All the while I was drawn to him, something deep inside me told me he probably wasn't that good for me. But he and his family came to our church so that should make him okay, a Christian boy. *Doesn't it?* Deluding myself trying to apply a reason that these things should make him okay.

It happened rather fast, getting caught up in the devious web of his charm. The first time he stopped in the morning in the road in front of our house and waited for me to walk to the school bus with him, my heart sang. *Maybe, just maybe in some small way might he like me?* That hopeful feeling would keep my heart singing through the school day even though he ignored me in the halls of school. He would every once in a while stop and wait for me to walk to the bus in the morning, just enough to keep me hoping, fantasizing, in the what-ifs.

Winter had descended with all of its snow and blustering cold air that nipped at our noses. On Sunday afternoons after church services and after we had eaten lunch while my parents napped, he started to show up at our back door asking for me.

He rakishly grinned at me when I came to the door. "You want to go sledding with me?"

"Ah okay" I turned around trying to hide the smile that wanted to erupt. "Just a minute I'll be right out!"

I would bundle up in all my winter gear to keep warm and we would go sledding outside on some of the hills around our houses. I thought my heart would burst with the possibility that he could like someone as awkward as me. Most of the time I don't think my parents even knew

A Simple Extraordinary Life

I had left the house since I usually returned before they had woken up from their nap. I sure wasn't going to volunteer that information unless they asked, but they usually didn't. It was on one of those sledding excursions when I became oblivious to the cold air that I felt the warmth of my first kiss. We had sled down the hill, crashed and tumbled and landed on top of each other when he gave me a quick kiss. I was hopelessly, having a full on crush and naïve as I was, I didn't understand that he was just starting to set me up to be used.

Maybe his first intentions with me didn't include what would become vile later down the road but it was as if he was testing the waters to see how naïve and gullible I was. He started to have girlfriends at school, never hiding it from me. It wasn't as if we hung out much but he would come around just enough, smile at me and give my hand the occasional squeeze or give me a quick stolen kiss that would have me smitten with his charm, again and again. I couldn't seem to pull myself away from it. I felt desperate for his attention.

Every time I would see him in school with these beautiful and cute girls, a part of me would die. I had become so good at keeping my feelings and hurt hidden from anyone that it just became par for the course to cry in silence at night. I found myself constantly caught up in comparing myself with these other girls, or for that matter any other girl, always finding myself coming up short. I had zero self-confidence. It was about this time I had finally started to develop, far behind most girls my age; uncomfortable with this new development, but also weirdly ecstatic that maybe it might make me more likeable. I had some pretty warped and confusing thinking going on around in my head. It wasn't that I wanted the wrong kind of attention, I just craved to feel that maybe I was worthy of someone liking me for who I was. My skewed and twisted mind told me now I was more like the other girls.

Months had passed with no more personal contact from him. There would be the occasional church attendance but even that was becoming rare. His school attendance was severely waning and I started to hear rumors of him getting into some kind of trouble. More and more I knew in my heart he was not the kind of guy I would eventually want to marry, sadly though, this didn't stop me from desperately wanting him to like me. I hadn't seen him around for a while and was really starting to wonder about it, wildly guessing where he had been. Out of the blue one day he appeared again at my house.

He ducked his head smiling at me his bright blue eyes twinkling. "You want to go on a walk?"

My heart started racing, hoping against hope that maybe he might just start liking me or maybe he already did a little. *Why else would he come by?*

"Umm okay."

I left with him and we wandered up the road not talking much. He started taking a path in the nearby woods and I hesitantly followed him. He had started talking a little; more like the carefree boy he was when I first met him so I felt myself relax some. He stopped walking and stole a kiss or two and then surprising me, his hands started to wander. He kept trying to joke with me, asking me what size bra I wore. Appalled and highly embarrassed, I kept grabbing his hands pushing them away. I didn't want this kind of intrusion or attention but felt helpless to know what to do to make him stop and just go back to talking to me. I was humiliated but didn't want to show him how stupid and naïve I felt, so I didn't say much of anything, looking anywhere but at him. Awkwardly standing there fully embarrassed as I tried to thwart his wandering hands, my voice locked in a strange and mute silence. He finally stopped trying to grope me and we walked back home.

He showed up a few times with the same pretense, charming me with his smile, getting me to think he was his old self again, but before I knew it I would be caught in the same predicament again.

I lay there in the dark in my bed, hurt and humiliated, embarrassed to have found myself yet again so easily taken in by his deceiving charm, stifling my crying in the quiet of night feeling incredibly ashamed.

You're so stupid! What makes you think he would like someone like you?

I wanted to hold out hope that maybe one day he'd be more like the boy he was when I first met him, back to when he would just talk to me, not grope and humiliate me. It would be the last walk in the woods I would take with him when I fell into the trap of remaining in an agonizing and tortured silence for the next forty odd years of my life.

Sheer panic was setting in.

That awful groping was happening once again, my hands furiously trying to stop him. Before I knew what was happening he had my pants and underwear down around my ankles and had pushed me to the ground. Sudden fear and terror ran through my veins. I froze, my virgin mind registering what he was trying to do, paralyzed with the thought this is how a person becomes pregnant. He was like a strong lion pouncing on a timid and frightened mouse. *Oh God please... make this stop!*

Silently I cried. *Please, please stop, I want no part in any of this!*

Humiliated and fraught with an agonizing emotional pain that was beyond anything my young mind could handle, all I could get out was a strangled and whispered no. My head pulsed and pounded with racing thoughts of how upset my father would be. The words I had heard many times in church of children are to be in order rang foremost in my mind like a loud clanging bell. The last thing I would ever want to do was disappoint my father. *Maybe this was my fault? I stupidly followed him into the woods.*

Desperately I wanted to scream. Screams clawed at my throat but I couldn't find the breath needed to push them up and out of my throat. Desperate cries that wouldn't make it past my lips. My heart pounded wildly. I couldn't figure out why I couldn't scream. *Why can't I fight?* Embarrassment, mortification, and intense confusion were swirling all around me in a terrible dark fear that was pulling hard at me with crippling thoughts. I felt strangely paralyzed, fighting like mad to be able to emit a sound, fight, anything but this crippling agony I found myself in. All I could emit were muffled cries.

He had rolled me onto my stomach. Humiliated, my face turned away as all I could think of was, hold your legs together as tight as you can. My mind was locked in an eerie place of escape that kept screaming. *No! No!* As he tried to force himself upon me my mind had locked down into full protection mode and had blocked out everything around me and went to a place that I no longer felt anything he was trying to do. My eyes squeezed shut as tight as my mind was, blocking this nightmare out.

He had never said a word to me this entire time when all of a sudden through the screaming fog of my tortured mind I heard him say something.

"Get up on your knees like a dog."

I refused and with those few uttered words, something deep inside me broke. Feeling no more worthy than a dog, a wound that felt like a hot knife plunged into the very core of my heart and lodged itself, leaving me so hurt I didn't think I'd ever recover from the searing pain. Through the eerie and dark gray fog of my mind I registered his frustration and he rolled off me.

The noise of the traffic from the nearby highway wafted through the woods as I rushed to pull my pants up and mutely walked back out of the woods behind him. My heart squeezed in excruciating pain, my eyes filled with hot silent tears that threatened to spill and drown me. Tears I felt I must never show. Screams burned like volcanic acid in my throat wanting to erupt, but my throat had closed up in a complete silence that would torture me for the next four decades.

I must remain silent, because no one, not one single person must ever know of my shame.

CHAPTER

11

One might wonder why I felt like I couldn't run to my father or mother and tell them what had happened to me that fateful day in the neighboring woods.

I've often wondered that myself. It was a varied combination of things that had already laid the rocky groundwork for me, feeling the way I did. I was already running amuck in self-pity, having bought into the deceiving lie that I didn't matter much and no one would really care. Afraid, lost in confusion, humiliated and embarrassed, my heart filled with shame, but most of all, I couldn't find my voice.

It's not that my parents didn't care or wouldn't care if they knew; on the contrary I'm sure because of their love for me they would have been there for me. My parents were probably very unaware of how different things affected me, and after all, how could they know if I didn't tell them. Sometimes the longer you keep a secret, especially if it's one you think is going to hurt you or hurt the ones you love, the harder it is to let your secret be known and besides, I felt like this was just too dirty of a secret a good little Christian girl should have.

My feelings and thoughts were always swirling around inside my head in a pool of confusion as to what it was I was supposed to think and feel.

A Simple Extraordinary Life

When we had first moved out to Peters Creek my father really wanted to promote fellowship within our little body of people. We had services Sunday morning and Sunday evening, Tuesday night Bible studies, and Wednesday night services. It started to become a habit that after evening services people in the congregation would wander up to our house to visit. We lived only a stone's throw away from the church so I guess it felt like common property to those who came to church. Many times tools from my dad's garage would get "borrowed" without his knowledge and eventually he would make an announcement from the pulpit about what tool he was looking for. Sheepishly, amid some laughter someone would usually fess up that they were the ones who had the missing tool.

My mom started making huge pots of coffee and serving dessert. Eventually people were starting to stay later and later into the evening much of the time. Since us kids usually had school the next day we would be sent off to bed right away while the adults visited. We didn't have a very big house so all the noise from the talking and laughing would travel easily through the thin trailer walls. My bedroom happened to be next to the living-dining room where all the adults were gathered. One night I was very tired but couldn't get to sleep because of all the noise from the visiting and laughing going on in the living room. Exhausted and craving sleep I got out of bed and went and stood in the hallway hoping to get my mother's attention.

"What are you doing?" my mom said as she came over to see what I was doing.

"I can't sleep! It's too noisy."

Secretly I hoped my parents would ask the people from church to leave. I was getting weary of this being a regular occurrence; it was getting on my nerves and I didn't function well with little sleep, especially as a young teenager. I could sleep the day away if allowed and still be tired, which of course I never was allowed to do.

My mom furiously whispered to me. "Get back to bed!"

"But I can't get to sleep, it's too noisy!" I whined at her.

She made a face at me and repeated, "Get back to bed."

My Journey from Anxiety to Peace

Well for me that one little statement said a host of things to me, she might as well have said, you're not important, it's these people, these others, the ones from church that are more important than you. What I heard was that they and their needs held much more significance than my own needs. I thought they were being rude and inconsiderate to not realize they were making it very hard for me to get any sleep. It was late after all and I had to get up very early to catch the school bus and get to school the next morning. This one incident was just one of many other little incidents that was fanning the flame and fueling the fire inside of me, telling me the lies that I didn't matter much.

I had this tangled up and false idea that it was much more important to keep the people of the church happy. Snippets of scripture would play out through my mind, the thought you must deny yourself for others. I must learn how to be a good Christian girl by denying myself and my own needs for the needs of others. I heard Bible teaching that is actually very sound but in my twisted thinking would lose what the true meaning really was.

My thinking, marred by my wounds was becoming very convoluted, and my trust in anyone in the church other than my father who I knew did love me, depleted. My father really did genuinely love people and people really loved him. He had a huge servant's heart, giving himself for others and by both example and deed really tried to instill that same heart in his children. I'm sure that he never would have intended that we would, or could feel that the people in the church came before his own family. It didn't stop me from sometimes feeling that way though.

A lot of these feelings were more perpetuated by the people in the church; their words and actions would and could speak volumes to me, sometimes much more than the unintentional actions from my father and mother. I was left constantly feeling under this intense pressure to live up to some certain standard that I must be held accountable for. I wasn't even sure what that standard was, but needless to say I didn't think I lived up to it. I was overly sensitive to the whispers from others about us kids when they thought we acted up too much or maybe didn't conform to what they thought we should be, or accusations that would come up of nepotism. Carrying around this impossible weight that I must never mess up, I already felt stupid and dumb enough that I could have ever entertained the notion that a boy could ever have truly liked someone like me. When the sexual abuse happened I couldn't forgive myself for what I thought was my blatant ignorance and foolishness, I had in some terrible way, messed up. *This is my fault.*

There was another key reason I kept silent. This boy was the son of one of the appointed elders, part of the leadership in my father's church. I wasn't sure I would be believed, and even if that wasn't true, I felt that somehow I had brought this upon myself. My naiveté and willingness to walk out into the woods with him made me think, somehow I had to be partially to blame, I just couldn't forgive myself for my stupidity. I was too humiliated to even think about the torture it would be for myself to tell, surely it would only serve to humiliate me further. The last thing I ever wanted to do was have my father be displeased with me and in my mind I was sure he would be displeased. I know now of course, he would have never been displeased with me, he would have been in anguish at the thought someone could hurt me in such a manner. Displeased by the situation? Yes. Displeased by me? No. But I couldn't see past the shame I felt.

I was positive, to say anything would be like upsetting the apple cart that would be sure to bring to light, a flaw in some of the church leadership's family. I was awfully sure this would be upsetting and painful to my father. So in light of my own flawed thinking, right or wrong, I stuffed and stuffed all my hurt, the pain and humiliation, way down in the deepest crevasses of my heart. I tried hard to lock it up, foolishly believing that I could control the pain, and never let anyone know of my private anguish. Wearing a heavy coat of shame that I couldn't seem to shed, foolishly I would try to control all the effects its weight had on me.

Little did I know what a futile effort this would become, it would later affect my every thought, compound my every feeling. Every situation in the future I was ever to face, this hurt and shame would rise to the glaring surface, and through every situation I found myself in, it would be the dirty looking glass that I viewed life through. Instead of cleaning that glass so I could see clearly I would resort to stuffing the pain down, over and over again, afraid of what it might take to get it clean. A private, closely guarded dirty secret that should never see the light of day. In bondage to the intense pain in my heart, it clouded my perception of who God was, and in bondage so deep to the pain, I couldn't truly believe His promises and love were for me.

For a while I managed to bury it deep enough that it didn't surface much for the next few years. I thought for sure I had gotten control of it, because I was able to think about new things and move on, I had put it behind me, and was moving forward.

In the tenth grade now, walking the school halls with my two friends I noticed a boy.

I pointed at a group of kids across the hall from us to my friend. "Cheryl, look isn't he cute!"

"Who?"

Covertly I tried to talk behind my hand so no one else could hear. "That one standing over there with the gray blue eyes and brown hair."

There was something about his eyes I dreamily thought, *look how they sparkle*. Deducing that he was somewhat older than me by the group of friends he was hanging around with I tried to figure out who he was. My friends and I, after lunch was over and in between classes, would make the rounds walking the school halls, trying to catch a glimpse of him. The only people I let know of my infatuation of him, were my two friends. No one, not even my friends ever knew anything about that other boy. That was a darkly held secret of mine. The infatuation I had on this new boy wore off by the end of the school year and I didn't think much more about him.

Our little church congregation was starting to grow some and get the occasional visitors. Somewhere in my eleventh grade of school a new family came to services one Sunday morning. I was surprised to see that one of their four children was that boy I would try and catch a glimpse of in the school halls the year before. They started attending services, and it didn't take long for me to take notice that he seemed to be a very kind person. My interest was piqued. His mother years later would say I turned around in the row at church and smiled at him, and it was over from that day on. Now I have no recollection of doing that, but I guess I must have, I don't think she would lie.

My sister who is only a year younger than me knew his younger sister from school. My sister had started to talk to me about what she knew about this family but I only listened to what she said about the oldest boy with them.

As we lay there in our darkened bedroom we shared I intently listened when she brought up his name. "His name is Larry, he's already graduated school." "I think his sister said he had a job, maybe with the State of Alaska."

It didn't take very long for their family to become pretty involved in the church and its functions, so I had the chance to observe him. I very much liked what I saw and observed of him. He was friendly to everyone, considerate, well-mannered, gentle, kind, funny, industrious, and had a servant's heart. He would show up at work parties, gladly pitching in and I noticed he knew how to work hard. Again, I noticed his eyes, they sparkled when he smiled and it seemed so genuine and come straight from his heart. All these characteristics very much attracted me. He mirrored a lot of the traits I admired in my father.

It was especially his kindness to others that drew me.

Love,
Fissures,
&
Cracks

CHAPTER

12

He confused me at first.

Larry owned a horse, a gray and white appaloosa; its registered name was Pepper Patch of Alaska. His horse was boarded down the street a couple houses down from where he lived with his parents, getting free boarding at the neighbor's house by helping her out with the horses that she owned. Late summer one day he invited me to go horseback riding with him. I had never even been next to a horse before so it made me nervous to think about even climbing up on an animal that size, but I thought I could swallow up my fears if it meant I could get a chance to be with him since I was starting to like him very much. I was ecstatic about the invitation; only to find out he had asked my sister to go too.

The plan would be, he'd pick my sister and I up and take us over to his house where we'd then walk down to the neighbors to saddle up his horse and then ride his horse around in some trails around his neighborhood. His younger sister would be there, my sister, him, and me. As the day wore on, he confused me even more when he was equally nice to both my sister and I, so I couldn't figure out if he liked me. I was sure hoping he did! The next invitation that came from him to go do something would again include my sister. I was really starting to wonder by then. *Between the two of us, whom does he like?* Maybe though, he was just a super nice guy and wasn't really interested in either of us.

Not long before I had become interested in Larry, my sister had confided in me.

"I like Larry" she whispered to me while we lay in our bed one night sharing secrets.

I have to say I wasn't very nice and laughed at her. It didn't take me long after her revelation to me to form my own interest in him. Things were getting a bit complicated, I didn't want to hurt my sister but I couldn't help it, darn it, I liked Larry too and wanted very much for him to like me back.

It became a little clearer for me one day, Larry had given me an extra special smile and look, and suddenly I knew. *Ooh, oh I think it's me he likes! Me? I can't believe it!* This super nice guy liked me! *Oh wow, me? Yes, it's me! How is this possible?* It was difficult for me to believe he could be attracted to someone like me, but thank my lucky stars he was! I wanted to be sure I wasn't just wistfully dreaming but he would do things that made me even more sure as the days went by.

Our little church had grown again and there were now quite a few babies and toddlers that needed to be taken care of during the services, so the church formed a nursery. The nursery workers consisted of my sister and I taking our turns watching the children up at my parents' house during the services. Since our house was next door, parents would bring their children before services then come pick them up after the service had ended. Larry started to make sure he always ran up to our house after the service to say a quick hi to me and talk for a few minutes before he left for home with his parents. No matter how quick his hi had to be, I looked forward to them, anticipating those few precious minutes or seconds I would get at the end of my babysitting duties that made my day seem worthwhile. He was winning me over quick with his thoughtfulness, never forgetting to come by and say hi. I wanted to pinch myself; this was so unbelievable to me that he would take interest in me.

That fall my birthday had rolled around. Larry showed up to my house carrying a long wrapped tube.

He handed me the tube. "You can't unwrap it until you guess what it is."

"I have no idea what it is!"

He smiled broadly. "Come on guess!"

"I don't know, what could be long and skinny?" I wildly threw out a guess. "A poster?"

"Nope!" he grinned, "Guess again!"

"I don't know, I give up!"

Laughing at me he said, "Go ahead unwrap it."

I tore off the birthday wrapping paper he'd taped around that tube, my curiosity high as to what in the world he could have possibly gotten me shaped like a tube. My eyes widened as I pulled out a brand new pair of shoes that he had stuffed down the tube.

I had a slight turned foot causing me to always walk on the side of my foot. I would wear out one side of my heel badly on one shoe, which would make me roll my foot even worse. Shoes never lasted long before I had a lopsided shoe but I would have to wear the worn out shoes a long time before the next new pair. He had noticed my damaged and worn shoe and without me saying anything about it, went out and got me a new pair of shoes for my birthday. Those shoes were better than anything else he could have gotten me, because to me it showed me he truly cared about me. It was the sweetest and most thoughtful thing someone had ever done for me.

By the end of November we were seeing each other more and more frequently. That Christmas Larry bought me a jewelry box. When I opened up the box, inside was a deep blue sapphire ring that had a white star in it. It was my birthstone. We were fast falling in love. Walking on air surrounded by beautiful clouds of good fortune, I wanted to pinch myself I could hardly believe it.

"Larry shouldn't be buying you so many things." My mother said as she took me aside.

She thought it was too much, too soon, but my dad, he just smiled and shrugged it off.

I was always amazed that Larry kept coming around. I think it was only the second real date we were going to be alone on that when Larry came to the front door to pick me up, my father the consummate teaser that he had always been yelled across the room.

"She's going to cost you!" he continued with his teasing. "Sixteen horses and twenty-four Indian blankets!" Dad giggled to himself thinking he was being hilarious.

I'm not really sure of the real number he said, but I was mortified! I turned a horrific shade of red and ducked out the door as fast as I could, grabbing Larry on the way. I was used to my father's teasing, but this was just too much, ever so sure Larry would probably never come back again. He came back much to my delight, again and again.

With Larry I felt safe. We would talk for hours. He was opening up a whole new world for me. Patiently he would explain things that I didn't understand. Never did he mean spiritedly make fun of my naiveté or lack of knowledge, of which I knew, was pretty limited. He knew how to tease me and make me laugh at myself. We dated for only about three short months when our talk started to turn to marriage. I was at the end of my junior year of high school. Larry bought me a promise ring and we started to make plans to marry. By now we saw each other every day, enjoying being together as much as we possibly could. I never tired of being with him and still to this day, we spend vast amounts of time together, working and playing. Some girls at high school asked me once how could I stand seeing Larry every day, didn't I get bored with that? *I don't understand their thinking, as far as I am concerned, twenty four seven would never be enough.* My father liked Larry very much and I knew he was happy for me.

I was always looking forward to the weekends when we could spend even more time together, it never got old being with him. My mother never let us sleep in much and on the weekends would wake us up with our list of chores for the day. It seemed like she could always come up with extra chores on the weekend, dusting, vacuuming, mopping floors and the never ending laundry and baking. I would complete my list of chores and then wait around for Larry to call to say what time he was coming over so we could go do something for the rest of the day. Sometimes if he hadn't called before noon I'd get up the nerve to pick up the phone and dial his number.

"Hello." His mom answered after a few rings.

"Hi, um is Larry there?"

"He's still sleeping, you want me to go get him?"

"Um that's okay, just have him call me when he gets up." I embarrassedly told her.

Never could I fathom how he'd sleep till noon or later before finally getting up, while I had already been up for hours and had already accomplished a lot of work. Even more surprising to me was the fact that his mother let him sleep! I was jealous of this fact for sure.

Since I would be ahead in the required credits needed for graduation my senior year and coupled with the fact I didn't like school much, we decided that I would do an early graduation in January. We made plans to marry that February following my graduation. Our wedding invitations were sent out to relatives in the lower 48 states and we started making all our plans for our wedding ceremony. Walking home from school one day trudging up the hill to our house, my father came driving by in his car.

Dad slowly stopped the car beside me and rolled down his window. "I need to talk to you in my office."

His office meant his church office. Immediately panic set in, because to be called into Dad's office meant for sure you must be in serious trouble. My trepidation was real. *Oh no, Dad must have found out about the small hickey I've been trying to hide on my neck. Am I ever going to be in trouble!* Larry and I weren't some of those squeaky clean Christian kids who had never kissed; we did a lot of kissing!

My feet felt like lead as I walked into my father's office.

A Simple Extraordinary Life

"You can't get married." Dad said to me as I entered his office.

I looked at him, thinking for sure he probably was teasing again since that was always my Dad's standard ammo.

"Yes I can."

"No, no you can't."

Exasperated with his teasing, I repeated more adamantly. "Yes I can!"

We went back and forth a few times.

Then I noticed tears in his eyes as he slowly says. "No - you can't".

I started to get worried, what was going on? He swallowed hard and with tears in his eyes told me he had just found out that the State of Alaska had passed a new law. Even with parental consent, the State of Alaska wouldn't issue marriage certificates unless you were eighteen or pregnant. I was neither of those; my heart raced, that was nine months away before I would turn eighteen. I started to cry as the realization hit me. *I wouldn't be getting married.* My dad hugged me and tried to console me as I cried in his arms.

Later that evening Larry came over and found out the sad news. Together we cried our hearts out, and then we decided to take a drive to Eagle River to the North Slope restaurant and get a chocolate milk shake to try and take our minds off our sorrows. It didn't work, we'd sip on our thick shakes then look at each other and our sorrow would make us tear up and start to cry again. I wondered how I was going to survive waiting nine long months. My heart was ready to be one with this man and start my own home with him, nine months seemed an eternity away.

My second thought that made me very anxious now was that I was graduating high school. *I am going to have to find a job!* Having taken office procedure and typing classes in high school I started to look for some kind of an office job. This sure wasn't in my plans; the last thing I wanted to do was go out into the big scary world and have to find work. It would mean for me having to talk to complete strangers, something that always made me anxious. I was extremely nervous but I got hired at the first place I applied, as a file clerk for Avis Rent a Car. Thankfully the job didn't require me to have to interact with many people, but still I would be a nervous wreck all day at work. I made the minimum wage, $2.10 an hour.

Since I didn't drive or have a car, Larry who had to double back just to get to my house would come pick me up in the morning and drop me off on his way to work, which was close by. I would pack a lunch for both of us and he would drive over on his lunch hour and we'd eat our lunch sitting and talking in his car. I worked at Avis Rent A Car for a while when they offered me the position of receptionist which I reluctantly accepted. It was just the accounting office and we didn't rent the cars out at our office so I had taken notice the phone didn't ring all that much. I was hopeful I could manage to answer the occasional phone call. My duties included sorting and handling all the incoming mail and doing some typing for the Vice President who was a middle-aged German man with a pretty thick accent. I always got really anxious when I had to bring the President of the company's mail back to his private office in the far back of our small workplace. It would be the only time I would ever interact with him during the day when I'd nervously hand him his stack of mail.

When things would be slow at the office for me I would go to the accounting manager's office.

Timidly I asked as I stood in her doorway. "Um, do you have anything for me to do?"

"Here you can check the addition of these," she answered through intermittent coughs of her scratchy voice. "Just double check my additions," she said as she handed me these large green columnar pads.

She was a bit of a crusty, but nice older woman who sat in her office chain smoking. I still remember how the smell of those stale cigarettes would waft off those columnar pads when I was handling them, trying discreetly to hold my nose so I wouldn't gag on the awful stale smell. It was long before the days of computers so everything was done by hand, laboriously adding the figures up with a ten key adding machine. I hoped and prayed that my additions were right when I handed back those columnar pads back to her.

A Simple Extraordinary Life

At the end of the workday Larry would pick me up, then we would either go to my parents for dinner or he would take me to his parents' house for dinner. We'd spend a few hours together usually talking about anything and everything. It would start to get late and if we were at my parents' house Mom would yell from her bedroom.

"Is Larry still here?" her voice floated from the back bedroom.

We'd roll our eyes at each other when we heard her not so subtle hint, it was his cue that it was time for him to go home. I was never ready for him to go home. I felt whole when I was with him, lost without him.

My father, along with others started writing letters to the state legislature. It was absurd to them that along with taking away parental rights it was like asking young people to go out and get pregnant. It didn't take but a few months and the state law was changed.

Ecstatic that we could now get married, we needed a new wedding date, so we chose June 6, 1975, Larry's birthday, he would turn twenty, and I would be three months shy of eighteen.

CHAPTER

13

either Larry nor I had much money but it didn't matter. Feeling much too excited and anxious to be married to care whether or not our wedding would be a very elaborate affair. I think I spent about $27 buying fabric to sew my own wedding dress. It wasn't very fancy or ornate, just a simple white gown with some lace on it which was okay with me. For a head dressing all I wanted was a very simple long veil that would attach to some flowers in my hair. My aunt who was so talented said she would make it for me.

The day she brought over my veil I thought for sure I was going to faint in panic. It was beautiful but nothing at all like I wanted. Layers and layers of netting attached to a very elaborate beaded head dress far fancier and bigger than anything I felt comfortable with. I smiled anyways and said thank you, taking the veil from her. There was no way I was going to wear it as is and feel the least bit comfortable. *What am I going to do?* The only thing I could think to do was take a layer of netting off and try to not make that thing be so poufy. *I hope she doesn't notice.* I knew I'd have to wear it even if it made me feel way too conspicuous, I couldn't hurt her feelings, she had gone to a lot of work. *I sure wished she'd listened to what I'd wanted.*

My aunt also arranged our flowers, daisies and white roses for our bouquets and made arrangements for the church auditorium where the ceremony would take place. Pale yellow and light green streamers hung from the ceiling in the church basement where our reception would be held. I find it funny now that I didn't spend much time antagonizing over my color choices, I was young and really didn't put that much thought into the details to care that much one way or the other, I just wanted to get married and have this whole public affair over with.

Food for the reception would be furnished by members of our church. My only friend from high school was my maid of honor, my sister my other bridesmaid. We had a young man that had recently gotten out of the military that had been going to our church and came to live with our family who had become like a brother to me and a friend to Larry. He was Larry's best man, his younger brother the groomsman. My youngest sister and my four-year-old brother were the flower girl and ring bearer.

The morning of my wedding day had arrived, a beautiful summer day. The first thing I did upon waking was run to the mirror to see if I had developed a cold sore during the night. *Oh good, there isn't one!* My relief at not finding one I thought was a good start to the day since I was very prone to them, especially if I was stressed and nervous. I had been so afraid my nerves would have brought on another one and it would be one of the huge ones I tended to get that there would be no way to hide, no matter how much makeup I slapped on it.

My sisters and Mom had gone down to the church to start decorating for my wedding while I waited to get my long brown hair done up by someone who came to the church who had previously been a hairdresser. I was glad that she had listened to me about not wanting all my hair put up in some ridiculous hairstyle that would be big and poufy and too attention getting for someone like myself. She kept it rather simple and left most of it down. After she styled my hair, which was stiff with all the aerosol hair spray she used, I wandered down to the church to check out how things were coming along.

"Where are the flowers?" I asked my mom as I looked around at what they were doing.

"They're in the refrigerator in the church kitchen." Mom said.

I wandered past her to go peek at the flowers. "It looks nice in here."

My Journey from Anxiety to Peace

Opening up the refrigerator door to look at our bouquets and the boutonnieres for the guys I swallowed hard, aghast at what greeted me. The white roses in my bouquet had turned brown from getting too cold. Everything else was fine; it was just my flowers that had frozen. Upset because we had no more flowers, I was resigned that it would have to do; hopefully no one would notice. I went back up to the house to get ready and try my best to apply my makeup and not mess up my hair.

By the time of my marriage the church had grown again and had added a new auditorium above that original old brick building. It was there in this new auditorium I was about to enter into the next phase of my life. The time came to start the ceremony; my nerves were off the charts. I hated the idea of having to be in front of everyone but knew I had to do this if I wanted to marry Larry, which of course I very much wanted to do. So with my cheeks which were hot and inflamed, my heart beating so loud I thought for sure you could hear it, my father who had just swallowed hard when he asked me if I was ready started to walk me down the aisle.

My eyes searched out Larry. The first thing I noticed, he sported a fresh haircut and for some reason that amused me and calmed me down some as I nervously walked up what seemed to be an awfully long aisle. He looked about as nervous as I was. He smiled at me and I knew then that I would get through this. My father handed me over to Larry, and then walked up the steps to the platform to officiate our wedding. He would eventually perform all eight of his children's wedding ceremonies. Standing on the platform now in front of everyone my first thought as I chided myself, *I forgot to hold in my stomach while walking down the aisle*. Then my thoughts turned to how lucky I was that Larry wanted to marry me.

Our honeymoon consisted of spending one night at the Captain Cook hotel in downtown Anchorage. It felt really awkward and strange to have my parents send us off with their blessing, knowing I'd never sleep alone again. The next day, which was a Saturday, we spent getting groceries and buying the things needed to set up our house. We were renting a small house on the property of the woman where he had previously boarded the horse that he used to own, having sold his horse when he no longer had time for it. His time had been taken up by courting me. We got to our little rental house and unloaded our groceries and I started to make tacos for dinner.

While I chopped up lettuce and tomatoes we heard someone knocking at the front door. Larry went to answer the knock to find his sister and brother standing at the front door wanting to come in and see us. As they stepped inside, again I felt very awkward. I had been alone and intimate with Larry and now that it was okay, everyone knew it. The next day was Sunday. A struggle ensued with me not wanting to go to church; embarrassed that everyone surely knew what had transpired between Larry and me. After all we had just gotten married that weekend, so surely everyone would be looking at me and that idea made me very uncomfortable. The notion that I was sure everyone's eyes would be upon me got me really worked up with anxiety wanting to stay home, but we got up anyways and went to church. I was much too afraid what would be said of me if I missed. After all, I was still the pastor's daughter.

Monday we went back to our jobs, settling in to what would be our new life together. That first weekend in our little rental house after we had finished out the work week we slept in till one o'clock that Saturday. At first I felt guilty and surprised when I rolled over and looked at the clock, but then ecstatic that I could now make my own decisions. *There is no one telling me now I have to get out of bed and start my chores!*

I found great satisfaction setting up our house. The first thing I did was clean it top to bottom, especially the fridge and kitchen which were extremely filthy. There was a back bedroom that the owner had raised baby chicks in and I couldn't get the smell out so we just closed off that room and never used it. I couldn't get over the fact that the owner had been a housekeeper by profession because it took a lot of elbow grease to make the place livable for my standards. Even though we didn't have much of anything, more important, it was that it was ours and it was a life with Larry. It didn't matter that our old used black and white TV picture would slowly flip over or barely work, or our clothes were in cardboard boxes beside the hand-me-down bed, we were together and I felt whole.

114

My Journey from Anxiety to Peace

I loved the serenity of having my own quiet place since having had so many siblings at home it was usually more chaotic and noisy than I would have preferred. It didn't take me long though to realize something. It wasn't very fun having to get up early in the mornings and have to go to work all day, only to come home tired and exhausted and still have to make dinner and clean up, then start that tedious process all over again the next day. The cravings for a family of my own didn't take long for me to feel, so three months into our marriage I quit my job, and became pregnant with my first son. Eventually I would have three more sons.

I was about eight months pregnant with our firstborn when we decided to buy our first place. We had moved out of that first little rental house into an apartment for a few months, but now an opportunity to buy something of our own had come up. It was a single wide mobile home trailer that we were buying from a couple with two small children from our church. It just so happened to be the young couple that had lived with my family previously. This man would soon become my father's associate pastor. Larry and my awkward pregnant self, moved in with them for about a month because the place they were going to move into next, wasn't ready for them yet.

We were still living with them when on a gorgeous summer Sunday afternoon after church there was going to be a bunch of people getting together to play softball on the church grounds. That sure sounded fun, even if I could only watch. I was much too cumbersome at eight months pregnant to try and play but I was dying to get out of the house, feeling cooped up there day after day. We had all gone home after the church service to have lunch first, since the game wasn't scheduled till later that afternoon.

"Don't take off without me, I want to go with you so I can watch the game." I hurriedly told Larry.

It was my turn to clean up the kitchen and do the dishes so I was frantically trying to get them done before it would be time to go. The guys had wandered outside when I heard car doors slamming, and then I heard the car drive off. At first I thought they must have just left to go get something. When they didn't return soon, I knew with a sinking feeling, they had left without me.

A Simple Extraordinary Life

It didn't take long for me to get upset. *I can't believe Larry left me!* I went to our bedroom, which was at the end of the hall in the back of the trailer and laid down on our bed. Soon waves of all those old thoughts of not feeling important enough to be remembered, especially by the one who I thought should love me started to fester. I cried uncontrollably for hours. Larry came home from the softball game to find me crying, my eyes swollen, my nose running profusely.

"What's wrong, why are you crying?" Larry earnestly asked me.

I sobbed repeating over and over, not wanting to look at him. "You left me!"

"I didn't know you wanted to go!"

Fresh tears poured from my eyes as I rolled over to look at him. "But I told you I did!" "I said, don't leave without me!"

"I'm sorry." He said as he tried to hug me.

He honestly had forgotten that I wanted to go, apologized profusely, but my heart wouldn't let me believe him. I was sure it was because I wasn't worthy of being remembered. *Someone who truly loved me wouldn't forget me!* It was just another new wound that I would hold close to me, letting it skew my thinking once again. I kept myself in our bedroom pretending to nap till I could get ahold of myself, stuff those feelings down where I could pretend I wasn't upset and finally wandered out to the living room to watch TV with everyone. Pretending like nothing had ever happened.

A month later we were on our own in the trailer we were buying, our friends having moved out into their new place. Immediately I threw myself into making the trailer our own. We picked out shiny yellow metallic wallpaper for the small kitchen that I put up, and then I started making curtains and a matching bedspread for our bedroom out of a really wild fabric that had gigantic orange and brown graphic flowers on it. Larry and I ripped up the flat brown carpet and replaced it with bright orange long shag carpet. To finish out the mod look we put in an orange metal free-standing fireplace and hung a big orange round string accent light. It was the seventies, so this was what was hip at the time. I even got Larry to stop wearing his Levi button up fly jeans and start wearing bell bottom polyester pants and silky long collared shirts, since that's what was now fashionable along with his long hair. Not long after we were alone in our new to us little home, on June 27th, 1976, I gave birth to my firstborn son.

That was a terrifying and scary experience for myself since I was still so timid around people; I never once asked a single question of my doctor, preferring to keep all my questions to myself. Here I was in labor and not completely sure what was happening to my body. As I lay in the hospital bed I became deathly afraid of what was in store for me when down the hospital corridor I could hear a woman, screaming and screaming. Hearing her screams did nothing to calm my fears. Frightened immediately I thought, *Oh no, this is going to be horrible, why did I think having a baby was a good idea!*

The hospital maternity ward was busy so they had put us in a faraway overflow room, Larry sitting on a cold, hard metal folding chair next to me. A nurse had come in to put an IV in my arm but my vein kept rolling on her. She would mutter and swear, finally leaving the room to regain her composure before coming back to try again. Eventually after many punctures and cursing under her breath, she had another nurse come in and that nurse finally got my IV in. By then my arm was sore and bruised. Yet another solemn and tired nurse came in who had left her compassion and what should have been gentleness at the door and prepped me for birth leaving me even more scared than I was before.

After a few hours had passed we were sure that we had been forgotten about, secluded in that backroom when yet a different nurse finally showed up and tried to give me some pain pills to swallow. I had never in my life been able to swallow a pill so I was nervous as she stood by my bed watching me.

"This is ridiculous." "I've never seen someone who couldn't swallow a pill!" she angrily muttered as I gagged on the pills.

Finally she gave up on me and stalked out. I felt scared and stupid; here I was again, another failure for myself. Several hours later, in incredible pain and increasingly scared I looked over at Larry.

"Look what you did to me, I am NEVER doing this again!" I hissed as I loudly exclaimed my outrage at him.

Finally the nurses thought I had progressed enough that they could give me something for the pain so they put some Demerol in my IV. Immediately, as the drug hit my veins I felt myself drifting into a foggy stupor. Feeling awful that I couldn't seem to talk right or get my brain to function properly it scared me even more. *If this is what it feels like to be drunk, I want nothing ever to do with it!* That feeling of loss of control scared me.

More panic hit me when the nurse informed me my doctor was not on call that weekend and I would have a stranger for my doctor who would deliver my baby. Strangers, how I hated them! They wheeled me off alone to the delivery room while they took Larry to another room to don a sterile gown, letting him in to the delivery room only to stand at the back of the room where I couldn't see him. Eventually my son was born and they put him in a bassinet next to me.

The doctor was still working on me when I looked over in wonder at my son, enthralled and stunned that this new little person next to me was my very own. Reaching over to touch him, the nurses immediately came over and strapped my arms down without saying a word as to why. Bewildered as to what I had done wrong and feeling even more stupid again, I remained silent. It put a strange damper on my new and budding feelings, that of a new mother's love she has for her baby, feeling conflicted and confused like I was supposed to somehow keep them under wraps. My feelings I had for my son felt complicated and made me frightened because I was a little slow forming that rush of love for him I thought I should have, afraid lest I be shut down again.

I was scared of myself when I had these complicated feelings, afraid that I wouldn't know how to love him properly. I chalked up for myself what would probably be another miserable failure in my life. Something else I wasn't worthy to be, a mother. Thankfully it didn't take too awfully long before I felt my love for my son start to fill my heart, though I did have bouts of doubt that would sometimes hit me hard. *Am I loving him right*? My head and thoughts were always rolling around in confusion and it was even affecting this new aspect of my life of being a mother, always second-guessing myself.

Two years later my second son made his appearance. It was quite the opposite experience than the first. After only feeling super uncomfortable which didn't seem that unusual, it made me think I probably wasn't really in labor. I talked to my mom who suggested just going in to the hospital to get checked out anyways. Good thing I took her advice, my second son made his sudden appearance fifteen minutes after I had gotten to the hospital. Now I had a new fear. Scared that I would be one of those women you hear about on TV or in the newspapers that give birth in their car, by the time I was pregnant four years later with my third son, I carried a packed suitcase with me in my car to be ready at any time.

The third time around I had gone into my last doctor's appointment before my due date where he told me he was pretty sure I'd have my baby that weekend. I knew my doctor wouldn't be on call that weekend and he hadn't been there to deliver my previous two sons so I nervously informed him of that fact. He sat there scratching his head. Having never missed that many births of the same client before in his career he suggested I just go ahead and check into the hospital and he would break my water. I of course very much liked that idea, so sure I wouldn't be able to tell true labor from false labor and I would have this child in the car and end up on the local evening news. *Frightened woman gives birth in her car, stay tuned, story right after the commercial break.* That, would just be my luck so fearful I was of this scenario. I left the doctor's office and went over to Larry's work and picked him up. We checked in to the hospital and my third son made his grand appearance five hours later. A bit disappointed by another boy but one look at his sweet little face and I quickly got over it.

Following the birth of my first son and most of the following year afterwards, is a blur in my memory, as I seemed to manage to keep most of my inner demons at bay. It was when the newness of married life started settling into the routine of housework, and bills, and taking care of a baby that I started to struggle.

A Simple Extraordinary Life

It didn't take long and much of my old worries and doubt would start to surface and haunt me again.

CHAPTER

14

*F*issures in my guarded heart were starting to bubble up and escape. Carefully stored away wounds that I tried hard to always keep hidden and under control were coming to the surface, feeling helpless to stop them from rising up. My husband I'm sad to say, would be at the receiving end. I started to become frigid. I would find myself freeze when more than just a kiss or two would happen, so sure he couldn't truly love someone as flawed as me. Whispers were always at the back of my mind that he just wanted to use me. *After all, isn't that what had happened to me before?*

I desperately tried to reason with myself but to no avail, crying myself to sleep at night, ashamed and distraught, angry that I couldn't control my reactions or myself and my thoughts. Still I couldn't seem to break my silence about the real reason why I felt the way I did, even to the one whom I felt the safest with. I became very worried that I was pushing Larry away, but felt powerless to stop my reactions towards him. Again and again, I would stuff the pain of my old trauma down hoping I could manage to keep it in a place where no one would ever have to know about it, not even him.

Eventually, too afraid that I was going to push my husband away and lose him, I gave him a very short and limited explanation. The pain of my experience was so intense I couldn't bring myself to tell him everything, just enough that I hoped he would understand and stay with me. He never once was anywhere near leaving me but my twisted sense of self-worth and doubt would tell me otherwise. It would take many, many years before I actually believed that he really did love me. So much time wasted and years spent; so sure that he desired something or someone else other than me.

That knife years ago had seared its way in. It was securely lodged into the very depths of my heart and the pain never left me. Every so often it would twist and sear, shooting its reminders of being firmly lodged there. Its reminders becoming more and more frequent through the ensuing years. I longed for something different in my life, freedom from this pain.

Why can't I find any solace?

The peace that I always longed for always eluded me. Deceived and caught up in the lies I believed, that I must never let anyone know and too afraid to let anyone know that I needed help.

Here I was, in church services over and over, felt the presence of God around me and knew he was a loving God, but it was a truth I couldn't transition from my mind to my heart. By now I had joined the worship team as a background singer and there I was standing on the platform singing songs about the peace of God, feeling like a monstrous fraud, because peace was something I didn't have. I could never bring myself to ask for help or prayer so afraid of exposing myself to others. My mind was so twisted that I couldn't even talk to God about it because of the shame I felt. I had placed my fears of performance and what I thought was expected of me as a good little Christian girl and a good pastor's daughter even onto God. I thought he must expect the same performance from me as everyone else expected of me. I wasn't taught this but I couldn't transition from one expectation to another. Imperfect love versus the perfect love of God, I didn't understand and couldn't seem to grasp.

So I continued to live my life smothered in fear and pain, remaining in a strangled silence and hiding, what was to me, my dirty little secret of shame.

Good Times,
Memories,
&
Happy Accidents

CHAPTER

15

*T*wists and bends in this river of my life were filled with periods of time, some short and some long, that I could conceal my inner pain deep enough and ignore it enough to manage to enjoy a lot of my life. I do remember having some good and very fun times.

Larry and I and our young kids went on a lot of fishing adventures with my dad. Every summer a group of us, friends and family, would embark on a week's long halibut fishing trip down on the Kenai Peninsula, at a place called Anchor Point, about a five hour drive from our home. We would fish out of inflatable Zodiac boats out in the ocean on the Cook Inlet. The men of the group would get together for weeks ahead, planning the much anticipated trip where they'd gather in my dad's garage and melt down lead to cast large fishing weights needed for their fishing gear. The one to two pound weights were used to hold their fishing lines several hundred feet down on the ocean floor bottom where the halibut would feed.

Part of the preparation included studying the tide tables and making trips in the early spring down to the banks of the Turnagain Arm near Twenty Mile River, where schools of hooligan would come in. The guys would wield these long poles with large nets on them, dip netting for the fish, scooping up the swimming fish as they came by, catching buckets of them that would later become the bait for their halibut fishing trip.

Sometimes us wives and our young children would ride along and sit and watch them from the banks as they put on chest waders or hip boots on and waded out into the cold and muddy waters with their cumbersome poles to catch their bait. We'd cheer them on when their nets would come out of the water yielding those wiggling silver fish.

Halibut fishing rods were brought out, and new heavy fishing line put on. Their Zodiac boats would be aired up and patched if needed. There was always lots of fellowship to be had and many stories would be told of all the previous halibut fishing trips they had taken. I always enjoyed sitting around listening to them plan their trip and tell their tales of the last fishing trip taken. Stories were always told of who caught the biggest fish, who turned a bit green fighting off sea sickness, how big the waves and swells were; they'd recount every last detail and it never failed, there was always something to laugh about.

We'd all go down to the camping grounds at Anchor Point near the beach and pitch our tents and hang out in the evenings around campfires enjoying the late midnight sun. The guys would fish around the tide schedule so sometimes they'd be launching their boats off the beach in the surf in the wee hours of the morning, usually being gone about 8-12 hours. Those of us that didn't go out in the boats would roam the beach during the day. I liked to find a pile of driftwood where I could sit peaceful in its shelter from the ever-present wind and stare out at the vast body of water and whittle the time away, watching the kids play in the tide pools and enjoy the beauty around me. It was here on these trips that I started to really love being by the ocean. The views in Alaska surrounding the ocean are absolutely breathtaking, the smell of the fresh salt air and wind whipping through your hair invigorating.

I did get awfully tired of tenting it though. Especially when it rained, standing in the drizzle trying to flip pancakes over the Coleman stove, making breakfast for my small children while Larry was out fishing. My kids were oblivious to their Mom's discomfort, having fun wrestling around in the tent while I made their breakfast. One particular trip a new family had come down and pitched their tent next to us, their young child cried all, and I mean all night long. Coming from another tent next to us the snoring was so loud from the man of the tent I thought I would go mad. Sleep ever so elusive with all these night sounds made for a very grumpy me the next day. By mid-week into our trip all I wanted was my soft bed at home and a long hot shower. Tenting it was just never my cup of tea.

The men got awfully jealous of Larry, his very first halibut fishing trip he caught a 100 lb. halibut, setting the record for the largest they'd hauled in as of yet.

The guy's excitement showed as we watched them haul their catch up the beach. We heard more than one of them ask the same question.

"Wow how much do you think this thing weighs!"

"I don't know, maybe seventy-five pounds or more!" Larry strained as he lifted up his fish. "It sure is heavy!"

"It's almost as long as you!" His friend exclaimed. "I can't believe it, your first time out!"

Larry beamed, happy to be able to break their record. "We'll have to measure its length too!"

His friend groaned as he held up the hand held fish scale with Larry's fish hanging from it.

"A hundred pounds!" a prideful Larry called out to the rest of the guys.

While we sat around the campfire those that went out fishing told stories of large sea lions trying to get in their boat after their halibut. Tales were told of falling asleep in the sun and waking up later to discover they had drifted miles past where they were supposed to be and stories of having to bring out the gun to shoot the larger halibut they had caught before they brought them into their boats so it wouldn't flop around with so much force they could get hurt. The way they told their tales made it sound like they had so much fun. I started feeling like maybe I was missing out on something rather grand, it just all sounded like quite the adventure. It set me to thinking. Even though I was deathly afraid of the water, partly because I'd never learned to swim, there hadn't been much opportunity to learn since there were no swimming pools around and most of the outdoor bodies of water in Alaska are freezing, I decided one summer I would be brave and see what all the fun was about. *I'm going to go out on the boat with them and fish!*

Only three people could fit in one Zodiac comfortably and fish. Larry, his friend that had been his best man at our wedding, and I, pushed out into the surf one morning. My excitement quickly turned into terror when that first wave hit us as we launched out into the ocean surf. My first thought was, drat, what have I gotten myself into! I knew once we'd launched the boat they'd never turn back no matter how much I whined. I was going to have to suck up my fears; I was stuck on this bouncing rubber boat in this vast body of water for the day! Part way into the forty-five minute ride out to the fishing grounds I felt myself get used to the feel of the boat riding the swells and waves of the ocean. Beneath me the Zodiac boat was riding the water rather smoothly so I started to relax, feeling relatively safe. We fished for hours, moved around some and fished some more. It was exciting to learn how to let your weight bob along the ocean floor and feel the tug of a halibut biting it, then reel the large fish up from the bottom of the ocean floor.

We caught fish, ate our packed lunch and then the dreaded thing happened.

"Larry, I have to go to the bathroom bad!" quietly but fervently I whispered to him.

Now the guys could just easily stand and pee off the side of the boat. My only option was to try to hang my derriere off the side of that moving, slippery, bouncing boat all the while trying to be discreet.

"I promise I won't let you slip!" Larry tried to assure me. "I'll hold onto you!"

"No, I can't, besides we're not alone!" furiously whispering in his ear my outrage at the thought.

I was far too embarrassed and scared to even think about trying it. That was not going to happen! I would have nothing to do with it. Visions came to my mind of myself sliding off the slippery pontoon, sinking to the dark depths at the bottom of the ocean. Finally they decided they'd fished long enough and we would go back in. I thought for sure we'd never get back in time before I wet my pants! That bouncing long, long ride skimming the waves as we headed back into shore was sheer torture.

It's always pretty cold out on the ocean in Alaska. So there I was all bundled up, long johns beneath my jeans, shirt and extra sweater, a dark green puffy vest for extra warmth, winter coat, knit hat, gloves, rubber boots, wool socks, and on top of it all an orange life vest strapped on. Just my luck when we landed at the beach, the tide was way, way out. It was going to be a long hike up the beach around and through the tide pools to the outhouse! As soon as our boat hit the beach I frantically leapt out of the boat, leaving a trail all up the sandy beach shedding my extra clothes in a mad rush to get to the outhouse in time. Everyone waiting on the beach for the boats to come back in were laughing at the long trail of clothes I had left up the beach. They knew exactly where I was headed in such a frantic rush. Deciding that had been more than enough adventure for me, I didn't go out halibut fishing with them again.

Several years later after having some pretty dangerous launching experiences in the ocean surf, my dad decided it was time to let his Zodiac go and build a bigger wood boat. I remember one particularly bad time the guys kept trying to launch their rubber boats in the pounding surf. Even though they had overturned some of their boats and lost gear trying to launch, still they stubbornly kept trying till they would finally make it out into the surf and past where they could motor off into the swells. My father was one of the first of the boats to come back in from fishing and when he came in trying to land his boat on the beach a rogue wave hit his boat in the back, flipping the boat over onto him and his passengers, carrying away in the waves a lot of their expensive fishing gear and soaking them in the process. He'd decided they'd finally had enough and we would move camp farther down the beach to a place called Whiskey Gulch where they hoped the surf would be tamer.

Some of us stood on the beach to watch for the other boats to come back in so we could yell at them to not try and land in the wild surf, but instead head back up the beach a few miles to Whiskey Gulch. Larry happened to have the smallest boat of all of them and when I saw him heading back in towards the beach for some reason he was alone in his boat. We yelled and yelled at him across the water, our screams being lost in the wind and waves while he attempted to bring his boat into the beach.

"Don't come in!" we yelled, "It's too dangerous!" "We're moving camp down to Whiskey Gulch!"

My heart leapt in my throat as I watched his boat, he was standing practically on end in the wild surf and swells, the boat not making it completely over a wave. I was sure he was going to go over backwards and drown. Finally after hearing our screams he managed to get back out farther into the ocean and took off towards Whiskey Gulch, where upon landing on the beach there, he realized he had lost one of his landing wheels in that wild surf.

I put my foot down; I told Larry in no uncertain terms no longer did I want to go on these week long fishing trips.

"I'd rather stay home than watch you guys take your life in your hands doing stupid things all over some stupid silly fish!" "It's not worth the risk!" "I won't watch, I won't!"

Larry sold his boat soon after, deciding it was much too small for the ocean. Funny how they always thought those were the best stories to tell, always soliciting chuckles among themselves.

"Remember when ..."

Many years later when Larry's work charted a large fishing boat taking their employees fishing free of charge, I thought I'd take the chance and swallow my ever-present fear and try going out on the ocean once again. This time though the boat was far bigger, had a large enclosed warm cab with heat and most importantly, a bathroom onboard. Taking this chance proved immensely successful, I ended up catching two extremely large halibut. One weighed in at 180 pounds, the other about 220 pounds. Only one other fish caught on the boat was larger than mine, and the rest much, much smaller. I was extremely proud of myself, especially since many had quit fishing altogether because they had gotten seasick.

I'll never forget how much work it was hauling those gigantic fish up from the bottom of the sea. The captain and some of the deck hands kept offering to take over for me but I staunchly refused, I wanted to do it on my own. The deck hands strapped a large thick leather belt on me that had a place to rest the end of my fishing pole in so I could reel in my line better. I worked and worked; slowly cranking on the reel inching those large fish up from the ocean floor. I'm not sure how long it took but as my arms burned it felt like an eternity. My body paid for the hard work later, never had I been so sore in my life. My arms and back ached horrendously but it was so worth it, just alone for the bragging rights. The next year again I went out on the company's charter boat with Larry, catching fish but nothing as large as before. Long after others abandoned their poles and went inside the cab I kept fishing, the captain letting me catch as many as I wanted since he did a boat limit not an individual limit. I started to love being on the water, feeling the wind in my hair and the sun on my back. As long as the boat was big and the waters not too rough I really started to enjoy myself and my newfound adventures.

In later years we took several tour boats out of Homer. One long weekend we took a camping trip down to Homer with our son's family where we charted a small private boat to take us out into the bay for a short sightseeing trip. When we all got down to the docks to the slip where we were to board the boat we noticed a distinct smell of French fries wafting from the rather rundown boat we were about to board. The friendly captain and his young son greeted us and welcomed us all on board.

"I sure hope this boat is sea worthy!" we whispered among ourselves as we stepped onto the weathered boat.

"It sure smells like French fries!" several of us mentioned to the captain.

"I have a side business where I turn used cooking oil into fuel, it's the fuel I use in my boat." The captain explained.

"Oh that makes sense for the unusual smell."

The smell of fried food coming from his boat as we made our way out of the harbor sort of made me hungry.

A Simple Extraordinary Life

We slowly motored out of the docks and into the bay, heading to a small island not far away called Gull Island where thousands of birds are. On our way to the island we ran into a pod of killer whales swimming and breaching around us. The captain started to follow the killer whales as they continued to swim all around us. He stopped the boat and just let us drift around out in the water while the whales started circling us coming closer and closer. It was a beautiful and rare sight for these parts of the waters the captain explained to us, so he asked us if we wanted to stay there with the whales instead of heading to the island.

"Yes!" we said with enthusiasm.

His young son had climbed up on top of the cab of the boat and was video recording the whales as they got closer and closer, his excitement very obvious as he kept shouting.

"How cool is this!" "DAD, can you believe it!"

I was standing outside watching them with my young granddaughter in front of me when suddenly one of the mama whales came swimming directly towards us. My poor granddaughter wanted to run and hide but we stood there as the whale came right up to the side of the boat, popped its head up with a dead seal in its mouth as if to say, look what I have! Next to her, a young calf popped up and the mama tossed the seal over to it. The distinctive black and white coloring of those whales as they surfaced near us took my breath away. They stayed around us for quite a while showing off as if they were playing a game with us till they finally tired of it and swam away.

Seward, Alaska is also another favorite camping spot of mine down on the Resurrection Bay. There are many large tour boat companies that take hundreds of passengers out on half day and full day tours to view the Kenai Fjords Glacier. One summer Larry and I had taken one of our young granddaughters and her younger brother with us to camp for the weekend there near the bay. We found a camping spot and popped up our tent trailer to find that our battery wasn't working so we didn't have any lights making us thankful for the midnight sun as we sat around a fire till way past the kid's usual bedtime while they pretended they were Indians on an adventure out in the woods.

My Journey from Anxiety to Peace

The next morning we boarded one of those tour boats for yet another ocean excursion. We saw whales and dolphins on our way to cruise by Fox Island and then they took the boat close to some islands where some caves had been carved out by the sea. The captain very carefully brought our large boat into the cave. We stood at the bow of the boat with my grandchildren watching as we could almost reach out and touch the sides of the cave.

"These must be the Jack Sparrow caves from Pirates of the Caribbean!" our young grandson announced to everyone aboard.

"Yep, they must be." An amused passenger said to him.

Everyone around us chuckled at his innocent admiration of what in his eyes he thought he was seeing.

Once while vacationing in California we took a whale watching tour, again seeing many whales. I thoroughly enjoyed being out on the ocean again but it was hard to not compare it to the beauty of the ocean bays in Alaska. I love to gaze at the majestic vistas that surround me near the bays in Alaska and marvel at the wonder of God's creation.

We had some other exciting and fun fishing trips, where we loaded our zodiacs on four-wheel drive trucks and went salmon fishing to a place we frequented a lot up The Little Susitna River. Back then just getting there to the river was part of the adventure. The road in, if you could call it a road was several miles of a slippery, muddy, and severely bumpy trail through the woods called the Burma Road that only a four-wheel drive truck could traverse. After finally making it to the river's landing we'd launch our boats in the river and go downriver towards the mouth and fish. We'd fish for silver salmon, which were very plentiful and so much fun to catch, especially when they'd put on a show jumping around in the river. Just when you almost had your fish up to the bank ready to net they'd make a screaming run back up river with the hook in their mouth and then you'd have to reel them in once again. I loved the thrill of catching them, but never cared much for eating them.

It seemed like once the state fixed up the road making the drive in to the river now a piece of cake, so many more fisherman started coming to the river to fish that our trips had declined. It just wasn't as much fun since much of the adventure was now gone and too many people were around with their boats on the river.

CHAPTER

16

*D*ad had built his new wood and fiberglass boat, painting it forest green and white. His boat was about twenty-two feet long and had an enclosed cab at the bow. He took it out a few times halibut fishing down in Homer but soon turned to a new adventure. He would launch his boat out of the port of Anchorage and go across the inlet to the mouth of the Little Susitna River where he would then head up river to salmon fish in the late summer, or take hunting trips in the fall.

My first and only trip I would ever take across the inlet in that green wooden boat of my dad's became the source of an embarrassing and many times recounted story, told repeatedly by my father across the pulpit.

There were always a lot of us wanting to go fishing with Dad, so one day my father loaded about ten of us up on his boat to take us fishing across the inlet. It was far too many people for his boat, but off we went anyways. I had three sons by now and had left my youngest son with my mom for the day and took my older two sons with Larry and me. Besides the four of us, three of my brothers, one of their friends, a sister, and my dad comprised the group.

Lunches were packed and our fishing gear loaded. Early in the morning we drove into Anchorage to the public docks where Dad could launch his boat. We all hopped aboard ready for a fun day of fishing for salmon. The forty-five minutes it took to cross the inlet went smoothly as we made our way over to the wide mouth of the river and then cruised our way upriver, anchoring the boat in the river. We got our poles and gear out and cast our lines into the river. While we all fished Dad ran around netting our catch as fast as he could, bringing the netted fish into the boat. The fish were so plentiful Dad was having a hard time keeping up. He'd barely get one in the net and into the boat and the hook out of its mouth when someone would excitedly yell.

"Fish on!" their fishing pole bent towards the river with the pull of their hooked fish.

My line tugged, I set the hook and yelled, "Fish on!"

"Hold on just a minute!" Dad said as he scurried around.

"Never mind Dad!" I yelled at him across the boat.

My fish had just jumped, hook and all and landed squarely in the middle of the boat on its own.

We had a fun day of fishing, catching our limit of fish when the weather started turning windy and the clouds were looking a little threatening, so we packed up and headed back to the mouth of the river. We planned to make our way back across the inlet to the docks where Dad would pull his boat out of the water and load it back onto his boat trailer and we'd head to our parked vehicles and make the drive home. The weather was turning bad rather fast as we headed downriver towards the mouth. The water was getting very choppy near the mouth of the river, the wind was howling, whipping around picking up force, and a light rain had started to fall.

By this time I was starting to panic, becoming really scared because we didn't make it all the way out of the mouth of the river into the inlet when my dad decided it was too dangerous and turned the boat around and back upriver. We found an old duck hunting shack out on the marshy flats close to the mouth of the river where we could take shelter in. Dad anchored his boat on the gray muddy banks of the river. The tide was going out which would leave us stranded so we'd have to wait till the next slack tide in about six hours, to try again to get out of the mouth of the river and back across the inlet. We all hiked up the muddy and slippery riverbank, through the windswept grass to the duck shack, which was pretty primitive. It did have two plywood bunks in it and a stove.

We were all hungry and had no food left, having eaten our packed lunch's hours ago. Because we wouldn't be able to get back down to the boat later due to the receding tide, the guys trudged back down the muddy banks to the boat and went and got some of our fresh caught salmon from the cooler. We cooked the fresh fish on the wood stove in a dirty cast iron frying pan that we had found in that old shack. We had no plates or silverware so we all picked at it with our fingers and tried to ignore our thirst because we didn't have anything left to drink either.

Listening to the never ending whistling of the wind outside that shack I was beside myself with anxiety about having to get back in that boat again. Afraid we were going to possibly sink out there in the waves in the inlet once we tried to make the crossing again. My fears were spiking out of control.

"Can't we just walk back upriver to the Burma Road and hike out." I pleaded.

"Don't be silly, it's too far!" Larry told me.

Everyone tried in vain to tell me it was way too far to hike, miles and miles away but I continued to beg Larry.

"Please, please can't we walk? They can take the boat if they want to but I want to walk!" my anxiety taking over any reasonable thought.

Frustrated with my insistent begging of him Larry had to get stern with me. "No we are not walking, I told you its way to far, it'll be fine!"

I didn't want to listen to reason. My fear was giving me a stomach ache, I positively dreaded the prospect of getting back on that boat when it came time for us to try and leave again. The wind continued to whip and howl outside that duck shack, the rain pelting the side of the old timber walls, only compounding my fears.

Hours later the tide had finally come back in and we all trudged back down to the boat. I wasn't very willing at all. My feet felt leaden in my rubber boots as I made my way through the tall grass and gooey mud, down the bank to the river. I had no other choice but to go. My younger brother, younger sister, my two children, and I were put in the cab of the boat while the guys rode in the stern. The door to the cab was kept shut by a lock on the outside of the door. Being locked in like that only served to heighten my anxiety even more. We made our way to the mouth of the river into the rough waves. There was a window in the cab at the bow of the boat, waves were crashing over and we could see nothing but a wall of water, which only made me more fearful. It was still very windy, not having calmed all that much, the skies gray with gloomy drizzling rain.

Dad's boat was bouncing and crashing hard in the waves as he drove it out of the mouth of the river and started to make our way across the inlet. We were bumping and crashing hard into the oncoming waves in the wide mouth of the river when all of a sudden my dad opened the cab door.

"Hand out the life jackets." He said rather seriously.

No one had been wearing any. My brother and I dug underneath the benches and handed them out, only to find we were short, there weren't enough life jackets to go around. Fearfully thinking to myself we had come across the inlet with no life jackets on, why is Dad asking for them now? *It's got to be bad, a sure omen.* Since I didn't know how to swim anyways I figured a life jacket wasn't going to help me any so I just sat there scared out of my wits going without one. I made sure to put my children's life jackets on and whispered a prayer we'd never have to put them into use.

Dad closed the cab door and locked it again after we handed out enough life jackets for the guys outside. My younger brother and I looked at each other, our eyes communicating how scared out of our minds we each were. Visions were dancing in my head. *I am going to be taking my kids with me down to the bottom of the sea floor and I will never see my baby again!* It sure didn't help my anxiety any that Dad had previously said we were overloaded with too many people.

Soon I could tell we started to go in circles, still bumping and crashing into the waves. I was going out of my mind, thinking for sure someone must have fallen over board. We knocked loudly on the door of the cab trying to get their attention so someone could tell us what was going on. Finally they opened it up a crack.

"Why are we going in circles?" my nervous brother asked.

Someone had lost their hat in the wind and they had circled back to get it. This did not relieve any of our fears in the least! My brother and I continued to look at each other, our individual fears feeding each other. They closed the door and locked us in again.

We slammed hard into another wave, walls of water crashing over the window when my brother scared as I was, jumped up and placed both hands on the window.

"Jesus! Jesus! Jesus!" he screamed.

My children's eyes were huge as I immediately started praying fervently that we would be saved, out loud, very loud, just as crazed as my brother. Our sister just looked at us rather calmly, like we had both lost our minds. We kept going and the waves calmed down a little, bit by bit, but it was still rough going. When we finally made it back to the dock as I hoisted myself over the side of the bobbing boat I vowed never to step back on that green boat of my father's again. Needless to say, from the pulpit, my father for some reason thought it funny to tell of mine and my brothers "*come to Jesus*" prayer meeting in the bow of the boat. It always solicited a lot of laughs.

Par for the course of being a preacher's kid is many times you get to be used as an example in their sermons. I would be highly embarrassed but learned to laugh about it. Our hysteria really had been a sight to behold. It wouldn't be the only story he told about me. I think my twin brother though was used as an example much more than the rest of Dad's kids. Like the time he decided he wanted to hang glide off the top of the church roof. My dad just watched him take heavy birch logs and staple visqueen onto them and then he hauled his contraption up to the church roof. My skinny brother grunted and strained as he lifted that thing up, took a running start and leapt off the roof, only to fall straight down flat on his face. My father just watched the whole thing chuckling. The drop wasn't that big so Dad wasn't too worried. Every time my dad told that story my brother would swear though that he got a few glorious seconds of hang time before he slammed into the ground.

A different time my brother decided he would build a dog house in the basement of our house. Dad again didn't interfere or say a thing; he just sat back and watched him build this huge and monstrous size of a dog house. When my brother was proudly done building his dog house he realized something, he had no way to fit it out the door.

Dad just laughed at him. "Bet you'll learn to measure the door first next time."

My unfortunate twin brother was always a great source of stories that would either make their way into Dad's sermons or be told in the circle of Dad's friends that would gather at our house. Hunting stories were some of his favorites. Dad loved to laugh and have a good time. He had a way of making you laugh at yourself if you happened to be the focus of whom the current story he was telling at the time was focusing on.

One such story he liked to tell was of a trip they had taken to Talkeetna to go hunting. My dad, my twin brother, Larry, and a friend were all on that trip. They had taken my dad's small motorhome and were sleeping in it close to a set of train tracks. While the men were all fast asleep snoring, somewhere in my brother's subconscious mind he was dreaming; the motorhome was stuck on the train tracks and the whistle was blowing as the train thundered down the tracks towards them.

He started screaming while everyone calmly slept. "Everyone out, everyone out!"

There they all were, standing outside in the dark and cold in the middle of the night in their underwear, rubbing the sleep from their eyes while looking at each other wondering what the heck was going on. Everyone that is, but Larry who had gotten up from his bunk to curiously look out the door at them wondering what all the commotion was.

"Why are we all outside?" "What happened?" Dad said as they all stood there looking confused.

My Journey from Anxiety to Peace

My brother sheepishly hung his head. "Aaah..."

He never lived that one down for sure. Turns out his subconscious mind had heard the actual train as it went by, rumbling down the tracks in the middle of the night.

My father who loved pulling pranks, one time decided while they had been out hunting it would be funny to try and scare my brother. They were hunting with some friends and of course as they sat around the fire at night there was always the requisite talk of bears and how to keep the bears away from their camp. They had finished up their hunt and were hiking back out to their parked trucks. My brother had gotten far ahead of the rest of the hunting party so when he got to the truck he laid down on top of the hood and promptly fell asleep while waiting for the rest to catch up with him.

When my dad approached and saw him asleep there on the hood of the truck, he silently crept up to him on his hands and knees and gently started scratching at his dangling legs. It was all he could do to suppress his laughter. My brother suddenly woke up startled, thinking it was a bear. In lightning speed he jumped up on the truck's hood, fists in the air ready to punch the lights out of it, while down at his feet his rifle lay there on the hood of the truck.

Dad rolled on the ground laughing at my brother. "You think you're going to scare the bear away with your fists?" chuckling at the absurdity of my brother. "I think he would have eaten you by now!"

When my father later told us the story we were just glad my brother had decided to use his fists instead of his gun!

There was always a lot of clamoring to get to be part of Dad's hunting trips. More and more new people were added to them till eventually he had to cut back on the amount of people that went with him; it was fast becoming just way too many. My father loved people so much it was hard for him to tell others no. One hunting party they took that was excessively large would include Dad, his sons, his new son-in-law Larry, my sister who had also starting going on his hunting trips and one of his new hunting buddies which also included his own two sons and his daughter. It took massive planning and gear to get them all to their hunting grounds where they would usually go hunt at the mouth of the little Susitna River. Several boats and several trips were taken just to get all their gear up there to set up camp and to ferry everyone upriver. Breaking down camp and ferrying all their moose out took many trips also, but it always resulted in many new stories to tell.

One of those new hunting stories came from my younger brothers when he won a free trip to Hawaii. That month Pepsi Cola Company was running a promotion, in your empty pop can there would be a printed letter and if you could spell out Hawaii you won an all-expense paid trip to the Island. While out hunting my brother managed to spell Hawaii with the accumulated cans he had been drinking of Pepsi that had been brought along for drinks for the hunting party. Secretly he hoarded his stash of cans inside his tent, holding them close so no one could take them from him. He couldn't believe his luck! Just as soon as they got back from their hunting trip he took his empty cans in and claimed his prize! At the age of 18, soon after getting home from that hunting trip he took that free trip to Hawaii he had just won. In his view, overall that was probably the best and most successful hunting trip he ever took!

Sometimes their hunting trips wouldn't yield any moose and other times they'd bring enough back to keep everyone's freezers full for the winter. One particular hunting trip the hunters told the story how they got a huge surprise on the first day of their hunt. It was early morning, opening season, when the hunting party crawled out of their tents that morning surprised to see a whole herd of moose standing close by. A barrage of shots rang out shattering the peace of the quiet morning as everyone simultaneously started shooting till they finally had to yell at each other.

"Stop shooting!" "Everyone stop!"

"We better do a count to see how many moose we have shot!"

Sure that Larry and those on the hunting trip would all be gone at least a week, I was so surprised when they showed up the next day starting to haul out all the moose they had just shot.

Our freezers that year were stuffed with moose meat. That was the part I didn't like much about those hunting trips, the endless hours and days of helping cut up and package the meat. It always grossed me out so much it would take me weeks to be able to eat the meat without gagging just thinking about it. The comradery and laughs to be had while processing the meat wasn't just our own family affair but always included the families of the hunting party. Of course the rehashing of stories of the hunt and previous hunts and the plans for the next hunt would ensue, making the whole process a lot of fun; even if I didn't like the smell of the moose quarters hanging nearby, ready to make their way to the tables spread around in the garage where we would cut it up into roasts, steaks, and grind up some of it for hamburger. They were good times laughing and joking with everyone.

Even my husband Larry had the should we say "unfortunate" experience of being used as yet another amusing example of a story that managed to find its way to the pulpit in one of my father's sermons. Dad wasn't even with us at the time the incident happened but because he had heard about it and what Larry's response was, I guess he thought it was fair game to tell it since Larry was his son-in-law.

Since fishing was a great past time of my dad's and he took us all with him a lot along with a lot of close friends, it made it much easier to participate in these excursions if you had your own boat and even your own four-wheel drive truck or SUV. We bought both.

Larry had just bought his new Zodiac rubber boat and new outboard motor. We decided to go fishing with our friends who also had their own rubber boat. There we were with our new shiny boat and brand spanking new motor, ready to go on yet another fishing trip to the Little Susitna River. We loaded up our young families in our four-wheel drive vehicles early in the morning, ready for another great day of fishing. Our two young sons were with us and very excited to go fishing. After the always exhilarating four-wheel drive ride down that rutty and muddy, bone jarring, teeth chattering so called road through the woods to the landing at the river it always made you feel like you had just accomplished a great feat. Just getting there would be worthy of some story telling later on.

Our excited kids watched, as their dads pumped up the boats with air, ready to get in and start our much anticipated fishing trip upriver.

A Simple Extraordinary Life

Our friends had their boat in the water and their motor running, waiting for us to get loaded into ours and start our motor. We pushed out into the current of the river, our rain jackets donned in the slight rain. A pair of very excited eyes from our youngest son looked up at us, he was wearing a grin ear to ear just happy as he could be. He was in the boat and what he thought, on his way.

Larry yanked on the pull starter for the outboard motor and nothing happened. He shrugged his shoulders as he looked over at our friends who were patiently waiting in their boat.

"What's the matter?" our friend yelled from his boat nearby.

"It won't start!" Larry answered.

He pulled and pulled, over and over again, it would sputter a bit then quit. As he tried to start the motor we slowly kept drifting down the river. Larry and his friend were yelling back and forth at each other.

"Do you have the choke on?"

"Not anymore! It just won't start!"

Sweat poured down Larry's face while he continued to yank on the pull start with no success. Yank, yank, it wouldn't start, Larry's frustration was mounting as we were drifting farther and farther down river. It was a brand new motor, but no amount of pulling would get the darn thing going when all of a sudden, through the soft drizzling rain we hear this little exuberant voice singing. An excited little boy sat at the back of the boat completely oblivious to his Dad's predicament. He was happily singing a song he knew from church, his sweet little voice floating through the air.

"This is the day, this is the day that the Lord hath made, that the Lord hath made."

Larry's mounting frustration I'm sure was telling him quite the opposite. We were drifting downriver and his brand new motor wouldn't start making him exasperated.

Furious Larry yelled, "Shut up Luke!" at our innocent singing son.

144

Trying to diffuse the situation I explained to my little son as I gave Larry a dirty look.

"Daddy is upset, he can't get the motor started."

I got him to sit quietly while Larry tried to control his mounting frustration. Realizing the motor wasn't going to start we had to get ourselves over to the riverbank, before we drifted too much farther. We knew we were going to have to pack the boat and useless motor back upriver through the woods to our parked trucks. Out came the oars and we managed to get ashore, unloaded and trekked back upriver, our fishing trip a bust. A disappointed but still happy go lucky little boy trudged along with us; though I made sure no more singing ensued. His Dad was not a happy camper!

Oh how my father loved to tell that story from the pulpit complete with Dad's boisterous singing.

"This is the day, this is the day that the Lord hath made, that the Lord hath made!" his voice ringing loudly through the speaker system.

Dad would giggle and laugh while he told the story and of course Larry would be embarrassed but he would get to laughing too. That was the thing about Dad, he never made you angry he used you as an example for his story telling, it was always in good-natured fun. He taught us the gift of learning to laugh at yourself and your sometimes unfortunate actions you'd done in the heat of the moment. In a way you were proud that your mishaps would become part of his story telling. We all loved him that much.

Now that I think about it, how he managed to weave them into sermons I'm really not all that sure. It was more than likely to lighten the mood and solicit some laughs. Even though he could embarrass me to no end, I loved him with a fierce love.

CHAPTER

17

$\mathcal{L}$ ife rolled on and surprise, I was pregnant for a fourth time. We moved into a new house we had just built when I found out I was expecting again. Honestly I wasn't happy about being pregnant again; I had been looking forward to a diaper free existence that was right around the corner. This wasn't planned and we had both been thinking three children were enough for us. I had a very bad attitude, I was upset and rather grumpy about this surprise especially since I had never enjoyed pregnancy and I sure wasn't looking forward to another one.

I had dreamed a lot about wanting a girl my first pregnancy, the second pregnancy I tried to not get my hopes up too much. I squelched my dreams for a girl the third time around and with the birth of a third boy I had resigned myself to not having any daughters. Having another chance at a daughter still didn't make me happy I was positively dreading the prospect of another pregnancy and delivery. After a few months of having a pretty bad attitude Larry told me I had better get used to the idea, this was happening. Trying to find something positive about the situation I tried to change my thinking. *Maybe this would be the girl I have always wanted which would help me learn to be happy about another child.* My hopes were escalating even though I was trying to control them so I wouldn't get too disappointed if they didn't come true. My eighth month into the pregnancy I was scheduled for a sonogram;

A Simple Extraordinary Life

Larry and I had made plans that I would pick him up at work after my doctor's appointment and we would go have lunch together on his lunch break.

I went alone to my sonogram appointment where they proceeded to tell me it was another boy. To say I wasn't very thrilled is an understatement. *Well that figures!*

Leaving my doctor's appointment I headed over to Larry's work ready to cry on his shoulder, only to find out, he had invited some of his co-workers to go to lunch with us. I sucked up my dismay and pasted on a happy face, determined to not let my crying that was just under the surface erupt in front of anyone. After giving Larry a peck on the cheek as I dropped him and his coworkers off at his office I drove home after lunch barely keeping myself in check. I unlocked the front door and went into the downstairs bathroom and looked in the mirror where disappointment radiated from my watery eyes, quickly turning away before I burst into tears.

"God, how could you do this to me?" my sudden outburst reverberated from the small room. "You know I have always wanted a girl!" I ranted.

Sudden visions came to mind of lightning bolts striking me down because of my ingratitude. Feeling guilty about my eruption of pent up emotion I determined I was going to have a better attitude from then on. *At least I'm going to try.*

Larry came home after work, I cried in his arms still simmering with letdown then pulled myself together and went to scrounge something up for dinner. That evening was a weeknight church service and I was short on time to make dinner so I decided to make something quick, grilled cheese sandwiches. I went to the bread box only to find no bread. Slamming the bread box closed I burst into more tears.

"Dad what's wrong with Mom?" the kids' worried voices inquired.

He shrugged his shoulders. "Oh nothing, she's just having another boy."

I glared at him, wondering why he didn't care.

My Journey from Anxiety to Peace

I can't remember what we did for dinner but off to church we went where I proceeded to paste on a fake smile, suck up my disappointment and feelings, afraid to let them show to anyone at church.

Now I can look back and find the humor in it all. A week or two after I had given birth to my fourth son he woke me up yet again during the night. I had been sick with a fever following his birth and was extremely fatigued. Exhaustion weighed down my heavy eyes, frustration bringing me close to tears. Since he had been born the nights had been grueling. Every time I finally had him asleep I would lay him back down and crawl back in bed only to have him wake up and fuss all over again. As I sat there in the chair next to my bed with him in my arms trying to stay awake enough to care for him I distinctly remember looking down at his little face as he dreamily slept away in my arms. I was captured by the sweet innocence that was so pure, as I watched his little pink lips randomly suck while he slept. I felt all my pent up defenses crumble. All the disappointment I had bottled up vanished as I looked at his precious face with the soft down of blonde hair upon his little head that felt so smooth beneath the palm of my hand. At that exact moment I fell deeply and madly in love with my fourth son.

He is, what I lovingly call, my happy accident. I loved to just sit back and watch him as he grew up. *How can this wonderful child be mine?* He was so very different from me, a super energetic child, funny, smart, independent, multi-talented, and so much more outgoing than I. His never-ending quick wit that developed as he grew into a young teenager would make me laugh and laugh. Some of my best memories are during his teenage years when his many friends would gather at our house, their laughter and antics a never-ending source of amusement for me.

The years I spent in raising children now are but a quick blur in my memory. In light of how many years I have lived now without any of my children living at home it's so easy to get caught up in regrets and want to go back in time and be granted a do over so I could have savored those precious times more. It really is so fleeting and to be as I was, so absorbed with anxiety about appearances, keeping up a perfect house, trying to always control everything around me lest I feel even more out of control with what was always going on inside me was such a waste. Overly worried and fretting about being at every church function lest people think badly about me, all of it, all the complexities that kept me from learning to live in and savor life's moments was at many times, at both my children's and husband's expense.

My problems and denial to truly confront those problems controlled my actions and responses much of the time. They wouldn't just affect me, but those close to me as well. A lot more of that wasted time I spent entrenched and weighed down with anxiety, fears and deep wounds that wouldn't heal.

Precious time and years that had gone by the wayside while I tried to ignore the real root of my issues continuing to vainly try and fix myself.

Advances,
New Outlets,
&
Hamster Wheels

CHAPTER

18

The meandering waters in the stream, which is my life, were picking up pace; the years of my youth and young adult life were rapidly slipping by. I was getting older, no longer that teenage bride and had moved quickly past being a young adult. Cracks were appearing more regularly in the carefully constructed hard shell of my wounded heart, threatening to spill out all of its contents. It was becoming increasingly harder and harder year after year, for me to manage and control, feeling like the weight of it was suffocating me. Wrapped tightly in my shame I still stubbornly clung to this idea I had to fix this on my own, manage it on my own, and repair it on my own.

It would seem that after all these years I would have found a way to put the past behind me but sadly that was not the case. Try as hard as I might, no amount of wishing it away would ease the pain I felt, temporary reprieves but nothing lasting. Finding myself fighting like mad to not let that old pain rise to the surface I would try and reason with myself, angry at my lack of control.

You're a grown woman; these things shouldn't bother you anymore! I repeated my mantra to myself over and over. *You've got to get over it already!* Angrily I would whisper under my breath. *Many other people have suffered worse things than I have, so why am I being such a baby about this?*

A Simple Extraordinary Life

Feelings of guilt would assault me that I let consume me when there were so many other people who had gone through much more horrific things, wildly thinking maybe this was just my cross to bear. Delusion had set in like hard concrete, believing I wasn't worthy of anything different. Shame wrapped itself so tight around me like a dark cloud, marring any view of the light I so desperately craved but couldn't seem to find my way to. So many times, and in many different situations when new hurts or offenses would come, I'd be back on what I can only describe as a monstrous hamster wheel again. Going round and round in a vicious cycle, letting the real deep reason for my hurt take hold of me, and overtake me yet again. Powerless to stop, but yet the pain so familiar, I didn't know any other way to live. Like a trusted friend, anxiety and fears were always right there, close by my side.

The unreasonable fear I had of other people was almost palpable. Through the years I managed to make small advances, breaking out of the tough shell of my timid and shy self that held me captive. Continuing to try and make more escape holes in that cardboard box of traits that surrounded me and held me back was a lot of hard work.

Larry worked for the State of Alaska as a draftsman when we were first married. We'd been married for four years when he decided he would rather work for himself. He had been doing a lot of work on the side for other people drawing up house plans and doing different drawings and plans for engineers. He discussed his idea of working for himself over with his father. Around that same time there was a very small office supply store in Eagle River up for sale. They decided together they would buy it and Larry would do drafting for his clients in the backroom of the store. Occasionally there would be times that Larry had to leave to meet his clients or run errands for the store, so he would work hard at persuading me into coming in and manning the store while he was gone running his errands. Not being too keen on this I hid out in the backroom while he was gone watching the clock for his return, fervently hoping no one would come in. If by chance the bell on the front door rang signaling a customer, my anxiety level would shoot through the roof. I had no choice but to drag my feet out to the front of the store and wait on these perfectly good strangers, hating every minute of it.

To converse with anyone other than family, or the people I knew at church instantly made me be in a state of panic. I'm sure our customers probably thought I was being rude with my lack of any kind of conversation with them. Accustomed to only being around mostly "*church*" people my circle of comfort was small, leaving me unreasonably afraid of anyone else. It was silly thinking on my part I know, but I had many unreasonable fears, this being one of them. Fears consumed me, rendering me almost useless much of the time. I couldn't even make the simplest of phone calls. Larry might ask me to call the telephone company to ask a basic question, and I would staunchly refuse. Slowly, very slowly I started to realize that people, especially ones I didn't know, were just like everyone else. I got used to helping with customers once in a while, making baby steps in my progress towards a less, albeit slightly less timid person.

After the first year or two of owning the office supply store we weren't making quite enough money to live on so Larry went back to work, finding a job with an engineering firm in Anchorage. We still owned the store so out of necessity because we couldn't afford to hire help; I reluctantly started to work there during the days. I learned how to order stock, do the accounting, display merchandise, and everything it took to run a store. Eventually, the store grew and financially we were doing a lot better leading me to hire help, family members or teens in the community to work some of the shifts.

This was something new for me, drawing me somewhat out of my limited comfort zones. I started to like what I was doing, finding some satisfaction in it. A slow confidence was building up in me that I could do more than just be a stay at home mom and wife. This new environment and new challenges were slowly forcing me out of my shell and giving me a new measure of self-worth, making baby steps of overcoming some of my extreme shyness.

By the late 1980's we had just moved our store into a brand new indoor mall in Eagle River, our fourth move due to our ever-increasing expansion. As soon as we made this move an unforeseen recession hit the state of Alaska. We had just signed a new expensive lease we couldn't get out of, resulting in a lot of money problems for ourselves over the next few years. The market was changing; you could now buy office supplies at many local stores and chain stores, no longer needing a specialized store like ours. We made another move after that lease was up to a different location where we downsized some and eventually sold the business.

I started to look for other work. I rather liked the thought of the extra income I could make that would help with our family bills or could be used for some family vacations. Extra income would also help pay for our children's tuition at the Christian school they attended, afford the occasional splurge of a meal out, and best of all I could have more choices of clothes in my closet to wear. The best thing extra money could buy, was not having to buy cheap powdered milk anymore, we could afford real milk. I hated powdered milk; it was what I grew up with.

On the lookout for a new job, a new opportunity had come up for me. My sister at the time was the full time secretary at our church and was about to get married. She wanted to go to part time work after she married so I started to work at the church as a secretary part time, essentially splitting the job between us. The church by this time had grown a lot and also had a Christian school of about 100 students. My sister's and my duties included being both the church and school secretary. We typed up sermons, made the church bulletins, answered the always ringing phones, and kept all the school records, which included the students' individual records. We typed up the teachers' tests and made copies and handled a myriad of requests from the staff, students and parents. We were always very busy. Eventually my sister quit to stay at home and raise her new family. I took over her duties which included keeping up three checking accounts, the church records, payroll for both the church and school, and all the other accounting. I added these duties to all the other things I had already been doing, going from working two days a week to three. If I thought my days were busy before, now they were extremely so, making the days whiz by. The church hired someone else to help out the other days I wasn't there.

My Journey from Anxiety to Peace

I enjoyed the years I was a secretary at the church but they also came with some new grievances I found I would have a hard time dealing with. One of my duties was accounting for all the tithes and offerings that came into the church. Being privy to this information of who gave money and who didn't to the church would be upsetting to me at times. When I knew those who never gave monetarily were also the ones who could whisper some unkind and untruthful things, especially if it pertained to my father and our family, it would hurt me and cause me to harbor ever increasing resentment. I already had enough trouble as it was with resentment, feeling like I always had to live in a fish bowl, having relegated in my heart that those feelings were the "*church*" people's fault. These new revelations would just add more fuel to the fire of my growing list of resentments I had, keeping track of them in my book of wrongs that had pages of an ever-increasing list of wrongs.

A few years had gone by and now my twin brother had joined the church staff as an administrator. He had come on staff, guns blazing thinking he'd shape things up. He didn't always use the best judgment as far as I was concerned. Not long after he came on staff he wanted to make some changes. Some of them pertained to me. He wanted to decrease the secretaries' pay by no longer paying for "*lunch hour*". I felt my anger start to rise. *How can he not realize that us secretaries never take a per say "lunch hour"*. We ate at our desk always answering the phones that never stopped ringing. We helped the steady stream of students, teachers, and parents. Lunch hour was actually one of the busiest times of the day because that was when the classrooms weren't in session. There were some other changes he wanted to make that I also felt were totally unjustified. I was having a very hard time feeling like I was being taking advantage of, just a doormat for someone else's wishes.

Well then, I'll just show him! I angrily muttered under my breath.

To be a bit of a stinker I had cooked up a plan to try to get my point across. Without telling anyone I started to leave at "*lunch hour*", let everyone else answer the phones I reasoned and they can see what it's really like!

A Simple Extraordinary Life

As I leisurely strolled in from lunch one day the phones were ringing off the hook. My dad, who didn't know where I went, was frantically looking around.

"Why aren't you answering the phone?" my father questioned me.

Needless to say, this didn't set too well with me at all.

Furiously I wanted to scream. *If you only knew what your precious son is doing to me!*

Pushing at my subconscious mind were all those feelings deep within of feeling unworthy and used from long ago.

Steaming I sat down at my desk and answered their precious phones with a fake cherry voice. "Peters Creek Christian Center may I help you?"

A few days later my brother came into my office and asked me to do something for him. I don't remember exactly what ensued but I do remember saying something snide to him and we got into a shouting match. I was near tears, the cracks in my wounded heart threatened to spill out what was in there. I was fighting like mad to hold all those injustices I had been keeping track of that had ever been done to me at bay, especially the worst one that always haunted me. I feared that someday someone might find out about the one that was so dirty to me that I had to hide it, the sexual abuse that was my private shame and deepest wound that had me browbeaten. It rose to the top of my list of injustices. My brother left my office, but he must have said something to my dad about our argument.

My father came into my office to ask what was going on between my brother and me. In an instant I became hysterical, crying and sobbing, highly embarrassed because I was so completely out of control. I ran out of the office, jumped in my car and went straight home where I immediately threw myself into furious cleaning and baking, crying and sobbing the whole time, still completely out of control. Awhile later my doorbell rang. Swiping at my tears, I answered the front door to find my father standing there. He had come to try and talk to me.

My Journey from Anxiety to Peace

My father tried to explain to me that my brother was eventually to take over the church because my dad would be retiring soon and he was worried for me, that I wouldn't accept my brother as a pastor. I tried to assure him that I would, but I couldn't stop my crying. While my father was trying his best to talk to me, I was giving him all kinds of excuses for my behavior. Dad stood on the other side of my kitchen counter while I furiously slammed bread dough around, trying to gain control of myself, and stop my torrent of sobbing. My thoughts were in rage at my brother, but most of all at that boy who made me feel so unworthy of being nothing more than his doormat, just something to be taken advantage of and I vowed, never would I let anyone hurt me like that again.

I was scared because I had lost control and full of an awful rage, angry that I held this awful secret. I couldn't bring myself to tell my father what my real struggles were and what secrets I was hiding, those I continued to keep silent about. I knew I was hysterical and my poor father was catching the brunt of it. Beneath the waterfall of tears and veil of anger it was hard to look at my father and know he was uncomfortable not knowing what to say or do with me.

"You know I love you," said my father as he turned to go.

I sucked in my breath and sniffed. "I know dad, I love you too."

As the front door closed behind my father a fresh wave of tears ran down my face. Tears of love for my father mixed with the angry tears of buried hurt. It would be many hours later before I got control of myself and yet again stuff the anger, fears and deep hurt away to a place far, far inside me that I thought I could again control. I steeled myself that once again I had to tamp down my feelings of unworthiness and continue to hide my pain. They must go to that icy place in my heart where the heat of those wounds would cool, if at least for a while, hopefully forever. *Maybe, just maybe this time I can truly forget and it won't boil up and rise again.* Eventually though it did, sadly it always did. Such a predictable cycle this hamster wheel I was on. Longing for escape but finding none.

A Simple Extraordinary Life

I had many uncontrollable episodes through the years; I never knew what might set them off. Sometimes it would be jealousy, other times it could be a slight innocent comment that made me feel invaluable. Sometimes the worst episodes would come when I felt my children were being treated unfairly. Looking back now I cringe when I think just how large my book, my list of wrongs, had become and to think how sadly I had only let that list of resentments grow in the future.

I felt bewildered, my thoughts were always jumbled trying to figure out if I was just acting out the role of a good Christian pastor's daughter most of the time or if I even had any true and genuine qualities or beliefs of my own. My father was such a servant and he had instilled faithfulness and servitude to the church in all of his children. We were on cleaning teams, worship teams, building teams and any and all activities within the church. Several of my brothers served as song leaders for many years. I struggled greatly with wondering if I had a true servant's heart or if I was just caught up in a works mentality. Like a yo-yo I went back and forth between each, burn out and guilt a byproduct of the two. *What is really at the core of who I am? Am I just a puppet pulled by the strings of guilt or am I pulled by the strings of genuine love? What convicts me to serve, is it guilt or is it an act of love? If my actions come from a place of love then why am I conflicted so much of the time?*

One of the things that drew me to Larry, his servitude heart; would also be something I would struggle with not resenting him for. Within his first year of attendance at our church he decided it would be nice for people if they could have access to recorded cassette tapes of all the sermons. On his own he took up his idea and ran with it. He sat on the back row with a reel-to-reel tape machine on the chair next to him and started to record all the services. Later during the week he would edit the recordings and put them on cassette tapes so people could check them out later from the church tape library that he also started.

Many times while we were dating I would sit with him in his bedroom at the end of the hall in his parents' house while he did the editing from the reel-to-reel tapes. We weren't always the best behaved when he was editing. Because he had to have absolute quiet during the editing process he'd hang a sign on his bedroom door that said don't come in, editing. His mother would leave us alone and we'd use the opportunity to do some covert kissing, which of course would only make us feel a bit naughty with the sound of preaching going on in the background.

Eventually advances were made at the church and new sound equipment was purchased. As the church grew new auditoriums were built and Larry had his own sound booth. For over thirty-five years he ran the sound booth during services and was in charge of setting up all the sound equipment before services and taking it down after all services. Right after services he would put the recorded service on tapes, which eventually became CD's for immediate checkout. It was just a part of all the many duties he had. The church had ordained him a deacon and one of his duties included counting and recording the tithes and offerings that came in every service and making sure it was put away safely in the church's safe.

Almost always he would also lock up the church building after every service. It made for many late nights during the mid-week evening services while our children and I waited with him for everyone to leave. We never drove two cars to church since just going to and leaving the church together was some of the limited time we were able to spend together. Our kids would be elated when the rare time came that the church building would empty out fast enough that we could run down to the gas station across the street before it closed for a bedtime snack. While we stood around waiting for their father to be done the kids would start their begging and plotting.

"Please Mom can we go get some donuts and milk?"

"You have to ask your dad."

They'd run to their dad and ask him the same thing. "Can we go get some donuts and milk?"

Larry looked at his watch. "I don't know they close in ten minutes."

"Come on Dad...please, pretty please? You know you want too." Their eyes pleaded with their dad. "We can make it in time!"

"Okay, quick get in the car while I lock the church doors."

A Simple Extraordinary Life

They'd take off running, grinning knowing they'd gotten their way because their dad loved donuts just as much as they did. We'd sit around the dining room table after we were home enjoying our donuts and ice-cold milk before I made them scurry off to bed and promise me they wouldn't be grumpy in the morning because of a late night when I had to wake them up early for school.

One of Larry's many talents is that he is gifted in graphics and design and knows how to do engineer drawings. He would spend many hours doing those kinds of things for the church. He did all the drawings for the church every time they made new additions to the church building. This included finding and being liaison for the required architect and assorted engineers needed; and overseeing the process it took to build the biggest addition to the church they ever did. He spent time drawing up house plans for relatives and different people in the church also. He worked a full time job that included many overtime hours so he was always busy with all the extra things he took on beside the commitment he had to his employer. I was quite proud of Larry's many talents and his heart to serve and his strong work ethic.

For a while the church had a team that would go out and clean up and harvest the meat from the many moose that would get hit and killed by cars on the highway. The meat harvested would go to needy families in the community. Larry was on what we called the "moose kill" team. It never failed that he would get called out in the middle of a cold winter's night to go help take care of the road kill standing in freezing temperatures for hours while they gutted and quartered it and then hauled it to someone's garage or shed where they'd hang it up before it was determined who it would go to. Many times in the wee hours of the morning after he had returned he would come crawling back into bed thinking it was funny to try and cuddle up next to me with his freezing ice cold bum.

I shoved playfully at him as he crawled beneath the sheets. "Don't you dare, get away from me, you're like ice!"

"Come here I want to cuddle!" Larry laughed as he squeezed me in his arms.

"You're mean!" I would giggle as I tried to squirm away.

He'd just continue to laugh at my mock outrage; he knew I was glad he was home as I settled down into his arms.

"Night babe," I whispered. "Love you."

"Love you too pet." His snores coming minutes after he'd settled in.

Even though I was proud of Larry's servitude it didn't always stop me from feeling resentment. Many times I felt like a widow sitting in the church pew with my four children always alone because Larry had to sit in the sound booth and run the sound. I sulked when he tried to get a break from it but the most anyone ever would take over would be a month or two then they'd decide they'd rather sit with their own families, so back to the sound booth Larry would go.

"I'll bet you a lot of visitors think I am a single mother sitting here all alone with all these kids!" I teased my husband.

My teasing though would turn into times of sitting there and stewing, *why must it always be us who have to sacrifice?* It would be just another thing I would add to my growing list of resentments and go into my book of wrongs where I was fast accumulating many marks. It was a mistake to foolishly think I could bury everything and not deal with things like I should have, wrongly thinking that they wouldn't come to light someday.

There was a reoccurring theme with me that always bothered me. I admired Larry's selfless heart but oh how I could begrudge it too. *Here we go again, the church and its people must always come first.* Coupled with the fact he was always busy with church activities besides working many overtime hours at his job, always finding it hard to say no to other things that took time away from us, he too just like me would struggle with trying to find the balance with learning how to put our own family first without having guilt and anxiety about it. It was easy to be weighed down with the pressure to have to uphold some ridiculous notion that we both had of having to sacrifice an unreasonable demand of our time to the church, reasoning that it was our service to God. *If the pastor's family which now included my husband and children, my brothers and sisters and their families weren't being everything the people expected, the example to follow, what then were we?* It always felt like an impossible weight to carry, one that caused a lot of anxiety.

A weight I didn't need to take on in the wrong manner I did.

CHAPTER

19

*L*ife was changing for me; I had more disposable time now. My boys were getting much older and independent, freeing up a lot of my time. No longer was it necessary that I was always home. They could easily fend for themselves and quite enjoyed the independence from always having mom around. I avoided the underlying fact that it was difficult for me to be still for too long lest I be reminded of the things that haunted my deep inside. I needed something more to keep my mind and hands busy.

Since I had always enjoyed making things, I started to make crafts and sell my finished products at local craft fairs. I liked the creative process of making things but didn't enjoy the part it took of selling my handmade items. It put me in that pesky situation that forced me into the dreaded position that made me the most uncomfortable, I would have to deal with strangers. The extra money I was making though spurred me to keep pushing through my discomfort and continue, feeling good that I could bring in even more money besides the income I earned at my secretary job.

More and more I was finding new and interesting things I liked to do. Ever so slowly the small and confined world created by myself from being riddled with so many fears and lack of self-confidence in any of my abilities was steadily evaporating.

A Simple Extraordinary Life

I had developed a new love of learning how to do different things when Larry and I had our first house built a few years prior by my twin brother. We were able to do a lot of the work ourselves on our new house. One job we did that I didn't particularly like was to insulate almost the whole house. Even with long sleeves and gloves the fibers from the insulation batts would work their way into our clothes and hair and make us itch horribly. The money we were saving doing the job ourselves spurred us on to just suck it up and get the job done despite our discomfort. By myself I took on the large job of staining all the woodwork and trim for our new house and together we learned how to install ceramic tile, tiling two bathrooms and the hearth and surround for our wood stove.

I beamed with pride at the willingness of Larry to learn to try new things. To save even more money on our new house, I encouraged him that he could make all of our kitchen cabinets. Never having done anything of this scope before he was a bit dubious but I had faith in his talents. He took the project on and ended up making beautiful cabinets; not only for the kitchen but for the bathrooms as well. He learned how to install Formica on the counter tops, doing a great job at that too. After we had moved into our house, eventually after much begging from myself, he made me a tiled kitchen island among some other things I also got him to make for our house.

Greatly intrigued by the building process of our new house and the use of all the power tools I stopped by almost every day at the building site and would hang out for a while, watching and learning. Wanting to start making things myself from wood I learned how to use an assortment of power tools like the band saw, pneumatic staplers, nail guns, a chop saw, drill press, and a circular belt sander. There did end up being one power tool I was banned from using, the circular table saw. Banned because once when I tried to cut a board on it, the board I was cutting bound up in the saw then cut loose and with incredible force shot up and hit me hard square in my stomach, leaving what would turn into a gigantic bruise.

"OUCH!" I yelled as I doubled over. Shaking I lifted up my shirt to find red angry scrapes and the telltale blue of a beginning bruise. I looked around the garage trying to figure out where the board had landed, it was clear across on the other side of the garage floor. Somehow I knew I was going to have to fess up when Larry came home.

"Oooh, that hurts." I grimaced as Larry gave me a hug when he got home.

"What's the matter?"

"Well..." nervously I lifted up my shirt to an even blacker and blue bruise than what it had been the last time I looked at it.

"What in the world did you do?"

Larry scolded me after I told him what I had done. "You could have really hurt yourself!" he warned me. "Do not touch the table saw again, next time you want a board cut wait till I'm home and I'll cut it for you!"

"But what if I need it right away?" I petulantly asked him.

He eyed me seriously. "You don't need it right away you can wait!"

"Okay!" *But I hate waiting, when I want it, I want it now!*

He knew I lacked in patience and was reading my thoughts, so he wrangled a guarantee from me. "You promise?"

"Yes, okay yes I promise!"

I despised waiting but that incident was enough to scare me from ever trying it again on my own to use the table saw. It was the one tool that I always feared anyways. The whine of the whirring, menacing and large exposed blade that threatened to cut off one of my fingers if I got too close to it. I did cut hundreds of different things out of wood on the band saw for the crafts I was making, my humming following along with the steady whir of the blade as it sliced through the wood.

Thoroughly enjoying this newly found creative outlet for myself, I spent hours and hours in our garage using the power tools. One time Larry had left and went hunting for a few days. Bored one evening I spied a stack of cedar boards in the garage and in the spur of the moment decided to panel a wall with them in the dining room. I had about three fourths of the wall covered and was sweating with the prospect if I had enough boards to cover the rest. I continued on hoping against hope I did. There wasn't anything but one small chunk left after I finished up the wall. Breathing a sigh of relief after I had cut and nailed them all up I got a bit nervous. *What have I done? What if Larry hates it and he wants me to take it all off, there will be huge nail holes all over in the wall and it will be a mess to fix!* I was relieved when he came home and saw what I had done and liked it. Regardless that the outcome ended up working out, I decided that next time I got a sudden whim I should probably think a little harder about it first. I've been known to repaint a wall or room though or rearrange the furniture in a sudden inclination to change something not always running it by Larry first, but after so many years together he just laughs at my sudden impulses.

Eventually I would have my own dedicated craft room in our house that Larry and the kids teased me about, calling it my crap room because it was stuffed to the gills with boxes and boxes of my assortment of craft supplies. Larry couldn't see the same potential for all my stuff like I did so he'd give me a hard time; but I knew he was just lightheardly teasing when he'd call it my crap.

Razzing Larry right back I had an answer for his teasing. "Well at least I turn this crap into money and we use it for vacations that I let you go on with me."

"Oh you let me, do you?" he laughed.

I slipped my arms around him. "Yeah I let you!" I teased as I tried to kiss him while he playfully acted annoyed, ducking my kisses.

The next house we would build fourteen years later we did much the same, doing even more of the interior custom work ourselves. We enjoyed the process of learning new things, being creative and working together. Larry and I had always tried to spend most of our available time we had together but now we were doing all sorts of different things together. This would eventually be the pattern of how we would live out our following years, working side by side.

I especially loved the process of picking out all the finishes for our new houses and seeing it come to fruition, spending hours and hours poring over my choices envisioning what it would look like in the end. Decorating became a passion with me, something I greatly enjoy. When we made the move into our newest house my passion would get the best of me much to the chagrin of my husband and kids.

My eyes looked frantically around at the mountain of boxes stacked in the living room trying to find the one box I wanted.

"Where are the boxes marked decorations, where did you put them?" I asked my tired and sweaty husband.

"Why?" Larry asked slightly annoyed.

I grunted as I moved boxes around trying to see the one I was searching for. "Because, I just want to find them."

Larry just shook his head wondering about my sensibilities. "For what?"

"Just give me a few minutes!" I answered wishing they'd just leave me alone and let me find what I was looking for without pestering me about it.

"Aren't things like the food or bedding more important to be the first things to unpack?" his irritation with me starting to show. He walked off and left me alone knowing it wasn't going to do any good until I did what I was intent on doing.

Quickly, finally finding what I was searching for I pulled out a few vases and pictures and placed them where I wanted them to go in my new house. Now I felt better and I could move onto the other boxes.

The kids shook their heads at me stating what they thought was the obvious. "Mom you're crazy!"

"Go help your Dad put together your bed then you can find the boxes marked with bedding and make your bed."

I'd quickly move onto unpacking the kitchen and bathroom boxes so I could get to the ones I really wanted to fully unpack. By the end of the next day my house would be fully decorated and order restored even if it meant I had to stay up all night to do it. I couldn't bear to live in chaos for too long.

My father started doing a lot of custom woodworking about the same time I started my little side business of selling handmade items.

A Simple Extraordinary Life

It wasn't long before he was doing the same thing, selling his wares at craft fairs. He made beautiful shelves, benches, and furniture out of oak. I loved it; I now had something in common that formed a bond with my father, a mutual like interest. I would randomly stop over at his house and hang out with him in the garage, which had become his workshop to see what he was working on. He'd look up from whatever he was working on and grin at me. I'd stand there while he finished cutting out the wood he was working on before he'd turn off the saw and dust off his hands.

"What are you working on?" I asked as I pecked him on the cheek.

He'd show me what he was working on at the moment and show me his finished projects he had sitting around. I'd ask him questions and he'd ask me what I was up to, then I'd just sit around and watch him for a while as he sanded smooth the wood he had sitting in front of him. Just being with him was always a highlight for me, soaking up some of the missed one on one time with him I didn't particularly have while a child. After hanging out with him for a while I'd wander into the house to say hi to my mother, but truth be told it was usually my father that I came to see.

CHAPTER

20

My life was no longer a stream but a river now. Life had a way of taking those years when my children were small and somehow overnight turned it into the years where they were now grown teenagers on the cusp of adulthood and having lives of their own.

My oldest son had moved out of our house and was now on his own. The day I came home to his cleared out bedroom, it startled me somehow. Slamming his bedroom door closed, I burst out in tears.

"I didn't just spend the last eighteen years only to have him leave!" I cried as I fell into Larry's arms.

I knew he was moving out, but my heart wasn't prepared for this monumental step. I knew things would never be the same again and his brothers would only be next. I think it surprises a lot of parents. We want our children to be independent but when it happens, our meandering creek of life leaves us breathless. We gaze at the waters that now seem to be rushing by, realizing those years will never be returned to us.

It was a cruel adjustment for me; I knew I had wasted some very precious time that I would never get back. *Why have I been so overly concerned with petty things?* It was hard to face myself, wanting to beat myself up for what I saw as a monumental lack in me. I knew that when it came to my children there were a lot of things I could have done better, should have done better. One of those things I needed to learn was to relax, but I always struggled with being uptight and too concerned about things that really didn't matter in the long run. Determined, I hoped that it wasn't too late to make some needed changes in myself. I strived even harder to overcome some of the many tendencies that cornered me into being someone I didn't like. With these thoughts always whispering to me in the back of my mind, it was time to move on.

I started to look for something different I could do. I still was making and selling things at craft fairs but I was getting weary of the craft fair circuit, all the setting up and tearing down. Since Larry was always helping me, he was quite tired of it too. Looking for a more consistent and steady way of selling my things I came across a small co-op gift store in the bottom floor of the JC Penny parking garage in downtown Anchorage. I garnered up enough courage to go in and ask them how a person went about getting their items in their store. The woman working that day told me they rented out their booth spaces, which also included you had to work one day a week. It just so happened they had a small space for rent that was opening and they would be holding their monthly meeting soon; so if I was interested, I needed to come to that meeting and present what it was I wanted to sell and apply for membership to their co-op.

Well shoot I thought. *Why does it have to involve something like that? Why can't it be something that would be easier for me?*

It had been baby steps for me. Years of learning how to actually talk to people. Even though I had made some progress I wrestled with the concept awhile, wondering if I could manage to get up enough nerve to actually go to their meeting. With Larry's encouragement I decided I would try, so I nervously took the plunge and went to their next meeting. My heart was beating like mad, my hands shaking like a leaf as I made my presentation that probably only lasted a few minutes but felt like hours until it was over with. Nervous and anxious but determined to push myself out of my box, I had made the decision I would join the co-op. My day to work at the co-op ended up being one of my days off from my church secretary job, so it worked out well for me.

It was very difficult for me at first; here I was again, in a new environment. Customers scared me, as did the other women in the co-op, but I was intent on making this work for me. Not long after I joined the co-op, the JC Penney parking garage was going to expand and remodel, forcing us to look for new retail space. We made the move across the street into the new 5th Avenue mall in the heart of downtown Anchorage. I was having pretty good success selling my things and was starting to supplement with wholesale bought items. I decided with this move to get an even larger space than I currently occupied. I eventually expanded even more, into two spaces within the co-op, which required two working days. I quit my job at the church and exclusively put my time and energies into the co-op. Finally after many years I was becoming more comfortable with people and learning how to overcome some of those pesky fears I had of interacting with others.

I started to travel to large wholesale gift shows to find new product I could sell in my retail spaces. These gift shows were held in different states, several times a year. Wanting an escape in the dead of winter I usually chose to go to the ones held in January or February. Larry always traveled with me even though he didn't enjoy the shows much; nevertheless he always willingly went with me. No way would I had ever have been able to fly alone, I had too many fears for that, let alone find my way through the huge complexes that these gift shows were held in. Having little to no sense of direction, I more than likely would have been lost for days wandering around those buildings trying to find my way out if it wasn't for Larry continually showing me the way. This might be a slight exaggeration, but it's pretty close to the truth.

He was always my guide, my companion. The poor guy would stand there bored out of his mind as he patiently waited for me to make my choices over what to buy.

"What do you think about this?" I asked my bored but patient husband, trying to solicit his opinion as I stood there staring at new products trying to make up my mind.

"I don't really like it."

"Well I do, I think I'll order some."

We'd laugh; I know I frustrated him some when I didn't always take his opinion.

173

"Why do you ask me then?"

"Well because, I want to know what you think?"

"Why? You just do what you want anyways!"

He would laugh some more and ask me again why I even bothered asking him. Then he'd look at me bleary eyed, bored with the whole process ready to go. But I was thankful that he put up with me because I was always so glad he was there with me as he patiently followed me around carrying my heavy bag of accumulated catalogs.

"Thanks babe for carrying my stuff!"

"Yeah that's all you want me for," he'd tease.

"No it isn't!" I'd say as I reached up to kiss him. "I also want your opinion!"

"Yeah right!" he'd answer as he kissed me back.

He would make me laugh at myself and at my no sense of direction, always lost and wandering off the wrong way. I think I was part of his entertainment because he loved to just stand there letting me take off in the wrong direction till I figured out by the look on his face, there I went again, off to who knows where. We had many laughs together about it when he expressed his wonder of how I could survive when I'm on my own. I'd giggle and say not without a lot of going around in circles first and backtracking, and then eventually I'd figure it out. His skepticism was apparent as he turned me around by the shoulders and led me the right way.

Fighting cabin fever when we were booking airline tickets for these gift shows we almost always ended up choosing to go to the ones held in Los Angeles, looking for some warmth since we were tired of the cold dark days of winter in Alaska. Once we had finished up at the gift show after a few days, we would usually tack on some extra days to spend on a mini vacation time for us. We took side trips to San Diego and Palm Springs, once a short three day cruise to Mexico, just enjoying having the rare time of being together alone and trying hard to soak up some of those glorious sun rays we had been missing.

My Journey from Anxiety to Peace

I stayed in the co-op for ten years. Even though I had expanded into even larger spaces within the co-op I was starting to get the itch to have my own retail gift store. There was always some kind of drama trying to get the group of ten women that comprised the co-op to agree on decisions. Who could carry what products and what they could sell in their booths that wouldn't compete with each other was always a hotly debated and divisive topic, and it was wearing me down. Another weary factor was that one of my working days was Friday and now that we were in the mall we had to abide by their rules, one of which, we had to stay open until nine o'clock in the evening, the late shift being mine.

I had two children graduated from school; the oldest son moved out of our house and on his own, the other one married now with his own life, and my other two sons who still lived at home teenagers who were usually busy with their church youth functions they were involved in on Friday nights. This meant Larry was usually home alone. *I want to be home with Larry, not stuck in this store!* The search began for a small retail space in Eagle River where I could have my own store and my own hours of operation. Finding a small space for rent on the second floor above the local Christian bookstore in Eagle River, I left the co-op and started the process to open up my own store.

Larry and I built shelves and display pieces for my merchandise, framed in a storage room, and made a sales counter, his cabinetry skills coming in very handy. I painted the walls and ordered new merchandise for my store that I had decided to name Heart & Home. Larry made a beautiful sign for me to hang on the outside of the building and soon after I moved into my own store and opened the doors for business. I loved all the freedom of being able to carry whatever I wanted in my own store, loved the process of buying and ordering, and displaying the new merchandise as it came in.

A sense of accomplishment and newfound pride in myself that I had come so far from where I had been filled me as I looked around at my new little gift store. Though I still struggled with a lot of things and had to push through on a daily basis to overcome my shyness, it was a major breakthrough for me. Through everything I did, Larry was always by my side. It helped give me the confidence knowing as long as he was beside me I could push myself to do more and be more, happy that he allowed me to be myself while he stood by me and my new endeavors.

Even as I was finding new confidence in some areas of my life, those buried old cracks in my wounded heart would rear their ugly head yet once again.

I must be honest and truthful here. Larry and I had our ups and downs just like any other married couple does, it wasn't always sunny and rosy. My biggest obstacle always came back to my lack of self-esteem, and incredible bouts of unbelief that he truly loved me. Every marriage has its share of bumps in the road that can and will threaten to derail the very fabric of your trust and commitment to each other if not handled properly. The very act of intimacy and vulnerability shown when you bare your soul to one another can sometimes cause your mate to be hurt and wounded. How each partner handles their hurt can either erode their trust or build that trust that is so vital in a marriage. Conflict or the inevitable wounds that come will either move us forward, backwards, or keep us at a status quo within our marriage depending on how we handle those conflicts. We, like many other couples had our own share of bumps in the road.

One such bump in the road for me caused me to move backwards, back again to that shaky place where once again I was questioning, not believing that Larry could possibly love someone as flawed as me. Close to twenty-five years of marriage and now that I was badly hurt by him, I was back on that cycle of major doubt that plunged me into a state of fear I couldn't seem to shake. I was upset with myself that I had let my defenses down around my carefully guarded heart, thinking maybe I had deluded myself and lapsed into a state of passivity, falsely believing in a security that he loved me for who I was. This was the thought that plagued me. I was hurt and wounded, on a downward spiral towards feeling unworthy of a lasting love. *Someone who loved me wouldn't hurt me this way.* Old patterns of thought were raising their ugly head once again.

One of my brothers at the time was taking some diet pills and was losing weight. I asked him what they were, maybe they'd be helpful to me I thought. Never having liked my body much if I could change it and get thinner, surely I would be more worthy of love. In my twisted thinking I felt sure this would keep Larry from maybe someday leaving me because he was tired of me. He would reassure me over and over, that was the farthest thing from his mind, but I had such a problem with self-worth it was a major struggle for me to believe anything he would say. These were all the lies though that my hurt, coupled with never dealing with all my inner wounds were falsely telling me. Constant and sinister whispers in my ear, *you're nothing of value, unworthy, full of shame*. Suffocating pain from a long ago, young and wounded heart still seeped through my veins.

Deluded that I had to change my appearance to be more loveable, I started taking those diet pills. Weight started to come off. The pills suppressed my appetite, which made me drastically cut back on my eating. They had a very nasty and dangerous side effect though, they made my heart race and feel like a quivering mass inside. I knew they were bad for me but it didn't stop me from taking them. Desperation to change something about myself was the driving force behind my awful bad judgment.

Arriving home from work, hours before Larry would, I started taking the opportunity to go on long and strenuous walks around our neighborhood. Grabbing the old and dirty green dog leash from the hook in the garage where it hung I bent over and attached it to our golden retriever's collar while she wiggled with excitement, then I'd take off heading down our driveway and into the street.

"Come on Sierra, let's go for a walk!"

Glorious sunny summer days that I didn't enjoy, oblivious to their warmth, my mind cold and dark, full of anxiety and fraught with an inexplicable urge to push myself to try to lose more weight. Then I would be more desirable to love. Arriving back home from my walks I'd feel like they had done nothing to calm the storm that was raging inside me. Losing weight and exercising had nothing to do with becoming healthier, but everything to do with trying to change myself into something I thought society's standards were telling me I should be. Surely this would be what would make me worthy of love. Frenzied thoughts that would have me out the door again with Sierra only a few hours after returning from our first walk. Hiding from Larry how deep my desperation was, sometimes I didn't tell him how many times I had taken off on my walks. *Why do I feel so guilty about telling him?*

Months of dangerous diet pills were shaping me into a different body but doing nothing for my internal struggles. Frequent heart palpitations were starting to scare me, warning me these pills were dangerous, but because I was dropping in clothing sizes I couldn't seem to stop. Every time I saw images of beautiful and thin women on TV, jealousy and anger filled me that I didn't look like them, strengthening my resolve to continue on my dangerous quest. Smiling on the outside when someone complimented my weight loss but I was crying on the inside because I felt so wretched at the core.

We started to hear the FDA was going to take these diet pills off the market because of people having heart attacks directly related to taking the pills. I knew in the deep recesses of my mind I couldn't sustain this new body of mine without starving myself. I was now at the lowest weight and smallest dress size since being a very young teenager. Larry kept reassuring me he loved me no matter what size I was and finally, I found the strength to quit taking those pills shortly before they were taken off the market.

I had wasted another year or more spent on trying to tame my inner demons by my own strength. I couldn't bear the thought of being completely vulnerable even to the one whom I most loved, my husband, always holding back a piece of myself lest I become too hurt again. Hurt like what that boy did to me, so many years ago. It took many years for me to become confident in Larry's love for me. One more area in my life of precious time I wasted, instead believing in the lies that plagued me. I had a choice to make, either believe in Larry's love or not. I would choose to believe, even if my heart didn't always follow suit. He wasn't perfect and neither was I, but together with hard work involved we grew even closer than ever before. Larry has always loved me regardless of myself, he is my best friend, and I can't imagine life without him.

Part of our commitment to one another involved supporting each other's endeavors. I had my own store about a year when in October of 2003, Larry again decided he wanted to go back to work for himself. I liked his steady paycheck his job afforded us and the thought of taking another leap of faith that this time he could make enough money to support our family drove me into having some sleepless nights filled with worry. Worry was always something I was good at.

Feeling conflicted because I knew he had always supported me; I had no option but to try and support him. He quit his job, opened up a small office across the hall from my store and started doing CAD (computer aided drafting) work for clients. One of his main clients turned out to be his former employer. A year later he was busy enough that he hired our youngest son who had been doing CAD work for a short time for a firm in town to come work for him. Having his office next to my store, I could wander over and see him and my son during the day which was something I loved.

His business was slowly expanding and he started offering the service of making banners and small signs for clients. Our youngest son who was working for him had formed a Christian heavy metal band with some of his friends and it wasn't long before he had a question for his dad.

"What if we could make t-shirts for my band?" He said as he leaned in the doorway to his dad's office. "Maybe we could start doing screen printing too, add that to our services."

Larry turned around in his office chair to look at him, thinking slowly. "I don't know, maybe." His question had piqued Larry's curiosity. "I wonder how much the equipment would cost."

"I don't know, but maybe I'd be willing to put some money towards it."

"Hmm…I'll have to think about it. We don't have the room now, I'd have to rent more space." The idea was gaining speed. "Maybe we could expand into the empty space next to us."

Before you knew it he had ordered screen printing equipment, rented more space and we all took a trip to Seattle where our son and Larry would take a class on screen printing. We took the weekend with our son and his new wife touring the city of Seattle, put his wife on the plane to get back to her job and Larry and our son went to take the screen printing training class, while I did some shopping. Not long after arriving back home from Seattle, the new equipment he had ordered came in.

Our son's band members hauled up the heavy machinery to the second floor for us. Our son printed their first job, t-shirts the band could sell at their shows. Larry's business continued to grow and eventually he started doing more sign and screen printing work than CAD work. A few years later we both had moved our businesses into a strip mall into larger spaces next door to each other. In the ensuing years he would add even more services, including buying a local embroidery and trophy shop that was for sale and adding those services to his ever-growing business. Soon I would put in my own time helping him out as his business grew and grew.

Years were passing by rather quickly now that we were both busy with our own businesses. I had some relatively easier years emotionally than some of the harder prior ones where I had crossed some major hurdles. Although somewhat more peaceful, I would still have my bouts of doubt and the occasional meltdowns and was still building up a list of resentments. It was more rare though that the knife still lodged in my heart would make its vicious presence known.

I had finally gained what I thought was a reprieve of its vicious reminders.

Bonds,
Loss,
&
Volcanoes

CHAPTER

21

*H*e never disappointed me; I could always count on Dad to tease me.

During the years I worked at the co-op if he and my mom were in town doing their craft fairs they would occasionally stop by and see me.

I looked up from the counter as my father walked into the co-op. "Hey everything in there is on sale!" pointing at my booths to the customers who were in there. He'd sheepishly look at me grinning as if to say aren't I being funny.

"Daaad!" I'd exclaim as I grinned at him slightly embarrassed.

They would just laugh; thankfully they could tell he was teasing. I could tell he was proud of me and my accomplishments. I knew teasing was just one of the ways he showed love so it didn't bother me too much. Later when I had my own store, I carried some of his tables and shelves he made. He'd deliver them to me so he would come into my store taking his time to visit with me a bit before he hurried off to finish his errands. I loved those times. Maybe because it was something that we shared that was completely separate from the church was why I found it so special.

A Simple Extraordinary Life

I had another bond with my dad through the years that was very dear to me. I had taken a cosmetology class in high school. The high school would bus students enrolled in the class into Anchorage, where in a trailer behind a local hair salon they taught us how to cut hair. It was pretty basic, but enough that my dad decided I should start cutting his hair. I became his barber.

The usual pattern that followed was my mother would call me up on the telephone.

"Hey, your Dad needs a haircut."

Arrangements for a time for me to do it would be made and I'd go over to their house and cut Dad's hair. I cherished those times; we would talk about so many things, my father and I, while Mom sat nearby joining in. He was always a sounding board for me. If I was having trouble with my kids and wanted to talk about it he'd listen, or we'd talk about what we were making, we would talk about anything and everything. Dad would just sit there and listen, never judging, only giving his advice if I asked for it. Depending on how much chatter we did those haircuts could take a very long time.

There was a very brief time when I didn't cut Dad's hair. A single father with a lot of children had started coming to church and his occupation was a barber. Dad went to him for a short time for haircuts, more to help out the man than anything else. It didn't last too long, I think he secretly preferred me to do it and soon, I was again cutting his hair. Privately I was very glad too, because it was one thing we shared, one thing I could do for him and I didn't want to share it with anyone else.

Quite a few years passed. Now it would be me that would be the one to notice Dad's long hair, it would start to curl around his ears.

"Dad you need a haircut!" I stated when I gave him my hug at church.

He reached up and touched his hair. "Yeah, I guess it's getting pretty long."

The calls from my mom ended and my father started to be the one who called me when he needed a haircut. One day this is what happened when he called telling me he needed a haircut.

I answered the phone replying to my father's request that I come cut his hair. "You know Dad, the only time you call me is when you need a haircut."

He snickered. "No it isn't, I don't think so."

I laughed at him. "Yes Dad, it is, I'm pretty sure."

Wouldn't you know it, the next morning my phone rings.

"Hello." I said as I picked the phone up.

Dad tried unsuccessfully to sound serious. "Hey Terry... what are you doing?" My Dad thought he was hilarious trying to make small talk. Again the next morning and the next, he called with the same question.

I smiled as I laughed at his antics. "Okay Dad now you're just bugging me!"

"Whaat?" as he tried to sound innocent, but I could hear him trying hard not to crack up, "I just called to talk to you."

"Sure Dad sure."

He always thought he was being so funny; he was like a loveable impish boy. Secretly I loved his teasing, it was one of the many ways that he showed his affection and it made me feel securely loved by him.

Dad's dark hair started turning salt and pepper. We'd both marvel at the pile of hair on the floor as I swept up, how much gray there was in it. Soon his hair would start to thin and turn all gray. He would get those long wild hairs in his ears and his eyebrows that many older men get and I'd trim those up too. Dad was a character for sure. He always wore his hair in a signature wave on top of his head. Since his hair was thinning, his "*do*" was getting harder to manage.

He sat there in the chair as I fastened the plastic barber drape around his neck. "Just cut it all off, you know short like a military haircut, you know a crew cut. Yeah, like a crew cut!"

Dubiously I looked at him. "You sure?"

I wasn't sure if he was really ready to get rid of his "*wave*" and more importantly to change how he had always looked was a bit intimidating for me. He finally talked me into it, so I apprehensively started to cut it all off like he wanted. Dad couldn't wait to get to the mirror that hung in the nearby dining room where he looked and looked at himself with the silliest of grins, admiring the heck out of himself. Turning this way and that with a wide smile on his face. Mom and I just laughed at his antics. He thought he looked pretty darn good with his new hairstyle.

Cutting his hair will always be one of the fondest memories of him and I that I will carry with me forever.

Overall, I felt things had been going pretty decent for me these last few years, I thought I was doing a pretty good job of keeping control of all the buried hurt deep in my heart. Soon though, I would receive one of the most devastating phone calls I have ever had that would start the spiral downwards to all that old pain and hurt that had never been dealt with resurfacing. Worse than it had ever before. The constant battle of trying to keep control of all the things that were buried there still lurking in my heart would be like a fierce losing battle.

My youngest brother, his pregnant wife and their two-year-old daughter had gone on vacation with my mom and Dad to Hawaii. My father liked to golf and he and my brother were going to do some golfing while vacationing in Hawaii.

Whenever any of Dad's daughters or daughter-in-law's happened to be pregnant, which there were many, he loved to tease them.

"You're going to have twins!" grinning with delight as he lovingly teased them.

I think one of his secret desires was to see twins born again in his family. He would endlessly tease my now pregnant sister-in-law a lot.

"Twins! Twins!" he exclaimed every time he saw her.

My own pregnancies always produced a fear that my worst nightmare would come true, and that was to have twins! Larry's sister's first children were twins and I had watched her struggle, having to take her laundry, which included smelly cloth diapers to the laundromat with not one, but two babies in tow. No siree, for sure that is not what I either wished for, or wanted, and no amount of loving teasing by my father would convince me to want twins.

Dad, Mom and my brother's family were scheduled to come home any day from their Hawaiian vacation. I was looking forward to their return, missing my father. Even as an adult I still felt a piece of me gone, a lot of my security in life missing when Dad wasn't around.

Dead asleep one night I awoke to the phone ringing beside my bed. Sleepily I rolled over and picked up the receiver.

"Hello?" I groggily answered.

It was my sister-in-law, calling from Hawaii. *Why would she be calling in the middle of the night?* My anxious thought now making me fully awake as I struggled to sit up in my bed.

"Um, I wanted to let you know, your Dad, he um collapsed at the airport and he's on his way to the hospital in an ambulance. I don't know anything else but I'm sure he'll be alright." She tried to assure me. "I'll call you back later, ok?"

A part of me wasn't too panicked. We had been in a church meeting a few months prior where Dad had been told by a guest speaker that God had many things left for him to do. Even though Dad was retired, by now having handed the church over to my twin brother, I had gone away from that meeting with the comforting thought, *Dad's going to be around a very long time.* He was seventy years old, always active and seemed very healthy. So in my heart I was trying to believe and trust that Dad would be okay, I tried to go back to sleep.

Several hours later the phone beside me rang again. It was my brother-in-law, my youngest sister's husband on the line.

His voice choked as he said the words that were hard to say. "I'm sorry, he's gone. I'm so sorry."

Horrific silence hung in the air as the news of what he had just said registered, permeating my numb mind. I hung the phone up, in disbelief and shock, overcome with such tremendous heartache I felt like I was drowning. I turned to Larry and he held me tight while I cried and cried.

A Simple Extraordinary Life

Never again would I get his special smile that was so dear to me, or touch his face and feel his hug. I had no chance to say goodbye. March 10, 2004, my beloved father, my pastor, my hero, my daddy, went home to be with Jesus. It didn't matter that I was forty-seven years old, I felt like a lost little girl whose world had just collapsed.

Several months later my sister-in-law would give birth to twin boys.

CHAPTER

22

*P*hones that rang throughout the night affected us all. Our entire family was raw with emotion, in shock and overcome with tremendous grief. Our father's death had hit us all very hard. He had been the center of our large extended family, much like the glue that held us all together tight. Dad was not only our physical father but also our spiritual father. It was a hard blow to us all, losing someone who filled two equally important roles in each of our lives. He was very much loved by his wife, my mom, all his sons and daughters, son-in-law's and daughter-in-law's, and his many grandchildren. His great grandchildren were only babies that would never have the chance to get to know what a wonderful man he was. Hopefully we can tell his stories as well as he could tell them and give them at least a small glimpse into the life of a man I'm sure they would have loved as much as we all did.

It was hard to hear what my youngest brother had to endure, witnessing our father's sudden death. When Dad collapsed at the airport after loading his suitcases onto the conveyor belt, my brother who had already started walking ahead of him heard the commotion around my fallen father and went running back towards him. He rushed over to him and knelt down beside him, but by then Dad couldn't speak anymore. As my brother held his hand he said that Dad with loving eyes looked directly into his eyes, communicating to him how much he loved him, then he was gone. I can't imagine the heartache that must have caused my brother.

In vain they tried in the ambulance to revive my father, but he had already left this world, he was now dancing with his Jesus. The state of Hawaii wouldn't release Dad's body until they performed an autopsy, so Mom and my brother and his family stayed there in Hawaii till the autopsy was done. Mom didn't want to fly home without her beloved husband.

It was dark and suffocating as I crawled from my bed the next morning. Suspended in consuming grief, the very air and light seemed sucked out of the gray morning that dawned. Morning light that couldn't penetrate the darkness of grief that had viciously left its shadows around my shattered heart and soul. Not knowing what else to do, Larry and I went to my twin brother's house where some of my other siblings were starting to gather, dazed and stunned with the news of our father's death. That morning while we were gathered at my brother's house, the pastor from a neighboring church came by the house to express how sorry he was to hear of my father's passing, then he asked if he could pray for us. Lovingly and heartfelt he prayed with us, asking God to help us find comfort as tears of sadness and loss rolled down all of our cheeks. It meant so much to me that he had showed up and shown us all such true compassion in our time of need. We would later hold my dad's memorial service at his church, since our own church we knew wouldn't hold enough people.

The next few days our family rallied together, spending the days and evenings at my parents' house, waiting for my brother and Mom's return from Hawaii. So many people reached out to us. The local pizzeria across the street from the church sent huge pizzas, enough to feed our entire family, which by now was approaching fifty people when we were all together. Our own church congregation took over making sure we had meals for the next few days while we all gathered, still reeling from the news, trying to cope with our sudden and great loss.

One of my younger brothers and his wife happened to be in the lower forty-eight states visiting friends when he received the same phone call everyone had, telling him of our father's passing. He had called me in the dark of that fateful night and we spent hours on the phone, our disbelief and grief heavy as we sobbed while we tried to find the words to comfort each other. His friends found him and his wife a flight home first thing in the morning so they could come home right away to be with the family. My oldest son was in Texas on vacation. I knew I had to find the strength to call him. I picked up the phone trying to control my emotions so I could make my own awful call to him and tearfully tell him his grandpa was gone. He too immediately found a flight home. Another brother and his family who live in Washington made arrangements to fly up to Alaska as soon as possible to also be with the family.

Everyone was going to be together to mourn and say goodbye to the patriarch of our family. We all gathered at my parents' house, a place that had held so many of our family gatherings. We reminisced, told stories, cried, and brought comfort to each other by just being together. It felt good to all be together once again, all but our beloved father, his missing presence a gaping hole in everyone's hearts. My parent's house held many memories. Over the years every time we had one of our large, boisterous, and noisy family gatherings we all would look at our Mom and Dad and tease them.

"Look what you started!" we'd tell them. "All this is your guys' fault!" we'd laugh at them over the noise of the squealing wrestling grandchildren on the living room floor.

"What?" Dad would answer looking slightly confused as to what we had just said.

Dad's hearing was especially bad, what with so much commotion. He became hard of hearing growing up around noisy farm equipment never having used ear protection. When he was older he broke down and got hearing aids, probably because of some persuasion by my mother.

"What's that noise?" he would ask looking around the kitchen.

"It's the refrigerator running!" mom said, "It always makes that noise."

"Huh?" he looked perplexed.

He couldn't get used to all the extra noises in the background that he had never heard before so he pulled out his hearing aids and refused to wear them.

"It sounds like fingernails on a chalkboard when I comb my hair!"

"Maybe you just need to have them adjusted." Mom tried to reason with him.

"Nah, I'm good." Dad stubbornly refused to wear them anymore, the hearing aids sat in their bedroom gathering dust.

Sometimes having to repeat yourself to Dad so he could understand what you just said was something we were used to, along with how fast he could talk. Our friends would look at us bewildered.

"What did he just say?"

We'd repeat to them what he had just said and they'd just shake their heads wondering how we understood him. Dad had to work on learning to slow down sometimes when he preached so others could follow what he was saying.

Dad passed away on a Wednesday. The following Sunday morning service we all assembled, sitting together on the front pews of the church. Since many of us, including myself were on the worship team of our church, a worship team from the church in Anchorage where our church had originated graciously came out to lead worship for our congregation so we didn't have to. It was hard sitting there in those pews; feeling like our grief was on display for all to see, especially hard for myself. Though it was incredibly hard, at the same time it was such an act of honor to be there. My father gave his life for the church, he loved God with all his heart, and to be anywhere else wouldn't have seemed right.

I'll never forget how during the worship that morning the song leader started to lead a song titled *Blessed be your Name*. When they got to the part of the song lyrics that say:

My Journey from Anxiety to Peace

Blessed be Your Name,
On the road marked with suffering
Though there's pain in the offering,
Blessed be Your Name

As the words rang out in song around me I knew that I really had a choice I was going to have to make. No matter how hard the pain of his death was to me, my dad's life and his legacy would cause me to rejoice again one day. There was solace in the fact that I knew my father was with the One whom he lovingly and faithfully served. When they later sang the part of the lyrics that say:

My heart will choose to say
Lord, Blessed be Your Name

My hands raised in surrender and worship to God, as tears of both sadness and joy streamed down my face. No matter the discomfort and pain in my heart, I would choose to believe that He is a loving God even if I didn't understand why God chose to bring Dad home to him now. This would bring honor to the God I served, to the God my father served and honor to the man who had so lovingly raised me.

Five days after Dad's death, on March 15, 2004, we held a memorial service at the neighboring church. While our family waited in an adjoining room, we could see out the window towards the road that led to the church a steady stream of cars, making their way into the church parking lot. The cars kept coming and coming. My stomach was in knots as we had to stand there in that room waiting, far past the allotted time to start the service because so many people just kept coming. Later we were told they estimated over 800 people had come to show their respect. Dad's life had touched so many throughout the years.

I was a nervous wreck. We were all to walk in together, Mom, oldest child to youngest, each with our respective families. As we entered the auditorium a solemn silence filled the air. We all filed into the dead silent room, making our way to the empty front seats that were being held for us. Suddenly as our large family was making our way down the center aisle, clapping erupted and we were given a standing ovation. Humbled, tears again streamed down my face as I was filled with wonder and pride, so blessed and honored that I got to be a daughter of this man who had touched so many lives. It was difficult for me to sit there during the service overwrought with grief that I couldn't control, my arm around my grown son next to me who was sinking into my shoulder as he tried to control his own sad grief. I hated that we were all so visible, on display so to speak. I'd rather be on display with laughter and joy than tears and sadness. Conflicting emotions were vying for a place at the table in my heart.

Several people in our congregation had put together a beautiful and moving video presentation for the service filled with pictures. Pictures young and old of our family and of our father. Pictures with some of his many grandchildren sitting on his lap. There were hunting and fishing pictures of him and his sons. Pictures of Dad preaching, standing behind the pulpit in the old basement that used to be the auditorium, back when his hair was still dark. Pictures of him and his old banjo he used to play. So many pictures, so many memories, they all chronicled his full and wonderful life. I loved all the pictures. Each one evoked different memories and feelings but the one that pierced my heart the most was a picture of Dad and my youngest brother as a boy. He was standing close in front of my Dad, the wind blowing through his blonde hair. My father was wearing one of his favorite hats he always wore, sweet contentment shining from both their faces as they rode down the river in my Dad's green boat that he had built.

Later in the service when they opened up the microphone for people who wanted to say something, the line of people waiting to pay their respects and say something about my father snaked around the auditorium. It was beautiful, poignant, and full of humorous stories. Dad would have loved the laughter of the funny stories told. Many expressed how he was like a father to them. How he never would forget to say hi and talk to them when they came to church. I was a bit amazed, so many people kept saying the same thing, a bit astonished that somehow my father managed to get around to everyone at church and yet no matter who you were, he took his time with you. I knew how much I always looked forward to my own special kiss and hug from him too, never once did he ever miss me. I always felt a bit prideful that I got to kiss and hug him in a familiar way that only family could. My heart held so much gratitude, amazed again that I had the special privilege to be this man's daughter, what a blessing.

Three days later we were scheduled to have a private family gathering at the funeral home where my father's earthly body would be, inside the burial casket my brothers had picked out for him. It was a beautiful oak wood casket that had a depiction of the Lord's Supper engraved on it. It was especially fitting for Dad and his life; reminiscent of the beautiful woodworking he did and his life spent serving the One whom he now resided with.

We were all gathered together again one evening a few days before we were to have our private service when my twin brother said he had a question to ask all of us. Someone had approached him, asking if they could come to our private family service. He said they expressed to him that my dad had felt like a father to him and that he was their good friend. We were shocked at this request and a bit outraged.

"No, definitely not!" several of us loudly exclaimed. We shook our heads answering again. "No!"

"Okay, I told him I would ask."

My heart raged, I couldn't believe it, I understood he was like a father figure to many, *but he was our father, our father, not yours!* Deep dark thoughts, angry that in just this one thing I wondered why can't people understand? *He was my daddy, our father and this was different.* He had a love for us and us a love for him, a precious blood bond that couldn't be shared. *Hadn't we already shared enough?* We had already had a memorial service for everyone, this one was to be for family and something that we all felt was to be very dear and private for just us. My heart cried, *please just this one time don't ask something like that of us.* It wasn't something I was willing or wanted to sacrifice. I was relieved when as a group we decided not to allow it. Yet again, this would be another thing that went into stirring up that secret resentment that resided in the dark places of my heart.

A Simple Extraordinary Life

The time had come for our private service. We all gathered in the room at the funeral home, my dad's casket front and center. Crazy and frenzied thoughts were going thru my mind. *I don't know what way Dad is laying in that closed casket, which direction is his head?* I desperately wanted to know, was I looking towards his beautiful and familiar face that I would never see again? *Where should my eyes look?* Not having been able to say goodbye was tearing me apart. The hat Dad usually wore was lying on top of his casket, a terrible reminder that he would never wear it again. I didn't know what to think, what to feel, my grief making it hard to stand upright in that room.

We started to go around the room and those who could, share what they wanted to say about what meant the most to them about Dad. It was my turn. I didn't have anything previously planned to say but I found myself saying the thing that I appreciated most was his love. How I had watched him over the years become softer and softer with age, and how I appreciated his unwavering love that he had for all of us and especially for the Lord. Leaving that room later was one of the hardest things I have ever done. I knew Dad wasn't really there in that room with us, but it felt like I was leaving a piece of myself there, back in that room where his body lay.

Dad died in the winter so the funeral home couldn't bury him till the spring. I didn't go out to his grave till later that summer. Larry and I walked over to where he was buried, on a hill beneath a tree with a beautiful view of the majestic snowcapped mountain, Pioneer Peak. Basked in the rays of the sun, I knelt on the ground next to his marker that us girls had picked out and wept with gut wrenching sobs till I was cried out. I have never been back. It is still too painful to think of him there.

I would rather think of him now, standing beside his maker where one day I will see him again, and he will give me that special smile that I know he reserved just for me, his oldest and firstborn daughter.

CHAPTER

23

*G*etting used to a loved one being taken from you is nothing I wish upon anyone. More than once I would find myself suddenly startled by waves of sudden grief. Standing in line at the post office waiting to pick up packages that had come in the mail, I glanced at the line next to me, only to see an older and fatherly gentleman standing in line next to me. His looks with his wavy gray hair and wily mustache, and mannerisms that would immediately remind me of my father. Blinking back tears, overcome as a fresh wave of grief and tears assaulted me, I turned and ran back out to my car, leaving my mail and packages for another day.

It's not fair I wanted to scream, *why my father?* Soon after his passing a man in the church had bought my dad's green and white truck from my mother. I could never get used to seeing that truck going down the road without thinking, *Oh, there goes Dad!* Then cruelly I would be reminded, he wasn't here anymore. Will I ever get used to this fact?

Life went on in the river of my life and I slowly found new ways to find joy. Some of the sting of loss had started to lessen. I had started to have more grandchildren by now and I found great satisfaction and delight in these new little people. I didn't feel quite as uptight with them as when I had my own children. The weight of fear I had that everyone was watching how I raised my own children had disappeared when it came to these new little ones. They weren't my own children so much of those old worries weren't bothering me anymore. I felt unusually free, a new light heartedness to be able to express my unbridled love for my grandchildren. I was relishing in this new role of being a grandma. Lurking down deep though was a quiet resentment that still resided in me. *Why had I felt this unrealistic weight of expectations in my own childhood and that of my children?*

Cracks in my veneer exasperated by the grief of losing someone that had been so vital to making me feel somewhat secure, the loss of my father, were making it harder and harder for me to keep in control of all the dark things inside me that threatened to spill out. All the old insecurities and the myriad of twisted thinking; some of which were feeling like I had to always play second fiddle to the church were rising up in me. I was fighting hard to put that resentment away but it was there, hiding deep within, ready to divulge its ugly contents. Old memories that had caused deep pain were coming to the surface. Still in a place where I was not ready to face them or admit to them, I would try hard to continue to repress all my hurt and wounds, and my ever increasing seething anger.

Quite a few months had passed since my father had died and I was still struggling with this incredible loss. One Sunday after the church service had just finished, I found myself talking with some of my siblings who were also struggling with their own grief and sense of loss. Overcome with our emotion we were standing there in the front of the church crying together. Several people had gathered around us. Leaving another blow, hurting me even more, someone said something very insensitive to us. They gave the impression that they were exasperated with our crying, they came over to us and told us in so many words that we just needed to get over it. Maybe they thought they were saying something well-meaning but I could hardly believe they had just said that. *How dare you belittle our feelings*! I wanted to lash out in sudden anger but I kept silent, those words that I badly wanted to say, reverberated in my mind as I looked away. Thankfully, another person had stepped up to us and very lovingly approached us.

My Journey from Anxiety to Peace

"Not only are you mourning the loss of your father, you are also mourning the loss of your pastor, your spiritual mentor. God understands your grief, let him comfort you." She gave me and my sisters a hug before walking away.

Those were encouraging words for my heart; feeling like someone understood the scope and depth this loss was to us. It helped take some of the sting of what the other person had just said to us and comforted us, instead of what felt like demeaning our loss. I was grateful for her kindness.

That little saying, *sticks and stones can break your bones, but words can never hurt you*, is so very wrong. Every insensitive word, critical or cruel word can cut you to the very core of your being. When these scars are left alone and not dealt with, cleaned up, they will fester and ooze. That is what was happening to me. Wounds that were rotting and putrid, their existence that only seemed to be magnifying and growing. I found myself shrinking back and trying to hide, so sure someone would find out how rotten I felt inside and smell the stink of my anger. Still trying to be that perfect pastor's daughter that I thought everyone expected of me.

Agitation was growing and swirling, pulling me into a very dark place. Nervousness, anxiety and confusion were getting the best of me. I thought for sure I was headed for a serious nervous breakdown. Determined by sheer force of my will, I wasn't about to open up to anyone, afraid of what would come out. I knew that I couldn't keep going on like this but I wasn't sure how to get myself off this hamster wheel. It was a cycle I repeated over and over. If I could just control what was going on outside around me maybe it would calm the storm that raged within, but intense pressure was building up, ready to burst.

I felt like those science experiments where you mix up baking soda and vinegar to pour in the kids' paper Mache volcanoes so that it will bubble up and explode. Only my baking soda was the accumulated resentments I was feeling that were mixed in with the acid vinegar of the biggest wound of all, the dagger that had lodged itself in my heart that fateful day in the woods. The final straw, the volatile combustion was getting to be more than I could take, afraid that I would lose my sanity and never be able to recover, feeling desperate and at the brink of despair. The fragile glass shell of my heart and all its hairline cracks that I was desperately running around in circles trying to patch and hold together with a will and strength I could no longer possess was about to shatter. I would barely manage to hang on for a few more years. Desperation for some kind of relief consumed my every thought, still stubbornly clinging to the belief I had to do this all on my own and in my own strength, it was still something I must hide.

Hide from everyone, including God because surely I would see nothing but condemnation and disappointment in His eyes.

Cracks,
Hope,
&
Mirrors

CHAPTER

24

*S*erious health issues had descended upon some of my family members. My twin brother was severely overcome with Parkinson's disease so debilitating, that the extent that this disease and its medications for it would be far reaching.

As you watch loved ones suffer, declining to the point that their actions take you to a place where you no longer seem to recognize them because of the choices they are making is agonizing and overwhelming, a new kind of grief. A loss of what once was. No longer could my brother be the pastor of our church. Confused and bewildered as to what was happening, a splintering of our family had started to take root.

Some of my family started to meet at my younger sister's house once in a while to pray for our family and for our brothers that were afflicted with health issues. I was filled with so much sorrow at what was happening but also filled with hurt and anger towards my twin brother because of some of his choices and actions, making me feel very conflicted in my thoughts. I knew that I loved him, but my love didn't stop the intense anger I was feeling towards him. Everything about the situation seemed to be spiraling out of control. Control, too much or lack of, a huge obstacle for me that I had never dealt well with. Void of any peace, more and more wounds were piling up a large part due to my always looking through every situation with my eyes clouded in the fog of pain I was never free from.

The impregnable walls I had built around myself were starting to crumble. My heart was pounding, my hands clammy and sweating. Haltingly and tearfully, I started to break my silence.

"I um… I um have something I need to share."

I told the family members present at my sister's house one night of the sexual abuse I had suffered so many years ago. Shock reigned on their faces. Still I did not fully let go of everything, tell everything. I had barely scratched the surface. My revelation was a small step but I had far to go. I wasn't completely ready to face the deep and painful origins of all that was pestering me. The cracks in my veneer were just starting to ooze with the stark reality that I couldn't keep trying to conceal all that was bothering me.

There was something my sister-in-law had said to me when I told everyone my secret; something that I really struggled with.

"Terry, you need to forgive yourself."

I wrestled greatly with that thought. I had deep-seated anger at myself for thinking I had been so gullible to walk out in the woods with that boy that day. I tried to justify in my mind though, *I'm not really angry with myself, I'm angry with that boy.* This wasn't true though; on the contrary it was just another lie I told myself. I wasn't quite there yet, ready to admit and face everything that was troubling me so. It was always easier to blame someone else, forgive someone else or reason in my mind that I was justifiably angry and hurt. Though those things may be true, *why is it so hard to forgive myself?* I had more breaking to do.

Living so many years in this bondage I had accepted and believed the lie that this was my portion in life. It became like a familiar blanket to me and even though I despised these feelings I didn't know how to let go of all my fears. When I chose over and over to tell myself I was unworthy of love, I became a willing partner in the lies. Every act of self-deprecation put another nail in the coffin of lies that would sink me to the depths of despair. I was sinning against Him, my God. My refusal to believe in what He said I was; beloved, worthy daughter of the King,

204

instead I kept making the choice to believe in all the lies. To be able to trust in God that He wanted to heal my pain and give me the peace I so desperately craved I would have to come to the end of my rope; quit striving to do it on my own if I was ever to find any solace. Like a silly fool, I fought hard entrenched in my fears, but that noose around my neck was tightening and tightening fast by now.

This constant living in a sea of hurt and pain was like a nasty habit that I couldn't seem to be free from, a scab on my heart that just wouldn't heal. I deluded myself into thinking I was successful at hiding from everyone my distress and my own sin; sin of my reaction to that pain, falling into the pattern of self-recrimination, soon followed by anger at the injustice. Living clouded in a mask of deceitfulness, trying to hide the ugliness that resided in my heart. Change wasn't going to come until the place I was in was so unbearable that I had to look at the truth.

Had others sinned against me, unjustly hurt me? Yes, I'm not denying the truth of that, but by staying in that place of being wounded, refusing to believe that I was worthy of anything different in my life, I had however unwittingly, partnered with the enemy of my soul. I was exactly where he wanted me to be; angry at being hurt, rooted in pain, devoid of any peace and was on the verge of having a nervous breakdown.

The enemy was delighted that he had rendered me so broken that I wallowed in self-pity and a suffocating silence upon my lips for so many long years. These emotions that I could no longer control, the total exhaustion, and desperation so deep it was driving me to seek freedom from the only place I knew was left, the only One I could go to. *What can I lose?* I knew in my heart of hearts it would mean breaking my silence and letting go. The ugliness would have to come to the surface and break free no matter how fearful I was of the pain and embarrassment I was sure I would endure. I needed guidance though and didn't know how I was going to get that.

Heightened agitation growing inside me so fierce, no longer did I feel I could stay at our family's church. I was wound tighter than a drum, like a rubber band being stretched to its max ready to break. I was getting so desperate to find freedom; feeling like maybe the answer would be that

I needed to go to a church where no one knew me. Maybe then in what I felt would be blessed anonymity, I could find the internal strength to be able to completely let go. It was one of the hardest decisions I have ever made. Feeling conflicted I agonized and agonized for several months over this decision. Rolling this thought over and over in my mind I had many fitful and sleepless nights about making this kind of momentous decision.

This was where I had worshipped for the last forty plus years, married and raised my own family. It was what was so familiar to me. So much of our lives had been fully entwined there, serving faithfully with our talents, our hearts and souls. My father's church, my family's church, my heritage. *How can I leave?*

It was also the place that I most associated with this suffocating pain I needed free from. If I could dis-associate, maybe I could find the freedom I craved, freedom to fully let go of myself.

By now both Larry and I were hurt and wounded. Unfortunate circumstances that had happened in our family and our church which were so interwoven had left us reeling and stunned. We felt guilty and confused about our feelings and thoughts that we were having about leaving our church; but also felt maybe God was moving us to a different place where we, especially myself, could find the strength to gain some healing.

The summer of 2014, we started to visit a church one of my sons and his family were attending. Immediately, we were overwhelmed at the love we felt there and moved to tears every time we visited. Everything, the worship, the preaching, the pastor and his wife's caring words and heart extended to us were the beginnings of a much-needed healing balm to my wounds. Embarrassed by my constant tears but feeling a huge relief, it was like a heavy burden was slowly being lifted off my shoulders. No longer did I feel like I was under some kind of scrutiny, mostly in part because these people didn't know who I was. I could finally have some of that coveted anonymity I needed and wanted. I know I had brought many of those feelings mostly upon myself, trying to live up to some kind of unattainable standard, but even that was a large part of all my problems. I didn't know any other way how to think or feel; I was so messed up, my thinking all twisted.

By October of that year we made the decision that this church we had been occasionally visiting would be our new church home. A burdensome weight had been lifted. Finally I was free from the ever-present fear of thinking that everyone knew me and my family and the expectations I thought everyone had of us. Here I didn't have that; I could be anonymous.

I know God is still God. Even though he could have met me at any place I was at or whatever church I was attending, my own ridiculous fears and inhibitions that had been so surmountable in my life had held me at bay from fully exposing myself to the extent I needed. How does one expose one's self, their wounds when they are also afraid that this exposure and what might come out will also hurt those around you? Afraid I would be misunderstood, afraid that to lay myself that bare would only cause someone else to be wounded, especially those I loved had kept me from it.

Many years prior, one of my siblings as an adult divulged something no one knew. They had kept a secret to themselves for numerous years. As a child they had been sexually abused by someone in the church.

I watched how that surprise revelation had hurt my mother and father. They, just like the rest of us, never knew anything about it. The questions that must have assaulted my stunned parents by this disturbing blow.

"Who could have been the one to do such a thing?" we whispered among ourselves.

This was just one of the many obvious and hard questions that must have floated around in their minds. To wonder and beat yourself up that how as a parent, you somehow failed to protect your child. How did such an awful thing such as this happen? Shock and disbelief ran through our entire family. I knew it greatly pained my parents to think that such sickening things happened under their watch.

Bewildered and confused, I couldn't, just couldn't bring myself to put my father through that same kind of agony again by letting my own abuse come to light. I loved him too much to want to contribute to that kind of suffering he would be sure to endure. It didn't matter that it was tearing me apart; I wanted to hold it tightly to myself, not wanting to wound the man I so loved.

In later years after he had passed, my reasoning changed into different thinking. *I don't want to tarnish or stain Dad's legacy.* I knew what had happened wasn't his fault; I didn't blame him. I always knew his heart was to love God with everything within him, his children and family, and to love all who were around him to the best of his ability. Circumstances for sure, could they have been different? Yes, they could have been. Was he perfect? Of course not. Dad's character and true heart I knew, was to never bring hurt or pain to anyone. I couldn't lay the blame on how messed up I was on him.

One of the very things in this new church we now attended that really drew me to it, was that the pastor reminded me a lot of my father. I could really feel the love he had for people emanating from him. I had been sorely missing that fatherly love, that acceptance a father has for his daughter. Through the pastor God was working, moving me to tears easily just by simple acts of kind and encouraging words spoken to me from him. Here I was coming apart at the seams; ugliness spilling out and I felt nothing but acceptance by him.

We hadn't been attending for very long when I was in a conversation with the pastor and I felt myself losing control of my pent up feelings. Our conversation had nothing to do with what was beneath the surface of my wary heart but I could feel this buried anger and old wounds rising quickly to the surface. I knew the pastor had all of his grown and married children and their families involved and in attendance there, at this church. I blurted out some inane and thinly veiled comment to him about making sure he was protecting his family. I'm not sure if even he, understood what I was saying, because I wasn't even sure, but my heart was loudly saying. *Watch out, you can get badly burned by the people in church and end up a mess like me!* Highly embarrassed and ashamed by my outburst and loss of restraint I headed to leave.

Wow, I am out of control! I can't stand myself! I silently muttered under my breath.

My Journey from Anxiety to Peace

These rotting and festering wounds were driving me to the brink of insanity. I wouldn't have blamed anyone for wanting to make a wide berth around me I felt so wretched, but without fail every Sunday the pastor would reach out to both Larry and I, instead of easily turning away. The small gestures that were so huge in my eyes, telling me things like you're going to make it, you have a wonderful heritage. He knew I was wounded but never once did he condemn me for it. He didn't tell me I just needed to get over it, instead he showed me love. Through his acts of kindness he was showing me God's heart and how God felt about me. My heart was being drawn to the light that would lead me out of the darkness that surrounded me.

December of that year the preaching at church was a series on hope. I felt like a lifeline was being thrown out for me. *Can I believe there is hope for me?* One of the pastors from the church was preaching one particular Sunday and some things they said spoke greatly to me, causing these gentle yet exciting stirrings of hope begin to rise up in me. There I was, out shopping the next day hurrying down the aisles headed to the grocery section of the store. Out of the corner of my eye I saw sitting in a display, a large wood cutout with the word Hope. Feeling this wasn't a random coincidence, I bought it, brought it home and put it on the bookshelf in my living room so I could look at it and begin to believe it. My thinking was starting to shift. Living in a constant struggle, never really believing that God loved me, I would yearn to be able to get that truth that He did to shift from my head to my heart.

I longed for something tangible. Something that would be tailor made for me so I could know; really know His love for me was real. My longing to receive something that would speak to me in just that way was soon met only a few weeks later.

CHAPTER

25

eing a parent can be a difficult road at times. It has incredible highs and sometimes its own shares of lows. You rejoice in your offspring's every accomplishment, wince at their mistakes and find you always want what's best for them hoping life somehow is easier and better for them than you; love that is so fierce for your children that much of the time their hurt easily becomes your hurt. Our natural instinct is to want to protect and shield them from any and all pain. The she bear can come out in a mother when she feels someone is threating or hurting her child. Caught between the places of letting our children learn from their own mistakes and shielding them from unnecessary hurt brought on by others is like walking through a minefield. It is so easy to constantly second-guess your own parenting choices. I struggled with all of these.

I especially grappled with wanting to protect my children. If I'm honest with myself I know there were times I should have protected them more. I never wanted for them to have the same kind of weighty burdens and anxiety I had felt upon me as a child, the expectations that frightened me so. Afraid of this would only be true for them, it produced in me even more anxiety worrying over them.

My children were my father's first grandchildren. It was very difficult for me to ignore how hurt and anxious I got when I thought my children, the first grandchildren of the pastor would more than likely have or feel the same kind of unrealistic expectations I did, or have wounding that would be hard for me to ignore in their lives. When I felt I failed to protect them from all this it took me to a place in my heart filled with anguish and deep anger. Afraid somehow my own wounds would become the same for them, I grieved that I couldn't always protect them from what was sometimes the harsh reality that they would more than likely face their own trials of wounds and hurts they would have to cope with.

My own expectations of what I thought other people, especially other Christians should be like and act like, were just as bad as what I thought the expectations they expected of me and my children were. Struggling myself with forgiving others by keeping a list of wrongs, things that were exasperated by deep and unhealed inner wounds; try as I might otherwise, I also knew that I could so easily teach this unhealthy way of living to my children by my actions and words. I was so bogged down with my own wounds and private struggle that watching my children have their own set of hurts to deal with was something that caused me a great deal of despair. Wanting for my sons what every mother wants, a life free of hurt and struggles, it was hard and painful for me to see them have to grapple with their own set of challenges life was throwing at them.

My heart was getting heavy, feeling the weight of my children's wounds. Though they were now adults, a mother's heart for her children never stops. It was in such a place that I found myself now, grieving for one of my sons. He had gone through a bad and painful divorce. His children, my very much loved grandsons were now living with their mother in another state apart from him. Long, long periods of time would go by where he would try and try, but receive no contact from his sons. He loved and missed them fiercely, visits were very infrequent, and being separated from them was taking a tremendous toll on him. Larry and I both greatly missed our grandchildren. Not seeing or hearing from them either was also taking its own toll on us as are hearts ached for them. *I want to see them again, hear their voices, and be able to give them a hug again!* I could only begin to imagine how painful it was for their father.

One previous Christmas plans had been made that the boys would be coming to Alaska for a much anticipated visit. Since it had been close to two years since I had seen them with only a couple of phone calls from them during that time I was beyond excited to see them. We were so eager because all of our sons and their families were going to be there that Christmas, including our youngest son and his family who lived in Colorado. Larry and I were joyfully looking forward to having everyone together, all our sons and wives, and all our grandchildren. We didn't know if there would ever be another opportunity again for such a family reunion.

In our excitement for Christmas gifts we got all our grandkids pajama pants and made thermal pajama tops for all of them with lettering on them stating their chronological birth order as our grandchildren, #1 grandchild, #2 grandchild, etc. for all twelve of our grandchildren. We couldn't wait to take a picture of all of them in their pajamas, youngest to oldest in front of our fireplace. The day before Christmas we got the devastating news; the boys didn't get on the airplane flight to come and they wouldn't be here. They weren't coming at all. I cried so hard, so very disappointed. Even worse than my own disappointment was knowing that my son's heart had been broken in two. It was a very sober Christmas.

Here we were going on another year of being separated from our grandsons and our son from his children. In January 2016, after just hearing the series of preaching on hope, with my heart still desperately trying to believe that there was a vestige of hope; I found myself sitting in yet again another church service. The guest speaker was talking about truly knowing that God loves you, and again, I found myself in tears because I just didn't have this truth in my heart. I longed to know, really know that He could love me. I wrestled with this so much and sitting there yearning within I found myself asking something of him. *God, if you could only give me something tangible so I could know this truth!* I tried to concentrate on what the speaker was saying while I sat there with this desperate longing in my heart.

Suddenly, I heard my phone ding from my purse on the floor beneath my seat. At first I tried to ignore it but then I had the thought, *I rarely get any texts or calls so what could this possibly be, maybe it's something important.* Reaching down on the floor I fumbled for my purse and took out my phone to inconspicuously look at it. There was one unopened message. Wondering what it was I opened it up. It was a question from one of my sons asking if I knew that his older brother was down in the states visiting his boys. Thinking there must be some kind of misunderstanding I noticed he had sent an attachment to the text. I opened up the attachment and staring back at me was a current photo of my son and his boys sitting in a restaurant eating pancakes with smiles on their faces that stretched ear to ear! *How could I have not known he was going for a visit?*

I had no idea that my son had somehow managed to take a trip to go see his sons, something that really puzzled me. One of the deepest cries of my heart had been that he could see his boys. Amazement filled me as there before my eyes at the exact time my heart was longing for a tangible evidence of God's love for me, He had answered. Joyous tears sprang to my eyes and rolled down my cheeks. I sat there and stared at the apparent and extreme joy on my son's face surrounded by his boys, letting it all sink in. God had answered my silent plea.

The next day Larry and I were able to Skype with our son and see the precious faces of our grandchildren, overjoyed that we were able to talk to them and hear their voices again and tell them again that we loved them. Awestruck, I felt humbled that God had answered my cry giving me more hope that I could find my way to the freedom I knew God had for me.

Will He answer that cry too if I can just find my way to Him and stop hiding my face from Him?

I despised how I felt. This nasty ugliness was always rearing its ugly head, rising to the surface where it was getting harder and harder for myself to keep control of and ignore all of its negative effects on me.

A few days later I found myself at church up front talking with the pastor's wife. Why I was up there talking to her I'm not even sure, maybe I was asking her in some kind of another veiled attempt at prayer for myself without revealing too much. I wasn't even aware or sure of what I was saying, but I remember being filled with confusion and shame as I knew some more of my uncontrolled ugliness had spilled out of my mouth, aghast that yet again I had let some of it escape. What I do remember clearly is that without any kind of condemnation, she asked something of me.

Gently she looked at me. "May I hug you?" Confused I nodded at her like I guess, and then she said something that was like a well-placed arrow to my heart. "I feel like I should just hold you like a mother would for a while."

Tears that were always at the surface streamed from my eyes as she held me while I sobbed and I felt some more of my carefully constructed defenses crumble and shed.

She didn't turn away from me and my ugliness at all, instead with so much love and gentleness she suggested to me that maybe I should go to a SOZO session, a ministry that is uniquely targeted for inner healing, getting to the root of your issues.

"You know I've been to them before." "They are nothing to be afraid of." She reassured me. "They are gentle and very healing, think about it, okay?"

I was at a place that I knew I could no longer sustain; wanting to be free of this merry-go-around I was on. Exhausted, I was tired of the fight it took trying to maintain control of myself and not let all the hurts I had buried raise up any farther where they would be seen. Smothered with their existence in my life I was caught up in the ridiculous notion that I must manage on my own and in my own strength control the effects they had on me. I wasn't managing anything at all. The wounds I had never healed. Instead by my burying them, stroking their very existence because I couldn't let them go on my own, they were steadily releasing their vicious poison, driving me to the edge of insanity.

Wounds, lies, hurt, and deception had me holding a mirror that I kept only at one hundred and eighty degrees; shining at everyone else but me. To turn that mirror three hundred and sixty degrees meant I would have to look upon myself where I would find someone that I had a great deal of difficulty looking at. Much of what I was and what I wore had worn me down into a useless angry and wounded person who wasn't very pleasant to look at. My eyes burned with regret and insight at the reflection I saw of myself.

Her heart isn't beating abundant life, it is instead leaded with hardness trying to protect itself.

She is wearing a heavy coat of shame that is buttoned up tight around her. A winter hat upon her head labeled unworthy, its thick ear-flaps that cover her ears, keeping her from hearing the truth that she is indeed worthy of the Father's love. Upon her feet are the heavy winter boots of self-sufficiency that she puts on, taking herself on a cold, wanton and barren path of trudging through wasted years of striving all on her own. Her hands wear thick mittens of fear that cover her eyes, too afraid to look into the light, the brightness of the Son, into the eyes of God, so sure she will find condemnation there.

My reflection in that mirror glared back at me. Dark and lonely years of my life which now stretched into most of it, sadly squandered by adorning garments I was never meant to wear. I had come to my breaking point, after all these long and wasted years, I had finally come to the end of my rope, forced to my knees.

God was moving me towards Him, using others and their unconditional love past my fears and inhibitions of the unknown, readying me to take the plunge and do something that was way past my comfort zone. I went home thinking about what the pastor's wife said.

At this point what can I lose? Finding courage in my course of thinking that I didn't know these people nor them I, if this was going to be a total disaster nothing could be worse than how I already felt. I had better do something before I lost my courage.

My laptop was open in front of me. I got online to request an appointment for a SOZO session. I sucked in my abated breath as I hit send, then immediately broke out in a sweat as my request was now out there in cyber world making its way to where it would be seen. It took all my will and fortitude not to turn back and cancel my request. My fears were ready to prevail yet again, but my desperation was so strong by now I surprised myself and didn't cancel.

It was time to leave the house; the time for my SOZO appointment had come. Nervousness had me so worked up that I was quivering inside. Alternating between cold and hot flashes I tried to control my body from the almost physical jolts of sheer anxiety.

I don't know how to do this, how do I start or begin to unravel the lifetime of hurts, wounds, and all the many lies I have believed?

Crushing defeat greeted me when I looked at the mirror of my life, realizing I had been in bondage to it all. It was a very hard pill to swallow; to confront myself with the knowledge that I had let it all render me useless and stay trapped in a world of deceit that I was okay, to think that I had wrongly believed I had to do all the work on my own to fix myself. Regret washed over me that I had wasted so many, many years living like this, failing miserably. Desperately I finally was now ready to ask Jesus to answer my cry.

Please free me!

Getting into my car, my mind was whirling, my stomach in knots as I drove out to my appointment. The entire drive I kept talking to myself over and over, reminding myself that I desperately needed this help while also trying to remain calm enough that I wouldn't drive myself off the road. I finally arrived at the place I was to have my meeting. The cold winter air assaulted my face as I got out of my car, doing nothing to cool the heat of fear radiating from my body. Hot and so cold at the same time, I trudged forward, forcing myself to walk in. I shook like a leaf ready to float off into the wind as I approached the reception desk. The lady receptionist behind the counter greeted me and immediately I sensed love emanating from her eyes, which slightly calmed me. She then showed me where I was to go.

Two ladies greeted me. They too just like the receptionist, held nothing but love in their eyes for me as they ushered me into the room. Soft worship music was playing in the background as they led me to a comfortable chair to sit in. They explained how they were going to let me talk and that anything I might say would be confidential and never leave that room. They continued to explain how we would stop periodically, pray about things that might come up and we would ask Jesus to meet us in that room and fill my needs. Most of all they kept telling me how much I was loved by Him, and had nothing to be ashamed of. Feeling no condemnation from them it helped me to relax and not turn around and run. I started by telling them who I was, my name, and brief information about me, how many children I had, and facts like that.

My defenses were on edge especially when I was simply asked if I knew Jesus. I shook my head feeling offended yet convicted.

"Yes, yes I do."

Afraid the mask of deceit upon my face was cracking open and these ladies might see the truth of who the real me was frightened me. I felt like I was losing control of my rock hard façade and it was turning into soft mud that was slipping precariously all around me, ruthlessly exposing me. Only seconds had gone by but I could see a lifetime of failure flash before my eyes. *Do I know Jesus? I've believed in Him for what seems like forever, but do I truly know Him? If I truly know Him why do I feel so ashamed and unworthy of His love?*

I could feel the heavy weight of my book that I always carried with me; my list of wrongs, like the dirt that rests upon a casket. I wasn't living that abundant life promised in Him. Instead I was smothered in my own sin trying to conceal the hurt that kept me from ever believing the truth that these ladies kept telling me; that I was loved by Him. How I wanted to know that truth.

We hadn't gotten very far into our meeting when one of the ladies stopped and said she wanted to share something with me. She said God had given her a vision of me.

"I see you floating in a pool of water with your hair floating behind you, you're void of any weight and completely at peace."

I looked at her totally skeptical trying hard not to roll my eyes and shook my head sarcastically. "Well, I don't know what to think about that, I don't know how to swim and I am deathly afraid of the water."

Softly she said. "Well that's what God is showing me about you."

Wanting to ignore what she just said because in seemed so ludicrous to me since it was more far reaching than anything I had ever felt, I just shrugged my shoulders nonchalantly at her. I was ready to move on. I really had nothing planned to share since I didn't really know how to unravel all that I was feeling.

"I grew up in a normal family, then everything changed when my father became a pastor."

I somewhat surprised myself with that opening statement, and just like that, the floodgates of agony deep within started to open. One of the ladies stopped me from saying anything further.

"What do you mean, you were a normal family then not?"

Suddenly as horrid resentment rose to the surface, I truly realized how angry I was at the church, how I wished my father had never become a pastor. I had deep rooted anger at people and what I perceived their expectations were of me. Anger at all the lies I had falsely believed and the confusion I felt. The most painful was the feeling, the lie that I could never tell anyone about the sexual abuse because good Christian girls and good Christian families just didn't have these kind of ugly and dirty things happen. I was upset, I had so much head knowledge of God and extremely mad that I had little heart knowledge, in part because I had chosen to believe the lies the enemy had fed to me all these many long years.

As I opened up my heart and let the ugliness spill out, they were so gentle with me, never condemning, leading me in prayers of repentance. The pain coming out was so intense I felt like I was drowning. I started to talk about the sexual abuse and found myself lost, back in that moment. Moaning with heartbreak and despair I cried out.

"This can't be happening, what will Dad think, I can't disappoint him!"

Suffocating, hot searing agony was rising to the surface breaking free. Rocking back and forth lost in the incredible pain, every muscle in my body was in severe tense knots. Through the desolate darkness I was lost in, I faintly heard one of the ladies speak to me.

"We're going to stop right here and pray." She started to pray, reverently, sweetly, boldly, asking Jesus to restore to me everything that had been stolen from me by that boy.

Immediately, instantaneously and miraculously as soon as she prayed that prayer over me, it was as if suddenly I felt the soothing hand of God reach deep into my heart. He ever so gently reached into all the dark corners and crevasses of my wounded heart and took all the pain and anguish that I was lost in away. As He took it away He replaced it, all of it with an overwhelming sense of peace, tranquility and light that I had never in my entire life experienced before. All the tension was gone. I felt my whole body and mind relax. Completely now filled head to toe with such a complete and utter peace that was surreal to me, a sensation of floating overcame me. Like I was floating, weightless, without a care in the world, in a pool of water that I knew without doubt was His love.

I knew I was practically falling over in the chair I was in, my body so relaxed it felt like rubber, but I didn't care! For the first time in my life I didn't care, I didn't care if I looked foolish, I didn't care what they or others might think of me, I just knew with every fiber of my being I wanted to stay forever in this place. This complete freedom and at rest, no more pain, no more anguish, just floating in the presence of His love and so at peace that I literally had to fight to stay awake. I was not imagining this; it was as real to me as the flesh is on my bones. God had miraculously and lovingly completely delivered me!

Fear and shame all those years had kept me from ever fully looking into His face, afraid I would see disappointment but all that had now melted away. Now I was unashamedly looking at His face, into His wondrous eyes that told me of His great love for me. The chains that had kept me in bondage for all those long years had fallen away, broken by His tender and fierce love for me. I was completely and wondrously set free! Even in the undying love of my husband or all of my striving to heal myself and lift off the heavy mantle of pain it couldn't be accomplished. I had strived and strived on my own and still could find no peace or answers but for One. I had needed the true healer, the One who could reach into the very depths of my soul. The One who would see me and embrace me, the One who had created me. When I finally took the chance to lay it all down at His feet and lift my eyes to fully look into His face that held no condemnation there, the shame I had always felt floated away in the presence of His love.

Why, oh why I asked myself. *Why did you let yourself be entangled in the web of lies of unworthiness, disbelieving in His love for you?*

It's a love so encompassing, so powerful that in the blink of an eye a life can be changed. My life is now changed, no longer do I feel the sting of those wounds. I marvel now at my long years of stupidity, but I also marvel in the undying love He had for me to never forsake me or leave me, just waiting for me, beckoning me to come to Him.

I found myself so overjoyed with this new freedom I wanted to tell everyone! I wanted to herald the battle cry, FREEDOM! FREEDOM! *I can't shout it loud enough.* Peace, such an undeniable and tangible peace like I'd never experienced before now floods me, reaching to the very core of me, and outward to the tips of my fingers and the soles of my feet.

How can I even begin to express to anyone what I know God has just done for me?

I am free from the enemy's accusations, free from expectations, free from all the pain, anxiety and fears, free to just be me. He loved me just as I was and because He loves me He had set me free! I know it was I that had held myself back, but just like the loving father He is, He continued to wait for me to come to Him, He never gave up on me. His compassionate love had freed me from the things that had bound me.

In the days and weeks and even months following, I find myself tentatively wanting to test the truth of this newfound healing, this peaceful state I now find my heart at. The wild erratic and painful beats that are no more; the hot searing pain that was always present now just a distant memory that no longer causes me any distress. Amazed that this can be true, my hand reaches out and almost gingerly my fingers run the length of my heart, sure I would find the sharp edge of a knife that had always held such a prominence in my life.

All I find is a completely healed ridge of a scar where once was a gaping and painful hole. Wonder fills me; so many years of pain and struggle miraculously now gone. The scar I feel now, a beautiful reminder of what once was. Tears that flow down my face now are that of utter joy and gratefulness to the One who has healed me. He was always there, patiently waiting for me to come and lay it all at His feet. Broken and weary of struggling on my own, year after year till the years had become so many that the weight of all that waste was crushing and suffocating the last of my self-sufficiency. It drove me to the only place, to the only One who could so miraculously give me this gift of peace.

Questions arise in me. *Why did you let your ridiculous fears torment you for so long?*

All those years that you tried and tried in your own strength to heal yourself, but never could you succeed. Is the answer because He had to show me, that it would be His strength I would need in my life?

It's a truth I now know without a shadow of doubt, that in my own strength everything is useless, any strength I have now is from God, and God alone. I had to learn the lesson, when I yield to Him, His love, His ways, He will give me all the strength I will ever need, He will be my rock, there can be no other. He and He alone is my peace that passes no understanding, just like the scripture says. I don't understand it, but I know I have it.

I was learning, that when I allowed myself to believe in who He said I was, worthy of His love, I can believe He's my provider, healer, all that I need because I'm worthy of those things. Striving to believe harder is just an exercise in infertility, I had to learn faith rises in the context of His presence and His love. Not only do I need to believe in these things, but I also need to rest in and have confidence in His love.

This lesson, this newfound freedom and peace was going to be tested and proved.

The
Proving

CHAPTER

26

*A*nticipating that summer will surely come after a long dark winter can be an especially hard wait. This was especially ringing true for Larry and I this year since we had cooked up some summer plans that we were really looking forward too.

This summer was going to be our fortieth wedding anniversary. Thinking we wanted to do something extra special to celebrate this milestone we tried to think what would be something we would both enjoy. Together we came up with what we wanted to do; we would take a long and relaxed six-week driving vacation. We would head down the Alcan Highway; spend some time traveling around the lower forty-eight states, then drive back up the Alcan Highway back home to Alaska.

We owned a travel trailer at the time but thought it might be a bit small and confining for that long of a time, so in the middle of that winter we started looking around at getting a bigger travel trailer we could take on our anniversary trip. Finding one we liked, we purchased the new larger one. Anxiously we waited for the snow to melt so we could bring our new travel trailer home. Snow can be frustratingly stubborn, it never melts very fast especially when you are ready for it to be gone. Which in our case, excitement for our trip made us feel like spring would never come. Finally the snow and ice started to melt, the steady drip of water in the rain gutters held the sound of the promise of warmer weather just around the corner. Early spring we put our smaller travel trailer we up for sale, eventually selling it shortly before we were ready to leave on our six-week trip. It was a huge relief since we were sweating at the prospect of owning two trailers.

In excitement over our upcoming trip we had spent many hours the last few months of a long winter dreaming about where we wanted to go and what we wanted to do. We decided we would leave May 1st weather permitting. We didn't want to drive in snow on the Alcan on our way to the lower forty-eight states. We also wanted to make sure we still had some summer left in Alaska that we could enjoy when we got back, knowing full well there were only about three very short months of summer before fall arrived and we'd be headed back into another long winter.

Plans were made to wander around the west coast first stopping in Washington to visit my brother and wife who live there, then leisurely we would make our way over to Denver, Colorado. Once in Denver we would see our youngest son, his wife and our very much missed young grandson. After spending time with them, we would make our way back to Alaska.

My son and his wife were planning on taking the opportunity to take a ten-day vacation, just the two of them to New York City while we were in Denver leaving their three-year-old son with us. Our grandson would go on a much talked up, big camping adventure with papa and gramma while mom and dad were gone. I could hardly wait, excited and very happy to have this highly anticipated babysitting gig. The thought of being able to spend all this extra special and rare one-on-one time with our grandson caring for and loving on him was something I was really looking forward to. I was super anxious for May to come and eventually getting to Colorado.

In the months prior to our trip while Larry and I had our heads together making our plans, I kept getting this overwhelming sense that we were supposed to take this trip for reasons I didn't really understand, it felt like it was more than just the mere fact that we wanted to go.

We still owned our own business and both of us worked there. I had given up my store years before to help Larry in his business. We had never been gone for this long of a period before as we were planning now so it worried Larry. Apprehensive and a bit worried he had doubts.

"I don't know, maybe we shouldn't go." He tried to tell me when he got worried about it.

I'd promptly screw up my face with a sternness, afraid he was going to change his mind telling him, "No, we are going, we are doing it!" I adamantly tried to get it across to him. "We need to do it, I just know we need this time away."

Little did I know what was going to be in store for us in the future, but God had a way of preparation, paving the way for what was to come.

We had two sons that now worked for us and the one that had worked for us the longest was going to manage our business while we were away. So that he could ease into his new role he would take while we were gone we started to give him more and more responsibility. I still planned on doing all of the bookkeeping, bill paying, and payroll while we were gone so we bought a small portable fax/copier machine and I made preparations to have everything with me I would need. He was going to fax or email me all the information I needed to keep up on everything and I would make sure to mail our employees paychecks back to the office in time to hand out on pay day. It was a little nerve wracking for us since this was going to be an extended absence from our business.

We had worked hard over the years building up our business to what it was now but felt fairly comfortable leaving it in the capable hands of our son. Larry also planned on being available for any phone calls needed and remotely do work if needed. We wrote up documents for our wishes how to divide up our business interests between our four sons in the event something happened to us while we were gone. It seemed morbid to me to even think that way but we wanted to be prudent. We were ready, we had prepared and laid out everything we could think of, hoping we didn't forget something important.

A Simple Extraordinary Life

Finally we had dry pavement in our driveway. Our new larger travel trailer got brought home and parked in our driveway and our other smaller one sold. Larry and I were like two excited little kids waiting for Christmas morning, spending many evenings sitting in our new trailer dreaming, packing it, and putting in little touches and upgrades so everything would be just how we wanted it. There were some evenings our kids would come over and find us in our trailer, waiting for the day we could leave. They'd laugh at our excitement and us because there we were again, sitting in our two recliners in the trailer out in the driveway thinking about the trip we were about to take. May 1st couldn't come soon enough.

Our departure day had finally arrived. The sun was shining brightly that early morning as we loaded up the last of our things. Hitching up the trailer to the truck we drove off, giddy with anticipation of being gone for a long period of time with little to no responsibility. We both have always loved going on long drives, love enjoying the scenery around us and the drive down the Alcan Highway on our way to the lower forty-eight states would be no exception. Part of the fun about a road trip through the wilderness is always being on the lookout for wildlife, which we saw plenty of on our drive down the Alcan. We spotted lots of black bears, had some grizzly bears strolling in the middle of the highway in front of us, saw herds of buffalo, caribou, moose, fox, swans, and Larry was sure he had even spotted a rare mountain lion.

About a week into our trip Larry was driving when he reached up stretching his arm a bit putting his hand on his neck and felt a large lump there on the side of his neck. He didn't say anything to me about it for another week and when he did, we didn't think much about it. He was prone to sinus infections and thought maybe it had something to do with that. It was probably just a swollen lymph node since he seemed to be fighting another sinus infection again.

Our first stop after making it through Canada was in Graham, Washington where we spent a few precious days visiting my brother and his wife. After a few days of fun visiting I had to say my teary goodbyes and get on with the rest of our trip.

My Journey from Anxiety to Peace

As we headed down the west coast the weather wasn't cooperating very well. We were looking for sunshine so we ended up leaving the cloudy, rainy coast and headed inland towards Redding, California. We spent Memorial Day weekend there in perfect eighty degree weather, the gloriously warm sun shining down on our lily-white Alaskan bodies. Time was flying by as we enjoyed seeing the ever changing scenery and new places. The most enjoyable thing of all was just being together. Our babysitting gig was coming up so we made our way over to Denver, Colorado. I was overjoyed at the prospect of getting to see my son and especially my grandson in just a few short days.

Feeling a bit nervous that our three-year-old grandson might be shy or hesitant around us since we don't see him very often had us worrying needlessly over nothing. Plans were made to meet our son after he got off work in a restaurant parking lot and we'd go to dinner together. I'll never forget, we were parked waiting for our son and when he drove up, there in the backseat in his car seat was our young grandson waving his hands excitedly about.

He squealed when he saw us. "Gramma, Papa!" The biggest grin ever upon his sweet little face.

Overcome with joy, tears escaped from my eyes as I watched him, he couldn't get out of his car seat fast enough, jumping up in our arms giving us the best hugs ever. My fears had been unfounded, he knew exactly who gramma and papa were.

He was so excited to go on his big camping adventure with gramma and papa while his mom and dad went on their vacation. They had bought him special toys just for his big adventure with us and he patiently waited till he was with us to open them up. We proceeded to have the best ten days of my life loving on that little guy. The memories made and the many pictures I took I'll always treasure.

We took him to the zoo, parks, played with his new nerf gun, read books and introduced him to the minion movies, which he wanted to watch over and over because he found them so funny. We spent hours with his new Lego set he got for the trip his imagination running wild, and every night after I had given him a shower and put his pajamas

229

on he would sit on my lap and I would read to him from a children's picture Bible while he listened intently. One of my favorite times with him would be in the morning when he'd cuddle for a long time with me, slowly waking up. We shared as many kisses and hugs as possible, knowing it would be a long time before I got to see him again. I tried to soak up all his smiles and laughed at his antics; he was such a delight, his constant chatter music to my ears. I felt sorry for him and a bit worried, enough that I called his mother to find out what to do for him, the poor little guy got a nasty cold and troublesome cough the last few days he was with us and Larry picked it up from him about a week later.

We had said more of our tearful goodbyes, my heart breaking just a little bit more every time, so precious were our visits with my son, his wife and my grandson. It was time to start our journey back up to Alaska so we started making our way from Colorado towards Canada. By the time we got to Canada we were both now sick with colds, Larry far worse than I. June 6th, on our fortieth wedding anniversary we were in Edmonton, Canada. We went out for dinner at a restaurant inside the Edmonton Mall, intending to go see a movie afterwards but we both were feeling pretty puny so we ended up back in our trailer after dinner, trying to get some rest. We still had a very long drive ahead of us.

Every day we had been driving many long hours, making our way back towards our home in Alaska. Larry continued to get really sick, and was getting weaker by the day. I was starting to get worried; he was coughing and extremely miserable, his sinuses were really bad, but what worried me the most was the way he looked, I don't think I'd ever seen him looking so sickly before. He couldn't stay awake. It was much worse than his normal sleepiness and it was really scaring me since he was doing all the driving. By this time we had decided to shave off a few days of our trip, not hanging around in Edmonton like we had planned to and get back home as quick as possible so he could go see a doctor. I knew he had to be feeling pretty puny since he rarely goes to the doctor and it's a fight getting him to go, him wanting to see one now had to mean he was really miserable.

I was on pins and needles trying to keep him awake while he drove. I was on high alert, afraid we were going to go off the road but too scared to do any of the driving myself since we were pulling a 24-foot trailer. I had never driven a vehicle before pulling something behind me. Constantly I tried to keep talking to him and shook his arm frequently, doing anything I could think of just short of punching him hard to get him to stay awake. Increasingly I was getting really freaked out and scared because he kept nodding off.

He was making me nervous so I asked him the question, "Do you want me to drive?"

"No, I'm fine." He tried telling me as he yawned again.

A few minutes later the truck dangerously swerved as he nodded off again.

"Larry, let me drive!" I said louder and more insistently.

"I'll be fine." He stubbornly said.

After a few minutes he was nodding off again. I was exhausted with trying to keep him awake. This wasn't working anymore, I couldn't keep him awake and I was scared.

"LARRY! Pull over right now!" I demanded. "I'm driving, you can't do it anymore, you're going to kill us!"

He never in our forty years together had ever wanted to be the one in the passenger seat, but he pulled over. Something in my tone made him realize I wasn't kidding. Deep down, he knew the seriousness of the situation, he couldn't continue, he was way too sick. Giving me a few short instructions after I had crawled into the driver's seat, I nervously pulled our rig out of the large dirt parking lot we had pulled into and out onto the highway. Within minutes Larry was snoring from the passenger's seat.

I ended up driving almost all of the last few days of traveling while he fitfully slept, thankful for the pretty empty roads we encountered on the way back up the Alcan Highway towards home. Secretly it was kind of fun to drive once I got over my skittishness, feeling rather bummed when Larry would wake up from a nap and want to take over driving for a bit till he got too sleepy again to continue. His wakefulness wouldn't last very long before he would be shortly nodding off again making me nervous all over again, especially when we could be talking and not five seconds later he'd be nodding off again. It was very stressful. He wasn't getting any better if anything only worse, and was extremely lethargic.

We went to the doctor as soon as we got back home thinking he had a severe sinus infection. The doctor responded with yes you have a sinus infection, but when he took one look at the lump on Larry's neck he immediately sent us to an ear and nose specialist, stating that the lump had nothing to do with his sinus infection. Worry was starting to take over. Within days we were thrown into many doctor's appointments, further tests, scans and biopsies. The word cancer came up as a possible prognosis causing our hearts to suddenly plummet.

It was still summertime and the weather was beautiful, coaxing us to enjoy it even though it was going to be a long weekend of anxiously waiting to hear the results of Larry's medical tests. Wanting to escape since we were reeling with the possibilities of what we might be looking at concerning Larry's health, we got in our truck, hooked up the travel trailer and headed to Homer, that peaceful and quaint little town by the ocean about five hours away from where we live and did our halibut fishing at. We were going to try and relax and not have to think too hard about what was going on, what the medical tests would reveal.

One of my favorite places to be and where I find myself the most content and relaxed, is by the ocean here in Alaska. Given the choice of where to go camping I will always choose to go anywhere where I can sit and look out at the water and listen to the lapping of the waves as they hit the shore. The biggest bonus I find besides the beautiful scenery is there are no nasty mosquitoes trying to suck your blood when you are by the ocean, so it was by the ocean we would go to try and find a reprieve from our worries.

I absolutely love Homer; it is so uniquely beautiful with its breathtaking vistas that always cause me to be in awe of God's creation. We were camped out on the Homer spit, which is a four to five mile long narrow bit of land that juts out into the Kachemak Bay. Surrounded by snowcapped mountains and glaciers and the smell of the salt air, the scenery and scents always take my breath away.

My Journey from Anxiety to Peace

One morning while Larry was still soundly sleeping, I got up, put on my sun glasses and headed out to take a walk on the beach to think and pray. The early morning sun glinted off the blue gray water in the bay while faint pink ribbons still graced the sky. The quiet sound of lapping water as it hit the sandy shore and the cry of seagulls as they swooped in the air filled my senses as I made my way down the beach in the gentle quiet of the early morning. Only a few people were out and about at this early hour. I walked down the beach a ways and sat on a large boulder now accessible with the receding tide. As I sat on that boulder, my eyes feasting on the sights and sounds before me, the wind was gently drying my tears as I cried out to God with my fears and anxiety I had about Larry's health.

I continued to sit there looking around at the beautiful morning sunshine that reflected off the unusually calm water, feasting on the beauty of the majestic snowcapped peaks that jutted up from the sea. Finding a peaceful serenity in the quiet morning it began to soothe my troubled thoughts. I felt God's hand in this glorious creation that surrounded me and it spoke to me of His love, His assurance. I knew that whatever the future was going to hold, He was going to be my anchor. The morning held a peace and calm for me that He was infusing deep within me. Just as He created this magnificent view I was looking at, He also created us, He knows the past, present and the future. *Where else can I put my trust but in the One who made it all?*

I remember having the thought, even if Larry was going to be taken away from me, I was determined I was going to trust that God would make a way for me to be able to handle it. I had witnessed my mother-in-law lose her husband and a year later my mom, my father. I didn't want to go through that kind of agony without having His comfort. I knew the only way I could handle something as devastating as that would be to me was to put myself in God's hands, because I would surely need Him. I let myself cry it all out and continued to look out at the beauty that surrounded me, letting it continue to soothe and comfort my soul.

Oblivious to the hardness of the boulder I sat upon, God was at work, erasing much of my fears. He continued to fill me with a peace that would carry me through the journey ahead.

A Simple Extraordinary Life

After returning home from our long weekend in Homer we were at the next doctor's appointment the following week when the doctor decided Larry needed to go into surgery to remove part of the lymph node on his neck to get a better and more extensive biopsy done on it. It was scheduled within the next few days.

We had just been gone from our business for six weeks on our anniversary trip, leaving our son in charge and now that we had only been back for a few weeks, here we were, constantly leaving our son shorthanded and in charge because of Larry's many doctor appointments, medical tests and body scans, and now surgery. All of this was taking a lot of time away from the office again, something we hadn't foreseen. I couldn't deny it, God had foreseen our need; our six week absence had paved the path for what the future was going to hold for the next five months. We knew this in the depth of our hearts, He had given us this assurance; God knew the future and had prepared the way.

When we got the final word that yes, it was definitely cancer, it was a bit like waking up from a startling and frightening nightmare and finding out it wasn't a dream, it was real. I won't deny that we were shaken and in disbelief. Cancer the dreaded big C, a word that was hard to believe that it was now attached to us. Following the staggering diagnosis, we were then sent to an oncologist where more scans were done to determine the staging of the cancer. Nervousness, fear and anxiety were at my front door knocking, trying hard to overtake me once again. I knew there was no way I was going to go back to my old ways, God had given me a gift of peace and I wasn't about to lose it. His timing, His bestowal to me of my newfound freedom would get me through this next phase in our lives, I would stand on it and rely on it, find strength in it.

In just a matter of weeks the medical bills were mounting, and mounting fast. Thousands and thousands of dollars had already stacked up in surgeries and tests and here we were, uninsured! I knew we would need a financial miracle. I tried to find rest in the fact that God had given me so much that I was so grateful for, I would try to trust He wouldn't abandon us now in our time of need. *I'm going to hold on tight to His promises.*

My Journey from Anxiety to Peace

Larry was sent immediately to start chemotherapy. He had been diagnosed with lymphoma, stage two. The cancer had spread to his lungs and it was an aggressive, fast growing cancer. We were reeling with this news and I will admit I did have bouts of sheer panic and fear. It was strange and surreal for me though; at the same time I had this underlying peace not of my own making. I knew we were going to get through this. I was fast learning where my strength and peace now came from, struck with the realization that I had never had this kind of assurance and peace before, having lived all of my life fraught with worry and doubt. I didn't know what it was to have peace before and to say I have it now is nothing short of a miracle. To say and know I have a strength that is not of me or my own doing is another miracle, this I know.

His perfect timing had been put into place. Assurance flooded me, I knew that it was in His divine timeline that I would have gotten to a place where I was finally driven to my knees and get to the end of my tightly held rope. Tired with the constant struggle of trying to fix myself, I had gained newfound freedom and peace that was without doubt found only in Him. I would hold onto it, and never let it go, it would be my lifeline. I had no illusion that without God first healing my deep inner wounds I would never survive this journey we now found ourselves in.

It would have sent me over the edge.

CHAPTER

27

*O*ur first visit with the oncologist was truly overwhelming. The doctor advised us not to wait on treatment. Her advice, he needed to start chemotherapy as soon as possible.

"How soon?" Larry asked a feeling of dread sitting hard in the pit of his stomach.

"My advice, two weeks would be the longest I would wait. Any longer and it would be risky." The doctor continued with her advice. "If you decide on this course I can schedule for you to have a port put in right away."

In shock with the sudden progression Larry looked at me first trying to gage my response, asking me what I thought. I think he wanted assurance from me that he was going to be okay. We both were in solid agreement.

His eyes clouded with unshed tears as we held tight to each other's hands. "Okay, go ahead and schedule the surgery for the port." I squeezed his hand trying to communicate my deep love for him as he gave his answer to the doctor. We were given a plan of attack and told how many rounds of chemotherapy he would need. We both exhaled the pent up air we had been holding, sighing as the door to the room closed behind the doctor as she left the room.

I reached over to hold his head in my hands, "It's going to be okay babe."

"Yeah it'll be okay." Larry whispered as our lips met in a kiss, "I love you."

My eyes were damp as I whispered back. "I love you too!"

We left the doctor's office after we were done and headed to the car, my head swirling with troubling thoughts.

At the mention of another surgery, quickly panic had started to rise, my heart doing major flip-flops. The biopsy they had just done on Larry's neck had already cost over $10,000. Before we had left the doctor's office social workers were brought in to talk to us, giving us a lot of different information on everything to support groups and programs for the needy. Other office personnel came in covering medications, nutrition, and what he could expect during the course of treatment. Still feeling stunned because it was all happening so quickly, it was hard to absorb, and I kept losing my focus on what they were saying. All I could think of was the money, the massive amount of money this was all going to cost us. *How in the world are we going to pay for all this?*

Because we were uninsured, our doctor had advised that we use the hospital's oncology unit instead of their own small one they had there in their office. Someone said something about a patient navigator at the hospital and maybe we would want to contact one. I couldn't think straight. Still grappling with just the idea of my husband even having cancer in the first place it was too much, too soon, feeling overwhelmed as I was. About all I could do right then was remember to breathe in and out and try to remain calm enough that I didn't return back to my old ways of deep fear and anxiety that would overtake me and return me to the pit I had recently been freed from.

Larry was scheduled for surgery in the next few days to have his port put in so they could start the chemotherapy treatments right away. To make sure his heart could survive the chemotherapy there were more tests scheduled. Every day it seemed that there were more and more appointments to go to. Both Larry's father and mine had died of heart attacks at the age of seventy so we were very glad when his own heart tests came back good, relieving some of our worry. Every doctor's appointment we had, for every procedure he needed, we would try to get an answer.

"How much is this going to cost?"

"It's expensive," they would say. "Try not to think about that."

It was difficult to get any concrete answers. We were getting a sinking feeling that it would be much more than we could ever imagine.

Within the week we were already at Larry's first chemotherapy session, which turned into an all-day affair. His room felt like it had a revolving door all morning. Besides the nurses coming and going, more social workers and several different hospital pharmacists were coming in, throwing even more information around making us feel yet even more overwhelmed. Not far into the treatment I looked at Larry and noticed a red rash starting to appear all over him, quickly rising up his neck, face and arms. He was having an allergic reaction to one of the drugs. The nurse came in and stopped the drip into his port then shot him up with a heavy dose of Benadryl. We then had to wait for another hour before restarting the drip at a much slower rate so his body could tolerate it, adding hours to the already all-day procedure.

I started to realize as I sat there bored with reading, at the next treatment I would have to bring something else to occupy myself with to help whittle the time away since the drugs were making Larry drift in and out of sleep all day. Wandering around the store a few days later looking for something I could bring to keep my hands busy, I decided I would try my hand at crocheting some hats. It had been years and years since I had picked up a crochet hook so I had to print out some basic instructions to follow since I couldn't remember anymore how to crochet. I armed myself with some yarn and packed a bag for our next trip to the oncology unit.

The way the hospital's oncology unit was set up, the children's unit was just down the hall from us, where the fresh drinking water cooler was. It wasn't till our second time being there that I wandered down there to get some fresh water to drink. Immediately my heart was gripped as I saw the parents sitting there in chairs holding their babies who were hooked up to machines receiving their treatments. Young children with large patches of hair missing, trying to play quietly while they were confined to the machines that dripped into their veins the chemotherapy drugs they needed. It grieved me to see the pasted smiles on the faces of the tired and worried parents that sat watching their children. Holding back tears I wandered back to Larry's private room, I had never felt more thankful in my life.

Who am I to think that what we are going through, though hard, is anything like what these parents are going through? They have to watch their beautiful children, so young and suffering. Wondering if they will even have a life to live ahead of them.

A new kind of gratefulness came over me. Larry and I had lived a relatively easy life, our children were healthy and we had shared many years together. I decided my time spent those long days we would have in that room would be ones of thankfulness, and while I sat there crocheting I would pray for the less fortunate ones around me.

We had started to do our own research about the costs of chemotherapy and it was staggering. We knew we didn't qualify for most of the programs the social workers had been telling us about and Obama care was no longer enrolling for the year. No extra money just sitting in a bank account for a rainy day, we didn't have any choice left but to trust that God would provide and try not to get too anxious about it. Sometimes it was easier said than done but He had already started to provide for us, we would pray He would continue to provide.

Not long into all the pre-diagnosis tests and surgeries, Larry's mother came to us and gave us a large sum of money that would have been his inheritance when she died. We had no inkling she had this money. New faith was arising within as God started to provide for our needs. I knew in my heart that even all those many years ago when his parents were putting this money aside, God knew the why and when we would have a need for it. It was enough money to pay for almost all of the previous tests and surgeries he had before starting chemotherapy. This provision was leading me to believe that He would somehow continue to provide for our needs. I could feel deep within, tremendous changes in myself. Previously in my life I would have been overrun with extreme anxiety and would have been dubious that we would be able to trust in provision. I knew that my thinking was changing and even my outward countenance had been changed with the peace I now felt.

Racking our brain how we could come up with some money, any money, we decided to sell my car since it was paid off and used infrequently. It would be fairly easy to get by on one car since we usually rode together to work. We lived about a mile from work and Larry could leave for the few minutes it would take to bring me home or pick me up if needed. I didn't put much thought into how we were going to sell my car other than putting a large two dollar plastic for sale sign in it with my phone number, then parked it in the parking lot at our place of business. I had a peace about it that God would send a buyer. *Where was this peace coming from?* Excitement filled me about these changes in myself. To be free from the never ending anxiety and worry that had always encircled me was like exuberantly walking on air now, instead of always trudging in the mud of the long and grueling previous years of before.

We were blessed with the many different people that were reaching out to us, letting us know they were praying for us. A lot of our business customers would tell us they were praying for us, and thinking about us. It was humbling to feel the love extended by those we deemed near strangers. I would get Facebook messages from people I hadn't talked to in years, the love and care that was being extended to us humbling. We could feel everyone's prayers lifting us up and sustaining us. Every Sunday at church without fail, our pastor would either pray with us or say encouraging things to us. I had a favorite encouragement that he had repeated several times to us.

Walking up to us he would put his arms around our shoulders. "Praying the Shalom of God over you."

Shalom is a Hebrew word meaning peace. When he said that, it never failed to bring more tears to my eyes and comfort to my heart, a reminder to never forget the precious gift of peace that had been given to me.

A Simple Extraordinary Life

My car that was for sale hadn't been sitting in the parking lot at work for very long when one day a longtime customer of ours came into our place of business. She came back to our offices, talked a bit with Larry and me giving us some words of encouragement, she herself a cancer survivor. Afterwards she went out to our sales counter and conducted the business she had come to do.

I watched her walk to the front door to leave. She had started out the door when suddenly she turned and said to my son who runs the sales counter.

"Oh by the way, do you know whose car that is for sale out in the parking lot?" "I've been looking for a car to buy for an employee of mine who really needs one. That car looks like a perfect one for them."

"Well, it's my mom's."

She came back in back to our offices and asked me a few questions about it and asked how much.

"$8,000.00." I answered a bit nervously.

Without hesitation she smiled at me. "SOLD! Take out the for sale sign!"

She went out to her car, grabbed her checkbook and wrote us a check for my car.

As I fingered her check I thought wow! *That was so easy!* Again brought to tears knowing full well that again God was providing without my even having to strive for it! *How is it that my faith just keeps getting increased? God I'm being blown away at how you are showing your goodness to us.* I'm starting to comprehend as I slowly walk towards the sure knowledge that God really does want to show His goodness to us. I'm not earning these gifts from Him, it's because He truly does love me. He loves us.

We were on to Larry's second round of chemotherapy and by this time had started to get an idea how much these sessions were going to cost. They were upwards of $50,000.00 each session with the cost of the drugs and all the hospital fees. Larry would need six of them. I hadn't done anything about seeing a patient navigator yet since I wasn't sure what all I would need to have to document and was even doubtful if they could help us at all, still feeling quite deluged with the whirlwind of how fast everything was happening. There we were in the hospital room, Larry hooked up receiving his second chemo treatment and in walks a strange lady, introducing herself as the hospital patient navigator. I couldn't believe it; I knew once again God was taking care of something I couldn't bring myself yet to do.

The patient navigator proceeded to tell us that there are drug companies that will give grants to the uninsured and cover the cost of the drugs.

"Do you want to apply?"

Skeptically we asked her. "Well what all does that entail?"

"Nothing much, tell us what your income is and just sign this form and I'll put the request in. The request will then go to two different drug companies, one for each of the two main drugs Larry is receiving."

By then our own research had told us, one of the drugs he was receiving was about $18,000.00 per session, the other around $19,000.00 per session. We signed the form, handed it back to her and that was it. We would hear in a few weeks whether or not we would receive the grants. I was a wee bit anxious, but still at peace waiting to hear. Within a few weeks the patient navigator called.

"Good news, you received both grants, the drugs will be covered!"

Close to $250,000.00 in provision had just been provided for us!

So many feelings flooded my heart and mind as I comprehended this news. I wanted to break out in a celebratory dance, but I'm pretty reserved so I just danced wholeheartedly and wildly in my dreams. Oh how God was faithful, continuing to meet our needs! Gratitude filled my being, my heart overwhelmed with thankfulness; I was grasping onto the truth of his love. No longer did it feel like just a fantasy of my mind but it was a reality felt deep in my heart. God really does love us, and He loves me, a person who had always thought she was unworthy of such love. He wants to supply all our needs. Humbled, my heart swelled even more with love for Him, in awe of all His goodness.

A Simple Extraordinary Life

There were still many other costs mounting up that we had to pay for. The hospital wanted us to start making monthly payments on our account. Like most folks we were already stretched to our max and had no budget to do this. We decided we would try to refinance the mortgage for our condo to get a lower interest rate and hopefully lower our house payment enough so we could start paying on our debt.

In order to also drop the extra $100.00 a month we were paying in mortgage insurance our appraisal had to come in higher than what the last two condos in our area had recently sold for, which was a pretty big stretch. I tingled with anticipation of what God could do. *Nothing is too big for my God, You have been faithfully showing me this. I'll just believe in this too.* I thoroughly cleaned the house and made it shine. Larry ordered the appraisal and when we got the appraisal back soon after, it came in higher like we needed. We were able to lower our mortgage payment by almost $400.00 a month, making a hospital payment now feasible. Again, God had met our needs! How do I say I was surprised, yet not surprised by this?

Other medical costs would come up with new tests and scans ordered that would somehow be provided for, the money for them showing up when we needed it. Trips to the post office would yield unexpected refund checks from the mortgage company or we would receive an occasional check from a friend. Our business did extraordinary well and we could draw more than normal to help pay for some of the extra medical costs. I had no doubt that it was God providing, it had nothing to do with what we did, it was because He wanted to lavish his love on us, He is just that good. He was etching His goodness deep upon my heart.

It was still a rough road to traverse at times. It is very hard to watch your loved one get weaker and increasingly tired from the rigors of chemotherapy, sick from the very thing that is supposed to make him well.

I did learn something new though; Larry had some vanity. He really didn't like the idea that he would probably lose his hair. I'll be honest I didn't either. I always loved his thick head of hair and now that it was peppered with distinguished gray, I liked it even more. I had talked him into growing a goatee a few years prior that I really admired and I just hated the idea he might lose that too. He kept telling me he was going to be one of those rare few, the small percentage the doctor said that don't lose their hair with these treatments. I was highly doubtful, so was the doctor. When we asked her about when your hair normally starts to fall out, she said right around the fourteenth day after your first chemo treatment, for which she apologized for.

One morning still asleep deep in the throes of dreamland all of a sudden Larry was standing directly over me, shaking me out of a sound sleep.

"Terry, Terry! It's happening!"

Alarmed, I awoke with a start; he had frightened me. My heart still wildly pounding, sleepily I looked at him through hazy eyes trying to sit up where I could get a good look at him, trying to read his troubled face.

"Whaat?" "What's wrong?"

Distressed, he put his hand to his head. "My hair!" he pulled at its strands, "It's falling out!"

I didn't know what to say to him, the poor guy, it bothered him quite a bit. He had been in the shower and noticed a lot of hair in the tub all around him. Sure enough it started to thin out badly to the day they said it would. I felt so sorry for him. Stubbornly we held out for a few weeks till it got so extremely thin you couldn't touch his hair without having large clumps of it left in the palms of your hands. He couldn't wash it in the shower anymore without it just falling out in massive amounts all around him, the evidence lying on the shower floor that had left bald spots on his head.

It was time, one evening while he sat in a chair in our kitchen I lovingly and sadly shaved off what little hair was left. I stared at his head, it was so white and his neck dark from a summer tan. I had never seen him bald before and neither had he seen himself this way before. It was a shock as he looked at himself in the mirror, one that neither one of us cared much for. Immediately we went out and bought him a hat he could wear when out in public. He was uncomfortable with having no hair and even the hat was peculiarly strange since he had never worn a hat before, except for a few times when he went hunting in our first years of marriage. At work he would sit in his office without his hat but if he had to go out front and talk to a customer or a client came into his office, he would put on his hat hiding his bald head.

It was strange, somehow the bald head and hat felt like a billboard that screamed cancer. My eyes were suddenly acutely aware of people all around me that wore the same billboard. The distinct look of cancer upon their faces; their head wrapped in colorful scarfs or obvious wigs upon the women's heads. The look of missing eyebrows beneath the rims of the hats that covered bald heads and the worn and tired look that screamed from their eyes.

It gave me pause every time I looked at that stark bald head of my husband. I was brutally honest with him. I loved him dearly but I didn't like how he looked bald. Neither did he, but somehow we were able to laugh about it, and laugh we did. The tears from our laughter a sweet release. Rubbing my hand over his bald head gave me comfort; *at least he is still with me!* I did tell him it was a good thing it wasn't me with the bald head.

"You would have a terrible time trying to console me!"

I knew my vanity would have taken a worse kicking than his did. I was ever so thankful he never lost his goatee. It thinned badly but stayed enough that we didn't have to make him completely clean-shaven, which made me very happy. We were in this thing together hair or no hair.

The chemo gave him a very upset stomach many days and he lost his sense of taste and smell. Things he used to like he could no longer tolerate to eat or drink. He'd go on binges, for several weeks cherry tomatoes were all that sounded good to him. I would buy cartons of them for him, only to have his taste buds change and turn to watermelon, or something else the next week. The strangest binge was coleslaw; I couldn't figure that one out. It was hard to figure out what to cook for him, his stomach so queasy much of the time. I felt like throwing my hands up in the air the day I lovingly made him some coleslaw, only to have him turn his nose up at it. The craving had passed.

Although he was getting increasingly tired and lethargic, he never missed much work. He'd use up what little energy he had and push himself during the day and then crash and sleep for hours and hours upon returning home. There were days we'd catch him nodding off at work or could see he was really fatigued, his cheeks getting really red or he'd turn white as a ghost. I'd make him go home early sometimes, having to really persuade him because he always felt so bad leaving our staff shorthanded. As soon as I got him home and tucked into bed he would immediately fall asleep, sleeping for the rest of the day and night. Several months had gone by and I was starting to feel really alone because he had no energy left for anything, having used what little energy he had for work. There was nothing left, not even for me. Feeling guilty and selfish about my feelings I tried to fill the quiet hours alone with other things, but I sorely missed him and the time we usually spent together. I missed my best friend. The fourth day after a chemo session would be the worst time he would have, being at his worst for the next few days. I was amazed how much a person could sleep, he always felt so incredibly wiped out. I understood he could do nothing about it but it didn't stop my loneliness.

To top off all the other side effects of chemotherapy Larry's short term memory was getting worse and worse by the day. Hard to watch for myself knowing he was struggling and equally hard for him to even realize that it was happening, making for some tense moments between not only us but those at work too. I remember one time going to one of his chemo sessions and we passed by a cork board at the reception desk that had a poster about getting what they refer to as, *chemo brain*. As lovingly as I could I pointed it out to him.

"Honey, look, it's a real side effect. We're not trying to demean you, but you really are forgetting things, it's not your fault, see?"

He finally accepted it even though it was hard for him to admit to. It was happening to him and we weren't just acting like he was a senile old man. It did get pretty bad at times, he'd quickly forget something just minutes after we discussed it, just positive that we had never discussed it. After he grudgingly admitted it, things weren't so tense anymore.

Feeling drained trying to protect and care for my husband the worst thing I struggled with was feeling really alone. *I want my husband back!* All these feelings were starting to get me down and I felt really guilty about them. I was having moments of weakness and doubt and fear for the future, whether Larry would fully recover, getting caught up in my old ways of thinking and letting anxiety start to creep back in. At my lowest point trying to hide my guilty and complex feelings, yet again, God reached out to me, showing me His faithfulness.

Sitting with Larry at church that Sunday while at one of my lowest points was proving to be a struggle. I was trying hard to keep my focus on the preaching and not on my feelings, but it was a losing battle. Without warning suddenly the pastor stopped in the middle of his sermon, walked down from the platform down the aisle and over to Larry and I. He put his hands on Larry's shoulders and started to pray for him and speak encouraging words to us. He prayed for complete healing in Larry's body then turned to me and said again, something that he had said to me before.

"You have a strength you do not know." He repeated this several times as he looked into my eyes.

At first I wanted to scoff at myself, *strength?* Tears were running down my cheeks, I felt so weak at the moment. Those words as he repeated them to me started to lift me up out of the places where I was struggling with self-sufficiency, and I knew that I knew, my strength comes from my God and Him alone. He was lovingly reminding me of it once again. Refreshed, renewed and strengthened again in my heart, soul and mind for this journey, peace, His peace was still there for me, I didn't have to lose it. The pastor turned around and went back up to the stage and continued his sermon.

I sat there and marveled. Here I am again, being amazed that God would meet me at those places in my heart where I needed Him most, astounded at how He continues to keep showing His love to me. Having wrestled most of my life to know that God loved me and to understand that truth, now here I am, being constantly reminded and shown that He does. It's not that He ever hid His love from me before; it was I who had hid my face from him, wearing the false garments of fear and shame that kept me doubting His love for me, it was there all along, just waiting for me to believe in it.

My Journey from Anxiety to Peace

We were getting close to the home stretch, the end of Larry's treatments. It was also the beginning of the fall holiday season. I usually did a large family Thanksgiving dinner but this year neither of us were up to it, we were just feeling too weary. Christmas that year was another holiday we just didn't have any energy for. Larry was way too tired and weak to even begin to help me out with any of our usual holiday preparations or do any gift shopping. Worn out, the decision was made, we wouldn't do anything that year, our hearts just weren't into it. I didn't even feel like doing my usual decorating for the holidays, it seemed pointless to pretend I was into it when my mind was engrossed with other things. I knew though that my grandchildren would still be coming over at times through the holiday and not wanting to be a complete big downer for them I thought I should at least do something, I put up a small three foot tree next to the TV and hung up a few decorations which was far less than my normal holiday decor. I went out on my own shopping for gifts for the grandkids even though I was having a hard time, my heart not into it like normal. Christmas shopping wasn't giving me the usual joy it normally did as I shopped for gifts for them. My mind was preoccupied. Larry had finished his last chemo treatment, and we were in the waiting stage for his last PET/Scan that would tell us if the cancer was gone.

It was when we were nearing Larry's last chemo treatment that I found myself in a place of doing some deep soul searching as I started to ask myself more new questions.

CHAPTER

28

*T*hings I didn't usually ponder much about were now foremost in my mind, crowding out my usual thoughts. I started to ask of Him. *God if we are meant to travel on this journey, what is the lesson or lessons that I can learn from it?*

What bad can You take and turn to good, what is it that You want of me?

I knew that I didn't want this newfound freedom I had to be only something that was just to benefit me.

God are You using this journey I have been on for so long for a reason? What about the current journey we are now on, navigating our way through cancer?

I continued to ask my questions of Him. *How can I be used to give You the glory, You the praise for what You have done?*

I wanted Him to take those wanton and barren years I had wasted and turn them into something beautiful and fruitful. He was chasing my regrets away and replacing them with new optimism that even in these later years of my life He could accomplish something much greater than I could ever imagine. I knew beyond any shadow of doubt, nothing I had gained could be credited to anything I had done. I hadn't worked for it or earned it. It was all because of God's infinite love for me that He had brought me to the place where I could now experience an undeniable peace and a freedom in my life that I had never walked in before.

I found myself furtively thinking that I was to start praying for people with cancer. Everywhere I turned there were images of cancer; TV, books I was reading that had characters in it with cancer, friends with loved ones with cancer, friends with cancer themselves. I know I had a heightened sense of being more aware because we found ourselves in the midst of our own battle with it, but it seemed more than just that. My heart was turning over with a different kind of compassion that was new and different for me and if I was honest with myself true compassion was something that was sometimes lacking in me. I could feel deep, but sometimes my compassion would be limited or wanting, dependent on the circumstances.

These were different and strange thoughts for me. It terrified me, my thought, *who am I?* Thoughts that were so very out of my personal comfort zone, but these impressions wouldn't leave. While lulling these thoughts over in my mind I started to get this strange and almost physical sensation that the palm of my hand held healing in it. Constantly God would bring to my remembrance the scripture, go and lay hands on the sick in my name and they will be healed.

Deep in my heart I knew this had to start at home. Conflicting thoughts mingled with the feeling of isn't that kind of selfish? I had to ask myself why I felt this way. I felt so impressed that I held this feeling in my hand and it was especially meant for my husband first and most of all. *Why would an act of faith and a prayer from me be what he needs? Surely there are more qualified people of faith who could or even have laid their hands on him and prayed for him.*

Even with Larry I had always held myself back, afraid of being too vulnerable. Dreams invaded my sleep, visions of myself laying my hand on Larry on his body in the spots the cancer had invaded it; declaring complete healing, that this cancer had no place in his body and was never to return. *Who is this bold and confident person in my dreams?* Not anyone I thought I knew! It wasn't as if I never prayed for Larry, but never like what was in these thoughts and dreams, it was more in my own private and quiet time. To become that vulnerable, there had always been something that held me back, fears that I struggled with; fearful of disappointment and always filled with an unexplainable nervous terror. Now though, a new and exciting desire that just wouldn't go away burned within. Still though I kept quiet about what was rolling around in my head and thoughts.

We were at the point where Larry had finished his last chemo treatment and was scheduled for a PET/Scan to see if the cancer was gone. Larry had the test done and our next doctor's appointment scheduled where we would hear the outcome of this last and final test.

We sat waiting for the doctor to come into the room. Finally she entered and sat down across from us.

"Well the test showed that there is still one hot spot showing up on your lung." "I'm not sure what it is." She tried to assure us. "I've never seen anyone have the kind of cancer you have and go through the treatments and still have cancer. Just to be sure I'm going to send you for another type of CT scan to see what we're looking at."

My heart sank as we left the doctor's office very disappointed. We had been so ready to be all done with this and now we had to do another expensive test and go through the required waiting to hear the results. On the drive home I was wrestling again with my thoughts that won't leave. *Pray for him, lay your hands on him!* I was pestered with the thought that I had waited too long by now to follow through. *Why would God want to use someone like me who questioned at every turn what I thought He was telling me?*

The following Sunday we were again sitting in church listening to a special speaker who was talking about laying all our disappointments down at the feet of Jesus. They were talking about how sometimes our answers come in the doing of things, taking a step of faith and getting off the ledge instead of being mired in our own understanding.

It's like I'm on repeat, yet again here I was, being stirred with the compassion of God that He would know just what I needed to hear. This seemed to be occurring on a regular basis with me lately. Here I was, regretting that I hadn't done anything about my thoughts; what I felt God was asking me to do. Admission that I was disappointed in myself and full of the stark realization that I was disappointed in even God hit me square in the face. We hadn't received the all-clear report we were hoping for at the doctor's office. I repented and made up my mind that I was going to take the initiative and do what I felt like I was supposed to do, lay hands on Larry and pray for him. I would step off that uncomfortable ledge.

Arriving home from church we sat down and ate our lunch. Afterwards, Larry went to lie down to take a nap. *Well, it's now or never.* I walked into the bedroom before he fell asleep.

Nervously I approached the bed. "Hey Larry, um… I have something to talk to you about"

By the look on his face I think he thought he was somehow in trouble with me, probably wondering, now what have I done? I summoned up the courage to tell him what was rolling around in my head and what I felt God had been telling me, about the burning sense that I held God's healing in the palm of my hand for him, and how I was to pray for him. It was silly and ridiculous to me that even after all these years with Larry, I even had these kinds of fears around him, but I did.

Larry looked at me with tears and love in his eyes. "Yes, go ahead, do it!"

I cuddled up next to him on our bed. I didn't feel full of faith, on the contrary I just wanted to be obedient to what I thought God was asking of me so I laid my hand on him, in both areas of his body the cancer had invaded and declared complete healing over him, speaking to the cancer that it had to go, never to return. He was a man of God and this cancer had no place in his body. It wasn't a long and drawn out prayer, rather simple but direct. We both shed some tears as we hugged and I left him to take his nap. As I closed the bedroom door I inquired of myself. *Why had I been so fearful? Hasn't God proven Himself faithful to us so far?*

He had healed my deep wounds, carried us in peace, provided for our financial needs, why was I still questioning that Larry would not be well?

The next day Larry was scheduled for the new scan and then we would go to the doctor's office that Wednesday, December 30, 2015 to hear the results. That Wednesday as we drove into town on the way to the doctor's office I kept repeating to myself. *God you are faithful, I know you are faithful!* Larry parked the truck and we headed across the parking lot towards the doctor's office, our hearts beating with anticipation. I felt somewhat nervous but at the same time also filled with an unexplainable peace that all was going to be okay. Side by side we sat there in the doctor's exam room, holding hands waiting for the doctor. She entered the room with a beaming smile on her face.

"Well, we don't know what that spot is or why it lit up, but it isn't cancer, no cancer!" she paused a second letting the good news sink in. "I just want you to come in and do a follow up blood test in three months, but today we are giving you the all-clear."

It was over. It would take time for Larry to regain his strength and for his hair to grow back in, but it was over!

We left the doctor's office walking hand in hand across the snowy parking lot, my heart aching with thankfulness. Tears burned behind my eyes ever so thankful to our faithful God! God wasn't done blessing us though. On the way home from the doctor's office we stopped and randomly went to check our mail at the post office and there in the mail was an unexpected check for over $1500.00 from our mortgage company from when we had refinanced our condo many months before.

It was the amount we needed to pay for that last unexpected test.

New Garments,
New Chapters,
&
A Life Worth Living

CHAPTER

29

*T*he calendar on the wall now read 2016, the fresh beginnings of a new year, a new chapter.

Leaning back, my feet setting my chair to rock I sat in my office at work and mulled over all I had been through the last year. I thought about everything we had just been through. There was no illusion or shadow of doubt in my mind that I would have never survived the journey without God first healing all my inner wounds and turning my bondage of fear and hurt into one of new garments of freedom and peace.

Gratitude I thought, may I never lose my gratitude that He never abandoned me while for so many years I wallowed in my own cesspool of bondage and sin, instead leading me patiently to the path of freedom and setting me on this road of incredible supernatural peace. Sitting there in my office chair, thinking on these things, I wrote down some of my thoughts on the computer, printed them out and handed them to Larry to read. He was reading them when I left and went to the bank to make some deposits for work.

In the drive thru at the bank waiting for the teller to finish my transactions, God brought something to my memory. Stuffed somewhere in the recesses of my purse was a note of encouragement a friend had handed to me close to two years ago. Much of what I had been personally going through for years, this person didn't know about. I hadn't read that note in a very long time. I couldn't remember much of what it said, so I rummaged through my purse till I found it. I took the note out to read again astonished at what words were there leaping from the wrinkled paper that I now viewed from a different light, piercing my changed heart and mind. This is what that note says:

"Terry, I see new garments placed on you. Old ones have been taken, many of those were not put there by the Lord, but by man. But know the Lord is separating out of you expectations by others and awakening you to HIS expectations. I see like you were trapped under a mountain, hidden, imprisoned. But today the Lord has destroyed the mountain and you will stand upon the very mountain that kept you bound. A stance of victory! Praise be to God!"

There in the drive thru at the bank, I started to cry. *How can I ever express my thankfulness, my love for Him?* I've been changed, no longer trapped within that cardboard box and never, will I be the same again.

Larry continued to get a clean bill of health and he no longer had to go back for more blood tests. We are confident in his healing. Looking forward with anticipation to the next phase of our life, we started to wonder what that would look like and be like. What would this part of our journey in our river of life look like? What about retirement? When will that be? We started to dream. The long anniversary road trip we had taken a short but long year before had really started us thinking about the possibility of living a full time RV lifestyle sometime in the future. After talking together a lot about the possibility of this and after going through the stress of the last year we just had, we decided we would like to retire in the fall of 2017, and accelerate our dream, making it our new reality.

We sat down with our son that had been the one to step up and manage our business in our absences to see if he wanted to take over our business, essentially selling it to him over the next course of our years of retirement. Not wanting to pressure him that he had to do this for us, we really tried to stress it was totally up to him. We had the option of putting our business up for sale to another buyer. After a lot of consideration and I'm sure nerves on his part, he decided he would take the helm and take over our business.

My Journey from Anxiety to Peace

The planning commenced, many hours were spent researching and pouring over what type of RV we wanted. Our current travel trailer we had, again we felt was not it. We wanted something with a larger kitchen in it and a different floor plan more conducive to full time living. This would be our new home, our only home, having decided to be able to do this we would have to also sell our condo. Decisions were made, we would take the year to sell off our possessions, our house, and our current travel trailer and start preparing for this new adventure. A new truck would be needed since our current truck wasn't big enough to haul the new fifth wheel trailer we had decided we would purchase. Larry and I spent many evenings pouring over the internet finding the truck he wanted and the brand and model of fifth wheel trailer we wanted. He found the truck at a dealer in Minneapolis, Minnesota, and a new last year's model of the fifth wheel in Lincoln, Nebraska. We would save thousands buying them out of state, so in April of 2016 we flew to Minneapolis, picked up our new one-ton diesel truck and drove over to Nebraska to pick up our new fifth wheel trailer.

Wow, were we excited! When we saw our new trailer, our excitement fast turned to nervousness. We glanced apprehensively at each other both exclaiming. "What were we thinking?" It was huge, never had we towed something this big. Then we went inside and fell in love with it.

Immediately as we explored inside, opening up cupboards and drawers, I started to visualize how I would turn it into my new home. My wheels were turning. *What can I do to it; I want to make it feel more like a home rather than a RV.*

We spent the day at the dealer getting a new hitch put in the bed of the truck and going through our walkthrough of our RV. Early that evening the dealer hooked up our fifth wheel trailer to our new truck.

"Okay guys, there you go, you're all set!" our salesman said as he waved us off.

Larry and I looked at each other, scared to death to even think about pulling this monstrosity out of the parking lot into the busy rush hour traffic. Away we went, our nerves at high alert, pulling out into the busy street. Reservations were made for an RV park only a few miles away for that night so we didn't have too far to go, but it was enough of a drive that it made us pretty uptight. We were afraid of getting into an accident that would damage our shiny new toy. We dubbed our new fifth wheel immediately *"the beast"* because it is thirty-eight feet long, far bigger and far nicer than any RV we have ever owned.

The next day we spent getting groceries, pots and pans and enough supplies to get us by for our quick trip back to Alaska. A few nights were spent in Colorado visiting our son and his family where we had a short but sweet visit with our loveable grandson who we always miss. We had to cut our visit short when it started snowing there in Denver; too afraid of being caught in too much snow while crossing the mountain passes we had yet to drive through. Larry slowly started getting more comfortable driving *"the beast"* as the days went quickly by. Only wanting to be gone a total of two weeks we didn't spend any other extra time anywhere else, instead heading straight up to Canada so we could get back home as soon as possible.

As we traveled along we were fast learning some new lessons about pulling something behind us this size. Lessons like we need lots of overhead room, we are 13 ½ feet tall so we can't just pull into any old gas station. Be mindful and cautious of not only our height but make sure there is plenty of room for us to turn around too! How did we learn that? One gas station we had pulled into we thought for sure we weren't going to get back out of without causing some damage. Embarrassingly cars had to be moved so we could maneuver and we managed to finally make it back out of the gas station without hitting anything. Lesson one learned.

Our next important lesson happened on our way while going through a very congested part of Canada. It was getting late and we were getting very tired. Looking hard for a RV park where we could spend the night, we couldn't seem to find one. We had been searching our apps on our phone and weren't coming up with much, resulting in us getting frustrated because we were ready to stop driving and have something to eat and go straight to bed. It didn't help our frustration that we were having a hard time even finding any spots large enough that we could pull off the highway to try and do a more exhaustive search on our phones for a RV park. By now it was dark and finally spotting a sign by the road for an RV park, Larry without much thought, pulled off the highway and started up the entrance to it, only to find it was extremely small and tight, and in the heavily treed woods on the side of a hill.

Oh no, here we are again déjà vu just like the gas station, finding ourselves not being able to make the turns. Huge pine trees with ominous branches were everywhere in the tight and narrow roads that wound around the heavily treed park. Besides the large trees that were in the way, RV's, cars and trucks were also in the way. We didn't know how we were going to get out of there. By now I was outside in the dark trying to warn Larry of the tree branches hitting us as we tried to maneuver our way out of there. We got to a point we couldn't go any farther without wiping the trees and us out. It was late and the last thing we wanted to have to do was go knock on someone's trailer door to wake them up and alert them to some fool's rookie mistake. Embarrassed and frustrated, we were thankful when a nice man who heard the commotion we were making moved their truck and helped spot us so we could try and get out of there. More than likely when he came out in the dark to find this monstrous rig stuck in the middle of the forest he probably wondered about the common sense of the two old people in it. Finally after a lot of backing up and pulling forward inch by inch we got out, just missing a big pine tree next to us by less than an inch to spare. We did have a casualty; one large branch hit our roof and put a small hole in the edge of our roof.

With our cheeks enflamed we hurriedly drove down out of there after thanking the man, our new mantra ringing in our ears. NEVER, EVER, do we randomly pull off the highway without fully scoping it out first and making sure we are going to have ample room to maneuver with our large rig. Another painful and very embarrassing lesson learned. One hour later we finally found an RV park that had plenty of room for us. We parked our rig for the night and after our nerves had calmed down, we had a good laugh at ourselves, cracking ourselves up every time we looked at each other; relief that it hadn't been any worse. Lesson two, now under our belts! We had better get used to what we were doing if this was going to be our new life soon!

A Simple Extraordinary Life

Our drive back home to Alaska was pretty much nonstop, driving long days, stopping to make a late dinner then off to bed rising in the early morning to start the drive again. Again we enjoyed the scenery and spotting a lot of wildlife on our way back up the Alcan Highway. After we crossed the border into Alaska the familiar landscape heightened my excitement to get back home. We spent the night in Tok and got up early the next day to drive the last six hours towards home. The closer we got towards home the more beauty that greeted our eyes. Majestic sweeps of mountain ranges, glaciers nestled in their peaks, rivers and lakes, their familiarity that told me I was almost home. We arrived home in one piece the first part of May.

Excited as I was about our new purchase and being home, I was even more excited with what had been unfolding within the last few weeks.

CHAPTER

30

My eagerness was making it hard for me to be patient and let the process resolve itself.

Recently our son due to unfortunate circumstances from a previous divorce and the circumstances he now found his boys in, was going through the arduous process of getting full custody of his boys. Everyone in our family was beyond excited; it had been a deep desire of all of us that the boys would finally come home.

It had been three long years of separation. They were terribly missed by their father, us their gramma and papa, and all their aunts, uncles and cousins. I had been fighting major disappointment; wondering when, and even if, God would ever give us this desire, this longing in all of our hearts to be reunited. Hoping that things would come to a conclusion before we left on our trip to go get our new rig it was hard for me to tolerate the delays without getting too anxious when that didn't happen.

There would be more waiting. Every day on our trip we would get several updates, one step forward, one step back. It was hard to be patient for me, trying to trust that God had everything under control. Patience never being my strong suit. I was worried about my grandsons and trying to trust that they would be safe during the interim. A few days after Larry and I arrived home we got a call from our son. Some unforeseen circumstances had suddenly come up. His lawyer had advised him there was a twenty-four hour opening, if he could get down to Texas where his sons were within this timeframe and get them on a plane back here to Alaska, he could legally gain the custody he was seeking.

He got the phone call from his lawyer late that morning. He left work and came to our office to figure out what to do. It was short notice and a lot of money for airline tickets, neither him or for that matter anyone had. Members of our family including us, a very elated gramma and papa, happily and generously quickly pooled our airline miles together to be able to get him tickets. Immediately we got online to see if we could find a flight for him right away, and a return flight for him and the boys to come back within this twenty-four hour window. It was the beginning of tourism season in Alaska, and the airplanes coming to and from Alaska are usually full, especially within such a short timeframe. We also knew there is very limited seats trying to use airline miles, if any at all at this quick of a turnaround.

We found a seat for our son to get down to Texas, leaving in just a few hours. When we went to book the return flight for the next day knowing we needed three seats, we were highly doubtful we could get them at this swift of a notice. We were shocked and rather stunned when we pulled up the first return flight that would work to find three empty seats in a row. There they were, the image of three un-booked seats highlighted on the computer screen in front of us, sitting empty while every other seat on the plane had already been booked. I started to weep tears of joy. It was so apparent to me, God in his infinite wisdom knew just when, how, and the timing that we needed. Those airplane seats were there waiting, available, because He knew just when they would be needed to bring our special passengers home. He had provided and was again meeting the desire of our hearts. It was no coincidence of that I'm sure, but an answer to prayer and tangible evidence of His great love for all of us. We quickly booked the tickets and our son ran home, packed a bag and hurried to the airport to catch his flight to go bring his boys home. I went out to the store and bought them each a few gifts of some needed clothing and a card for each of them where I wrote down notes of love for them telling them how much we missed and loved them, placing the gift bags upon their beds where they would see them as soon as they got home.

Less than forty-eight hours from the time we made those airline reservations, my son brought his boys to our office to come see their gramma and papa. My heart full, my eyes could hardly take in the difference in them. My how they had grown in the last three years, especially my son's oldest.

"Wow, look at you, you're so tall!" I exclaimed as I hugged him. "I can't believe it!"

"I missed you!" I said with tears of joy in my eyes.

"I missed you too Gramma." He shyly said.

I kept staring at him. "I can't get over how tall you are! How tall are you?"

"I don't know, I haven't measured myself in a long time." He shrugged his shoulders a shy grin pulling at his lips.

"You must be close to six feet now!" I marveled as I continued to stare at him trying to take in all the differences in him.

He smiled at me, those eyes so familiar. "Nah, I don't think so."

I couldn't get over how different he looked, his hair which had always been short now hung below his ears, and he had drastically filled out his small frame. "You've changed so much!"

His younger brother had grown some but his looks still the same. His goofy grin still just as sweet to me as the day he left. We hugged and when he told me he missed and loved me too it warmed my heart. It was my sons oldest that had shocked me the most.

In three years he had changed from a young boy to a tall teenager that now towered over me. I hugged him again, I couldn't help it but when he hugged me right back I knew he was still the same child that I loved and knew. How glad I was that we were able to take right up with both of them where we had left off, three long years ago.

I have a picture of me with them that day, a reunion that will ever be dear in my heart. Even though there was heartache and pain in the waiting, I couldn't help but see how God had provided for us just what we needed, when we needed it, and again he gave me one of the greatest desires of my heart. The boys were back home with their father and back in our lives. Two weeks after they got here we took our grandsons camping with us in our new RV for a long Memorial Day weekend at my favorite place, Homer, Alaska.

As I sat there on the beach in Homer watching my grandchildren play in the sand, digging for creatures in the low tide of the ocean and surrounded by nature's beauty, I couldn't help but reflect back to the previous year. When we had last taken a trip to Homer we were in the midst of learning whether Larry had cancer or not. I sat there remembering, reflecting on how while I cried out to Him with my fears, He infused me with peace and met me right where I was at. I continued to reflect, contemplating on the differences in me now, how my outlook has been changed and how God has answered our prayers this last year.

That year, although it is something I don't want to repeat; I can also honestly say I wouldn't trade it for anything. God took me to places in Him I'd never been before. He filled me with a peace that passes no human understanding and refined me with that refiner's fire that got us through the trials of cancer, chemo, and gave us blessed assurance that all was going to come out good in the end. Today Larry walks in health. I've seen answered prayer that God is good and He knows the desires of my heart. I rest assured that this time, this trip with our grandsons to Homer is a fulfillment of His promises to us, His promises to me. *Not only is Larry healthy but here we are, reunited with our grandsons and we are getting the great pleasure of bringing them with us!*

Another son of ours and his family joined us for the weekend camping with us. I spent a lot of time that weekend just watching my grandchildren play for hours on the beach. They chopped wood for the fire, made driftwood tepees, and looked for shells and sea creatures while they played in the tide pools. The splendor of the magnificent views surrounding us, the sound of all their laughter, it all spoke volumes to me. *How can I not be grateful and be filled with wonder?* God and His infinite love for me would be with me no matter which road I traveled, in the past, in the now, or in the future in my life. He turned all the pain and heartache I have ever faced, or am yet to face and will turn it into something beautiful if I let Him.

We took a few more camping trips in our new fifth wheel that summer and were sad when we had to store it for the winter; anxious for the coming new year when we would retire and make it our full time home. Many evenings that winter were again spent dreaming and making plans for our future. YouTube became one of our favorite pastimes. We found there is a very large full time RV community out there and we would watch many videos to learn about what this life would be like. Of course my favorite videos were the ones where people would remodel their interiors to make it feel more like a sticks and bricks home. Larry, now he liked the ones that were boring to me, how to hook up solar power, what do to for better internet services, things like that. Since I have always loved turning whatever home I lived in into something that suited my tastes, my new home was going to be no exception.

Although I was excited for our new life I had conflicting emotions about it. It was hard for me to think about selling our condo. I had spent many hours painting walls and painstakingly decorating it and finally after living there for ten years I had gotten it to just how I liked it. I knew I would have to sell off almost all of the things I loved and had accumulated. Glad that I had a year to adjust to letting go of everything, the time consuming process would start that winter. Many hours were spent taking pictures and posting our things on local virtual yard sale sites, constantly answering questions and making appointments for people to come and buy our stuff. Even though I was never much of a hoarder it was amazing how much a person can accumulate in things over the years.

It was becoming easier and easier, week-by-week, letting go of all of it.

Just when I thought I had gotten rid of a lot, I would look around and realize more had to go. We had a two-car garage, storage shed, and almost 1500 square feet of household goods, furniture, tools, and decorations, decorations of which Larry couldn't believe how much I actually had.

Endlessly he would tease me. "Just how many vases and pictures do you have?"

We would have to pare down all our possessions to fit in about 350 square feet and it would have to withstand the jostling of going down the road. This meant most of what I had would have to go since it would be sure to break.

The most stressful thing for me was going through my closet of clothes! I think it took me five or more rounds of going through it, slowly letting garment by garment go. It was a painful process trying to decide which article of clothing I wanted and which one I could do without. Larry on the other hand as never had a problem, jeans and plaid short sleeve shirts are all he has ever worn, besides those few years of polyester in the nineteen seventies. He's happy with only a few pair of pants and a few shirts. When he'd tease me trying to make me conform to what amount of clothes that he thought was acceptable I'd quickly respond.

"I'm not the same as you, this girl likes to have her choices!"

He just laughed at me knowing it was a useless argument. I was determined on finding a way to fit as much as I could inside my RV closet.

I'm glad he knows what is going to make me happy. He knows me well enough that if I was going to be able to adjust to this knew lifestyle, part of that would be letting me have some leeway and decorate my new home. I watched a lot of videos and got on Pinterest researching how to paint the interior walls of an RV. Deciding that I wanted to do just that, he warned me.

"Okay, but you'll have to do it yourself."

I quickly responded. "I have no problem with that."

It was exactly what I planned to do, along with making new curtains, recovering the ugly brown vinyl headboard in the bedroom, and making a colorful wood panel to cover up what I considered to be an ugly brown fake tile that was in part of the kitchen. I also had a few other things up my sleeve that I would tackle, hopefully by myself. I didn't want him telling me no I couldn't because he didn't want to particularly help me, even though I knew he eventually would. He did wind up helping me with everything else but the painting since he has always hated painting. I had to wait until spring though before I could start on my renovations since our rig was in storage so I spent a lot of time daydreaming and planning on what colors I was going to use.

Our plans included that we would put our house on the market in the early spring of 2017. We would spend the summer in Alaska, leave that fall, spend our winters roaming around in the states and return every year for the summers, making us what they call snow birds every year. One of our sons thought it ridiculous that we would spend a lot of money parked in an RV park over the summers so he generously offered for us to stay on his property in the summers.

I kept asking him over and over. "You sure?" playfully teasing him. "That's an awful lot of togetherness with Mom and Dad!"

Plans were made that's what we would do, stay on his property in the summers when we came back, so in the fall of 2016, we put in an RV parking pad and utility hookups for us in his backyard. Our plans were coming together.

Our condo sold within a month of putting it on the market. In early May of 2017 we brought our fifth wheel out of storage and moved it onto our son's property. Immediately I started in on painting the interior, loving that I could now quit daydreaming and see my plans come to fruition. We sold off the uncomfortable RV furniture it came with and replaced it with some of our regular house furniture. I was starting to fret about selling off the bed in our house in time before the final closing date on the sale of our condo. We would have to be out soon so I put it up for sale, thinking it might take some time to sell. Surprising me, it took only a few days to sell so we moved into our fifth wheel earlier than planned since we no longer had a bed in the house to sleep in.

The rest of the month I spent doing a lot of final cleaning, emptying out the house and selling the last of our stuff, taking the last little bit of unsold stuff to the Salvation Army. The final day when I had the last of our possessions out of the house, everything cleaned and the wood floors polished, I was surprised to find myself overcome, sudden tears springing to my eyes as I took one last look around. A chapter of our life was closing and even though I was excited for this next chapter, I did love that house. Memories sprung before my eyes of it being filled to the brim with family dinners and Christmases with our grandchildren. Peaceful memories sprang to my eyes of many evenings spent just Larry and I, relaxing in our recliners in front of the fireplace. Such a large part of our life had been spent there and knowing life was going to be different was a sobering thought.

The tears didn't last too long though, it was a good thing I had a year to process all the changes in our life we were making. I locked the doors, closed the garage door one final time, excited for the coming years. I left and headed back to our new tiny home that was parked in my son's yard.

It wasn't until weeks later as I stepped into my RV that I realized why I had been drawn to the colors I had chosen to paint my walls. The main body of walls I had painted a very soft glacier blue, clear and calming at the same time, reminiscent of that pool of water where I had found my healing in, not so long ago. On one side of our RV is a slide out that our recliners and a small dining table sit in. These walls I painted a brighter yellow called appletini. The color reminds me of a vibrant golden and green delicious apple. When I look at these colors the blue is the calm peace I now feel, the serenity that now lives inside me. The yellow is the newness I feel as I come alive, a new person, no longer weighted down by the wounds I once had wrapped around my neck, drowning me. Now when I enter my RV, my new home, these colors tell me I am finally home, finally at a place where I was always meant to live.

We are just shy of a little over two months left before we leave for our new adventure, this next chapter in life. I am starting the process of trying my hand at writing down my story. I now sit here writing and reflecting, pondering, what is it I want to say, what I should say.

Memories both good and bad come to my mind. Pieces in time I would surely love to repeat and pieces, I would have liked to slow down. Pieces in time that were incredibly hard and pieces in time that were wonderful and will be told in stories over and over again. I can't help but think, a simple ordinary life, but yet, I did have experiences worth telling. Most vivid to me is that the work He did in me wasn't just ordinary but His works are extraordinary. The most worthy of telling is the one that without Him, my life would not have been worth living. Everything I've experienced points me to Him, for without Him I can do nothing; I cannot survive on my own. He makes my life worth living, fills me with incredible joy, and loves me like no other. There is a freedom and peace I can find only in Him. So it is with excitement I'm ready to start this next chapter in life, this next passage of time that chronicles the winding river of my life.

Larry and I are settling into this new life. It's a slower pace and as I savor each day, I marvel and find delight that we are able to live it. I am learning new things, experiencing new things as we go. We're meeting new people and making new friends along the way. I take endless delight in the ever-changing scenery. I especially enjoy feeling the sun upon my face as I rock myself while sitting outside, in my nice new rocking camp chair. There is a quiet camaraderie between Larry and I that comes from being together for so long, words unnecessary as we just sit and enjoy being together, our love strong.

Sometimes as I sit and rock, I travel back in time in my mind remembering; holding my children as babies, their precious weight in my arms but a faint and distant whisper. Sometimes our phones will ring with grandchildren wanting to skype with us, so thankful for this technology for I miss them so, anxiously looking forward to seeing them again in the summer. Then there are the times as I sit and think, grateful that my father said yes to his master, his Lord and Savior. His life, his devotion and his unwavering love that he had for me. He gave me an earthly father's love that pointed me to the one and only true heavenly father's love.

Then most precious to me are the times when I've gotten up in the middle of the night when I don't sleep too well. How when I return to bed in the wee hours of the morning, the feeling I get when I cozy up to my husband and feel the heat of his body, feel the touch of his skin and listen to the soft breathing of his sleep. It never fails to calm and soothe

273

me. I put my arm around his sleeping body and know that this man is a gift to me, his very life a gift. As my body starts to relax, ready to return to sleep, my fingers rest upon the healed scar upon my heart, yet another beautiful gift. My lips curl in a smile, grateful for these gifts that only One can give. As my eyelids flutter and close, I drift off to sleep filled with peace, such an undeniable and sweet peace that can only come from Him and I know, *I am finally home.*

Epilogue

I do not tell my story to garner pity, but rather to bring glory to the One who can change a lifetime spent in bondage to one of freedom in the blink of an eye.

A restoration so beautiful and life changing I can't help but tell of His greatness. He brought me from suffocating darkness into His glorious light, changed forever more.

Would it be that what I have lived and experienced, my tears, my joy, be for the purpose to bring glory to the One who makes my life worth living? My wish is that if even just one can find that my story points them to Him, to the One who can heal their wounds, make their life worth living, and restore their soul, then it is a life well lived.

There is a scripture that comes to mind when I think upon my life's journey and what I have learned about myself along the way, both the good and bad. There is such a deep truth in it.

> "There is no fear in love. But perfect love drives out fear, because fear has to do with punishment. The one who fears is not made perfect in love." 1 John 4:18 (NIV)

Another translation makes it even clearer for me.

> "Love never brings fear, for fear is always related to punishment. But love's perfection drives the fear of punishment far from our hearts. Whoever walks constantly afraid of punishment has not reached love's perfection." 1 John 4:18 (TPT)

A Simple Extraordinary Life

Who is the one that is perfect in love? No one but Him. When I fully look into and fix my eyes upon that perfect love and let it heal me, the shame, fear, and anxiety disappears and is driven out, replaced instead with His peace. In contrast when I had fixed my eyes on everything else but His perfect love I constantly walked down the path of hurt and shame, fear and anxiety becoming what overtook me.

Dear one, know that you are loved by the one who carries perfect love. Let it wash over you, cleanse you, and heal you. Dare to look fully into His eyes of love and be changed.

Acknowledgments

When the first soft whispers came to me to write I wanted to ignore it. With those whispers also came a yearning that was building deep within I couldn't ignore. So I started to write. Learning to listen to the still small voice that spoke to me during the night was a process and the writing took on new form as I learned to listen to that still small voice. What an incredible journey this has been. Heart wrenching, reflective, joyous, healing and incredibly exciting.

I could have never attempted something like this without the support of my loving husband who has always been by my side in everything I have ever done. His encouragement kept me going through the arduous process of getting my story down on paper. He is my champion, my best friend, my better half. His patience to always be my computer guru and answer my never ending questions, fix my mistakes, and be my technical guy is something I'm always grateful for. I always think I couldn't love you anymore but another day, another year goes by and I know I love you more than the day or year before.

In the beginning, during the very rough drafts as I wrote I knew I was missing something vital that I couldn't quite put my finger on. Through the encouragement of some of my brothers and sisters and other relatives to write stories of my father, I knew this is what I was missing. My father always played a huge role in my life and I loved him deeply. I can't wait till the day I get to see him again.

I am very thankful to have the upbringing I had. To have the chance to grow up and experience the beauty of Alaska while doing so only made it even more special. I am rich to have been blessed with the love of all my brothers and sisters; I love each and every one of you.

A Simple Extraordinary Life

My life has been incredibly enriched by my four sons. Micah my oldest, I love to hug you and stand beneath your arms and feel your height that towers over me. I am so proud of the man you are. Your passion and selflessness for your children whom you have sacrificed much for, speaks volumes. Your heart is soft and huge. Luke, you have a heart large enough to love your own naturally born children and still have love to adopt more and also open up your home to foster care and love those hurting children like your own. Makes me proud. I'm so thankful you thought of me and asked Jamie your friend about my writing. I was floundering not knowing where to go and what to do next and within days I had God appointed connections. Caleb, your heart to want to take care of us, your parents, makes me want to cry, it is so special to me. I love to watch you parent. You parent leaps and bounds above where I ever was. You're a servant and for that I'm grateful. Zach, my youngest you will forever hold a special place in my heart. I couldn't be more proud of your drive and determination. You are gifted and talented and I can't wait to see how far you will go. Your encouragement to me to keep writing meant the world to me and your tip that google is my friend, priceless. I love all of you from the bottom of my heart, my wonderful boys who have now blossomed into fine men that I'm proud to call my sons.

To all my daughter-in-laws, you are like the daughters I never had and I am blessed by each one of you. You're all unique and have such great hearts. A mother's greatest joy is to see her sons loved by such special women. The grandchildren you have all given to me I consider to be one of life's most priceless gifts. I love them all so much, such joy they give my life.

I would be remiss if I didn't acknowledge my pastor and his wife. Dennis, the first time I encountered you my first thought was that something about you reminded me of my father. You showed me true and real Godly love when I was at my lowest and worst point and it was the lifeline that kept me from drowning. You are God's faithful servant that helps bring healing to the broken. Brenda, what a blessing to me you are and have been. You were a light when I was sinking in the darkness. The love and compassion you showed me was a divine appointment I'll never forget. Thank you so much for being willing to read my writing and encourage me to share my story.

Thanks to Andy at 5 fold Media for your quick response to my inquiry and giving me insight into the publishing world. Your help answering my questions and giving me direction and encouragement meant the world to me. When you didn't want to hang up the phone until you prayed for me, which was a passionate and honest heartfelt prayer, I knew I had found the help I was looking for. Everyone who has helped along the way, including my editors and my wonderful husband for his many talents doing my book cover, I am most grateful for all the work you all have done.

My greatest thanks goes to the One who gives me life, makes my life worth living, my wonderful Lord and Savior.

Made in the USA
San Bernardino, CA
14 January 2019